RECLAIMING AMERICA

through

"SINGLE ISSUE"

Federal Conventions

Charles Kacprowicz

RECLAIMING AMERICA

RECLAIMING AMERICA

through

"SINGLE ISSUE"

Federal Conventions

Charles Kacprowicz

Markets
Global
Publishing

Spruce Pine, North Carolina

RECLAIMING AMERICA

Visit http://CitizenInitiatives.org

RECLAIMING AMERICA – through SINGLE ISSUE Federal Conventions.

Markets Global Publishing
P.O. Box 523
Spruce Pine, NC 28777-0523
Support@CitizenInitiatives.org

Other books of excellence from Markets Global Publishing are available from your local bookstore or direct from the publisher.

Kacprowicz, Charles

RECLAIMING AMERICA – through SINGLE ISSUE Federal Conventions
Charles Kacprowicz. – 1st ed. (Amendment Introduction)
Includes Index. Bibliography
Edited

ISBN: 978-0-9723007-4-2   (soft cover)

Library of Congress Control Number: 2010923999

Books by Charles Kacprowicz

RECLAIMING AMERICA
through "SINGLE ISSUE" Federal Conventions

THE ELEVENTH NATION
America Identified In Prophecy

UNBORN CHILD AMENDMENT
A National Strategy To Amend
The U.S. Constitution Through State Legislatures

HOW TO CONTACT THE AUTHOR

Charles Kacprowicz frequently appears on local/national radio and television programs as a guest speaker. Requests for information, as well as inquiries about availability for public speaking, lectures, and seminars should be directed to:

CITIZEN INITIATIVES
P.O. Box 523
Spruce Pine, NC 28777-0523

http://CitizenInitiatives.org
ckacprowicz@CitizenInitiatives.org

Readers of this book are also encouraged to contact the author with comments and ideas for future editions and Amendments.

RECLAIMING AMERICA

TABLE OF CONTENTS

About the Author   9
Preface   11
Introduction   13

CHAPTER 1   A CONSTITUTIONAL DISCUSSION   23

CHAPTER 2   SINGLE ISSUE FEDERAL CONVENTIONS   33

CHAPTER 3   INCREMENTAL LEGISLATION   47

CHAPTER 4   STATE AND NATIONAL STRATEGIES   55

CHAPTER 5   OTHER ASPECTS OF THE AMENDMENT   65
                 STRATEGY

CHAPTER 6   CONGRESSIONAL PREROGATIVES IN   67
                 THE CONVENTION PROCESS

CHAPTER 7   WE HAVE THE VOTING POWER   71

CHAPTER 8   PROPOSED AMENDMENTS TO   77
                 THE UNITIED STATES CONSTITUTION

CHAPTER 9   BALANCED FEDERAL BUDGET AMEND.   79

CHAPTER 10   LEGAL IMMIGRATION AMENDMENT   105

CHAPTER 11   TRADITIONAL MARRIAGE AMENDMENT   127

CHAPTER 12   SCHOOL VOUCHER AMENDMENT   151

CHAPTER 13   CONSTITUTIONAL HISTORY AMENDMENT   175

CHAPTER 14   UNBORN CHILD AMENDMENT   197

CHAPTER 15 TRUTH IN EDUCATION AMENDMENT   219

CHAPTER 16 TRUTH IN MEDIA AMENDMENT   241

CHAPTER 17 PARENTAL RIGHTS AMENDMENT   263

CHAPTER 18 FREE MARKETS AMENDMENT   285

CHAPTER 19 ENERGY AMENDMENT   287

CHAPTER 20 AMERICAN SOVEREIGNTY   289
                AMENDMENT

CHAPTER 21 AMENDMENTS BEING CONSIDERED   291

CHAPTER 22 UNITED STATES CONSTITUTION   293

CHAPTER 23 UNITED STATES BILL OF RIGHTS   305

BIBLIOGRAPHY   315

INDEX   317

ABOUT THE AUTHOR

Charles Kacprowicz is the founder of CITIZEN INITIATIVES which presently is advancing 19 Amendments to the United States Constitution through "Single Issue" Federal Conventions.

Charles has been working to reinstate righteous laws in America for 38 years. The *Balanced Federal Budget Amendment* is a top priority for Charles because he is persuaded that no debtor nation can long remain free. He has been fighting for the Unborn Child's right to life since January 23, 1973. After hearing the news about the Supreme Court's Roe vs. Wade decision the night before, he addressed an outdoor audience at Akron, OH. His message was simple : "We must overturn Roe vs. Wade! . . . We must not give the American woman the right to decide who lives and dies in America".

He has authored multiple position papers, the *UNBORN CHILD AMENDMENT – A National Strategy to Amend the U.S. Constitution Through State Legislatures, THE ELEVENTH NATION – America Identified In Prophecy* and *RECLAIMING AMERICA through SINGLE ISSUE Federal Conventions.*

No stranger to media attention, Charles has appeared on many radio and TV talk shows. He conducts prophecy seminars, has been the guest speaker before 200+ audiences, lobbied Congress on behalf of the Unborn Child Amendment and Late Term Abortion Bills twice vetoed by President Clinton, and has received support from United

States Senators, United States Representatives, State Legislators and Pro-Life Groups.

He has served in the Church as Preacher, Elder, Deacon, Teacher, Jail Ministry Director and Youth Director. Charles has been recognized by Entrepreneur Magazine for founding one of America's top 500 entrepreneurial companies and has been awarded the coveted "Authority Author" status by EzineDirectories.com.

Charles has been married to his first love for 45 years. He has two sons and four grandchildren. He's a graduate of California State (Government/Political Science), with 4 ½ years of post graduate work at Loyal Law School and Moody Bible Extension Studies. He also served honorably in the U.S. Navy.

PREFACE

By dying today, we leave for posterity a cesspool of moral, economic and legal perversions that are becoming increasingly more difficult to reverse. We are condemning our children and grandchildren, through our selfish indifference, to a future they will find impossible to change. Will you join us in this righteous battle for America and our posterity or will you wait for our enemies to enslave us making reclamation impossible?

> "To my last resource and final breath, I will fight to reinstate America's righteous laws that honor God, human life and human dignity."

Charles Kacprowicz
National Director
CITIZEN INITIATIVES

> "Who will rise up for me against the evildoers? Or who will stand up for me against the workers of iniquity? . . . Shall the throne of iniquity have fellowship with thee, which frameth mischief by a law?"
>
> PSALM 94:16,20

> "If thou forbear to deliver them that are drawn unto death, and those that are ready to be slain; If thou sayest, Behold, we knew it not; doth not he that pondereth the heart consider it? and he that keepeth thy soul, doth not he know it? and shall not he render to every man according to his works?"
>
> PROVERBS 24:11,12

RECLAIMING AMERICA

THE STATES ALONE HAVE THE AUTHORITY TO RECLAIM THEIR STATES RIGHTS AND REINSTATE CIVIL LIBERTIES

The States alone determine the purpose, agenda and terms of a Federal Convention, not Congress. Even the Convention itself does not have final authority to control the deliberations at the Convention. When the Calling States enter into a binding contract through their Legislative Calls on Congress, the parameters of the deliberations at the Convention are predetermined. This Constitutional authority, which rests in State Legislatures and given to the States by our Founders, is the States most powerful vehicle for *RECLAIMING AMERICA through "SINGLE ISSUE" Federal Conventions.* The States are, in fact, the final arbitrator of selected Constitutional issues. I pray that the States will not be deceived by flawed legal and Constitutional reasoning and continue to ignore the authority they have in Article V and Article IV, Section 4 of the United States Constitution.

FEDERALISTS PAPERS

Approximately 15,000 copies of this book will be mailed to individual State Legislators in all 50 States. We are also planning to mail follow up books containing Legislative Calls for individual Amendments. This mailing campaign will be CITIZEN INITIATIVES' 21st Century equivalent to the *Federalist Papers* which were used by our Founders and Constitutional supporters to persuade State Legislators in the Colonies that they should adopt and ratify the new Constitution. Our purpose will be to convince State Legislators that SINGLE ISSUE Federal Conventions, for individual Amendments, will empower the States to regain their Constitutional Rights and reinstate civil liberties for their citizens.

INTRODUCTION

The central theme of this book is to show how and why "SINGLE ISSUE" Federal Conventions can and should be used to reclaim our Constitutional Rights, States Rights, economic health and moral high ground in America. The concept of "SINGLE ISSUE" Federal Conventions is not well known to Americans. For decades the concept has been maligned by many politicians, Constitutional lawyers, profit and non-profit organizations. However, it is a valid and safe Constitutional strategy that our Founders provided for us in Article V and Article IV, 4 of the United States Constitution. When Congress and the Courts refuse to address an egregious wrong suffered by the people, Article V and IV, 4 empower the people to amend the Constitution one grievance at a time. It was the Founders' way of providing a peaceful resolution of irreconcilable differences as a last resort.

Our analysis will compare the differences between Open vs. SINGLE ISSUE Federal Conventions and why the SINGLE ISSUE Convention has been shunned by the greater majority of churches, tax exempt denominations, political parties and political action groups. We will also explain why *Incremental Legislation* as a strategy to achieve social and Constitutional justice has, for the last 50+ years, become the strategy of choice and why it has failed Christian Conservatives.

After studying the evidences and arguments in this book, it is my hope that you too will recognize that only through "SINGLE ISSUE" Federal Conventions can the American people reclaim the moral and economic high ground in America. We are in a life and death struggle for the survival of Constitutional government, our Christian/Judeo heritage and our posterity.

The United States Supreme Court on January 22, 1973, in its Roe vs. Wade decision, asserted the existence of a woman's un-enumerated right (i.e. a right not enumerated in the Constitution) to reproductive privacy in which she can abort, at will, a father's Unborn Child, without State interference. In effect the Court amended the United States Constitution without ratification by the States. The anti abortion laws in all 50 States were nullified by 7 Justices with this decision. Other Court decisions that have amended the Constitution without ratification by the States are School Busing, Prayer in School, removal of the Ten Commandments from government property, annulling States Rights regarding 2nd Amendment protections, etc.

The States have also lost a great many Constitutional powers through Supreme Court decisions that either restrict or invalidate State police powers, regulatory powers, legislative powers, judicial powers and commerce powers.

There are numerous Supreme Court decisions that either asserted an un-enumerated right in favor of a petitioner or denied a Constitutional Right of the people.

The Supreme Court's authority is defined in Article III:

"The Judicial Power shall extend to all Cases, in Law and Equity, arising under this Constitution, the Laws of the United States, . . .".

The task the Supreme Court has been given is arduous and its decisions rarely satisfy all parties. However, the cardinal rule the Court is required to follow is to protect the Constitution of the United States and to confirm the original intent of the Founders in its decisions. Over the last 60 years the Court has become decidedly more radical in its decisions. It has often viewed the Constitution as a living document that can be altered based on circumstances in each case. This practice in effect means the Constitution has no absolute mandates for the judicial or legislative branches to follow. It is instead vulnerable to the interpretations and imaginations of men in each succeeding generation. A prime example of this is found in Amendment V:

> "No person shall be held to answer for a capital, or otherwise infamous crime, unless on a presentment or indictment of a Grand Jury, . . .".

The Constitution protects every "person" against capital punishment, except Unborn Persons who should be protected through Amendments V and XIV:

Article XIV, Section 1:

> "All persons born or naturalized in the United States, and subject to the jurisdiction thereof, are citizens of the United States and of the State wherein they reside. No State shall make or enforce any law which shall abridge the privileges or immunities of citizens of the United States; nor shall any State deprive any person of life, liberty, or property, without due process of law; nor deny to any person within its jurisdiction the equal protection of the laws."

How did this happen? Seven Justices on January 22, 1973 decided that an Unborn Baby is not a person protected by the Constitution and granted American women an un-enumerated right to reproductive privacy, which right she already had. In this twisted, flawed, costly and unconscionable decision seven men held the lives of 48 million plus American Babies in their hands and chose to waste them by giving the mother the Constitutional right to decide who should live or die in America. [1]WE LIVE IN THE CONSEQUENCES OF OUR CHOICES:

- 48 million fathers are now without children
- 192 million grandparents are without grandchildren
- 42 million American mothers have committed murder and have to live in the memory of their decision especially after they give birth to other children who they learn to love
- America has lost 16% of its population through abortions
- The black community has lost 45% of its population through abortions

- $38 trillion in Gross Domestic Product has been lost
- $15 trillion in tax revenue and other government income has been lost
- Social Security has been ravaged because the tax bases that should have supported it have been killed
- Social and Economic costs include:

  i. millions of families don't exist because of abortion
  ii. no birthday celebrations
  iii. no precious moments between mother and baby
  iv. a father's pride in his children has been destroyed
  v. personal family moments lost
  vi. no weddings
  vii. no church outings, confirmations, Bar Mitzvahs
  viii. no graduations
  ix. no Scouting, athletic and music events
  x. 48 million potential entrepreneurs, scientists, statesmen, pastors, laborers, etc. have been lost to America
  xi. trillions of dollars in family incomes have been lost
  xii. development and growth of new industries have been lost

(Go to http://UnbornChildAmendment.com/abortion_statistics.htm for the real costs, State by State, of this flawed decision)

If it were not for this terribly flawed and evil decision America would today be a creditor nation, not a debtor nation. The Supreme Court destroyed God's and America's heritage by foolishly catering to feminists and abortion rights advocates.

Roe vs. Wade is one of many flawed decisions by the Supreme Court that have changed the legal, political, economic and moral climate of America. This is why we MUST boldly use the authority our Founders gave us in Article V and Article IV, Section 4 of the United States Constitution and Reclaim America through "SINGLE ISSUE" Federal Conventions.

"But . . . , ,ye have sinned against the LORD: and
be sure your sin will find you out."
NUMBERS 32:23

"The way of the wicked is an abomination unto the LORD: but he
loveth him that followeth after righteousness."
PROVERBS 15:9

"There is a way that seemeth right unto a man, but the end thereof
are the ways of death.:
PROVERBS 16:25

The United States Congress has also usurped the authority of the States through Federal statutes and regulatory laws that rely on flawed applications of the Commerce Clause, the Full Faith and Credit Clause and other Articles in the Constitution. The latest Congressional debacle is the Health Care Bill that is over 2,000 pages long with multiple mandates requiring the American people to "purchase" health insurance. As of this writing, there has been no reconciliation between the House's version and the Senate's. The fact remains that no matter what provisions are in a final bill there will almost certainly be constitutional protections violated by Congress.

The political climate in Washington, D.C. is so divisive that it is virtually impossible to secure the necessary majorities from both Houses of Congress in order to pass Constitutionally sound legislation. It is even more difficult to persuade two thirds of both Houses of Congress to send any of our proposed Amendments to the States for ratification. In addition, **Incremental Legislation**, a strategy foolishly opted into by many in the Christian and Conservative movement, has failed. You cannot overturn Supreme Court mandates with Federal Court decisions, State Court decisions,

Congressional legislation, or State legislation. In the case of Roe vs. Wade, even if the Supreme Court overturned its 1973 landmark decision and left the matter to the States again, the legislative and *State Constitutional* battles for the Unborn Child's life would be expanded into all 50 States. However, even if State Constitutions were amended to protect the Unborn Child's life, the United States Supreme Court could overturn all of them as it did with State statutes that once protected the Unborn's life before Roe vs. Wade. Only a United States Constitutional Amendment can give the Unborn Child the legal standing of a "Person" which would then give him the same protections the rest of America enjoys in the 14th Amendment.

Another Constitutional conundrum develops when special interest groups such as those advocating Gay Rights or same sex marriage secure favorable legislation or judicial decisions in one State and then work to impose those decisions on other States through Article IV, Section 2:

"The Citizens of each State shall be entitled to all Privileges and Immunities of Citizens in the several States."

Efforts to oppose the application of another State's legislation or judicial decision is never ending. On a national basis organizations have to be set up in each of the 50 States to counter such efforts. An arduous task!   SINGLE ISSUE Amendments to the Constitution can prevent this.

While these political deadlocks continue to play themselves out in States, Congress and the Courts, the American people are now in debt to the tune of $14.3 trillion. This means that every family in America owes $142,000 plus interest. If they paid this out over 30 years the total amount they would have to pay would be $426,000. A 30 year payout assumes that other nations in the world would still be interested in loaning the United States money to fund this debt. This likelihood would diminish as the dollar loses value, inflation increases and interest rates to fund the debt rise.   Today our unfunded liabilities have been projected at $60 trillion.   These are truly staggering numbers and for you and I to look the other way is unconscionable. We must stop this insanity with the *Balanced Federal Budget Amendment* and restore sound fiscal policies that Congress would be mandated to follow.

The President has no Constitutional role when amending the Constitution. He can lobby members of Congress to send an Amendment to the States for ratification, but he has no authority to authorize such action nor can he veto it. He can lobby State Legislators, but again he has no power to force them to vote his way.

The Constitutional Convention remains the only way left to the people for amending the United States Constitution when Congress and the Courts refuse to address an egregious wrong suffered by the people. There are available to the people two types of Federal Conventions: one, an Open Convention that would allow the delegates to alter, replace or nullify the Constitution; and two, a "Limited" or "SINGLE ISSUE" Convention in which the States define in their Calling instrument on Congress the terms, conditions and agenda of the Convention thereby restricting the business at the Convention. All CITIZEN INITIATIVES' Legislative Calls are for a "SINGLE ISSUE" Federal Convention that gives delegates the authority to decide only one issue – Should the proposed Amendment as written be sent to the States for ratification? No other business can be discussed or proposed for discussion by delegates at the Convention. In either case, the States still have to ratify whatever the Convention proposes. *The "SINGLE ISSUE" Federal Convention, as defined in the Legislative Calls of 34 States, becomes binding on the Calling States and prevents the Convention from becoming an Open Convention. Because 34 Calling States control the business at the Convention, rogue elements will not be able to redirect the Convention. Non-Calling States can send delegates to a "SINGLE ISSUE" Federal Convention, but the delegates must agree to the terms, conditions and agenda at the Convention, as mandated in the Calling instruments, before they will be admitted to the Convention. Non-Calling States will have full voting and participation rights at the Convention as long as they do not violate the terms of the Legislative Calls. Non-Calling States will not be able to extract from the Convention powers that the Calling States did not grant in their Legislative Calls.*

CITIZEN INITIATIVES is providing to the Several States a 13 page Legislative Call for each of 19 proposed Amendments.

We can protect and install righteous laws through "SINGLE ISSUE" Federal Conventions. We can regain the economic and moral high ground in America. What is most promising about "SINGLE ISSUE" Conventions is the fact that once a proposed Amendment has been ratified by ¾ of the States both Congress and the Supreme Court are bound by it. We *can* control the direction of the Convention and government. Because we are a Republic (Article IV, 4), the States control the direction of our Constitutional Republic. Later in this book you will learn how the States actually controlled the direction of the Constitutional Convention. You will also find a copy of a Legislative Call that 34 States must approve for each proposed Amendment before a "SINGLE ISSUE" Federal Convention can be convened. Once 34 States complete their Legislative Calls on Congress for a "SINGLE ISSUE" Federal Convention, Congress is forced to convene the Convention.

The following list shows the names for each proposed Amendment that is to be voted on by delegates at each of 19 "SINGLE ISSUE" Federal Conventions:

Active Amendments:

- **BALANCED FEDERAL BUDGET AMENDMENT**
- **LEGAL IMMIGRATION AMENDMENT**
- **FREE MARKETS AMENDMENT**
- **TRUTH IN MEDIA AMENDMENT**
- **TRADITIONAL MARRIAGE AMENDMENT**
- **ENERGY AMENDMENT**
- **SCHOOL VOUCHER AMENDMENT**
- **TRUTH IN EDUCATION AMENDMENT**
- **CONSTITUTIONAL HISTORY AMENDMENT**
- **UNBORN CHILD AMENDMENT**
- **PARENTAL RIGHTS AMENDMENT**
- **AMERICAN SOVEREIGNTY AMENDMENT**
- **PROPERTY RIGHTS AMENDMENT**

Future Amendments:

- **RESTORING THE 2ND AMENDMENT**
- **HEALTH CARE CHOICE AMENDMENT**
- **STATES RIGHTS AMENDMENT**
- **PRAYER IN AMERICA AMENDMENT**
- **TERM LIMITS AMENDMENT**
- **POLITICAL CORRECTNESS AMENDMENT**

CITIZEN INITIATIVES will be studying other Amendments that may be added to this list. The reader (regardless of political affiliation) is invited to help us by sending comments and ideas to director@citizeninitiatives.org. In the following Chapters copies of each of the proposed Amendments are presented along with explanatory notes. We still have available to us a peaceful way to redirect the affairs of our government. We *can* protect existing righteous laws and install new ones through "SINGLE ISSUE" Federal Conventions. America's moral compass and God fearing sensibilities have not been destroyed by our adversaries. The people have the ability to revive this nation by restoring righteous principles through its Constitution. We can reignite the torch that has for 200 years been the envy of nations.

DECLARATION OF INDEPENDENCE

"When in the Course of human events it becomes necessary for one people to dissolve the political bands which have connected them with another, and to assume among the powers of the earth, the separate and equal station to which the Laws of Nature and of Nature's God entitle them, a decent respect to the opinions of mankind requires that they should declare the cause which impel them to the separation. We hold these truths to be self-evident, that all men are created equal, that they are endowed by their Creator with certain unalienable Rights, that among these are Life, Liberty and the pursuit of Happiness. That to secure these rights, Governments are instituted among Men, deriving their just powers from the consent of the governed, That whenever any Form of Government becomes destructive of these ends, it is the Right of the People to alter or to abolish it, and to institute new Government, laying its foundation on such principles and organizing its powers in such form, as to them shall seem most likely to effect their Safety and Happiness..."

DECLARATION OF INDEPENDENCE July 4, 1776

CHAPTER 1

A CONSTITUTIONAL DISCUSSION

In the late 1700's conversations about religion and politics were commonplace in America. Farmers, statesmen, preachers, teachers, professionals, writers, journalists, politicians, common laborers and others thought it quite proper to discuss the future of the Colonies and the risks associated with declaring independence from England. Underlying much of the rhetoric of that day were concerns over religious freedom and political independence. The word "posterity" was frequently used by our Founding Fathers in their treatises and letters. In fact, America's future generations were addressed in the first paragraph of the United States Constitution:

"We the People of the United States, in Order to form a more perfect Union, establish Justice, insure domestic Tranquility, provide for the common defence, promote the general Welfare, and secure the Blessings of Liberty to ourselves and our Posterity, do ordain and establish this Constitution for the United States of America."

Posterity to our Founding Fathers was of primary concern and it was their intention to provide for future generations the Blessings of Liberty that they themselves fought to secure. Future generations would carry their names, their physical, emotional and psychological characteristics, their religious faith, their philosophies, their dreams, their ideals and more. Their children and grandchildren would be recipients of their love and devotion. Protecting their posterity was central in their planning. There was immense pride, for both men and women, in their heritage. Leaving for their posterity a $14.3 trillion debt, legalized abortion, removal of the Ten Commandments and prayer from the public arena would have been abhorrent to them.

There are fundamental Rights given to men by God that are not negotiable. The Right to Life is one of them. No individual has been authorized by the Lord to kill another human being, whether born or unborn makes no difference. Government's first duty is to protect all human life. Another fundamental Right is the Blessings of Liberty to ourselves and our Posterity. What has happened to America? That we have so lightly regarded our heritage by allowing 1/3rd of our Unborn babies to be killed in the womb is inexplicable! That we have allowed each child who survives the womb to inherit a debt of $47,600 is unconscionable! That we have stolen from our posterity their Constitutional and Christian/Judeo heritage is damnable!

" . . . We hold these truths to be self-evident, that all men are created equal, that they are endowed by their Creator with certain unalienable Rights, that among these are Life, Liberty and the pursuit of Happiness. That to secure these rights, *Governments are instituted among Men, deriving their just powers from the consent of the governed*, That whenever any Form of Government becomes destructive of these ends, it is the Right of the People to alter or to abolish it, and to institute new Government, laying its foundation on such principles and organizing its powers in such form, as to them shall seem most likely to effect their Safety and Happiness..."

DECLARATION OF INDEPENDENCE July 4, 1776

Reclaiming our God given Constitutional Rights is still possible, but it won't be done through the Courts, Congress, Executive Branch or politicians. It can only be done *by the people through prayer, confession of our sins and repentance before Almighty God* and through "SINGLE ISSUE" Federal Conventions.

"If we confess our sin, he is faithful and just to forgive us sins, and to cleanse us from all unrighteousness."
I John 1:9

"If my people, which are called by my name, shall humble themselves, and pray, and seek my face, and turn from their wicked ways; then will I hear from heaven, and will forgive their sin, and will heal their land."

Consider the God fearing heritage of our Founders and early leaders:[3]

"My God! How little do my countrymen know what precious blessings they are in possession of, and which no other people on earth enjoy!"
THOMAS JEFFERSON

"Indeed, I tremble for my country when I reflect that God is just, and that His justice cannot sleep forever."
THOMAS JEFFERSON

"The first and almost the only Book deserving of universal attention is the Bible"
JOHN QUINCY ADAMS

"No people can be bound to acknowledge and adore the invisible hand which conducts the affairs of men more than the people of the United States. Every step by which they have advanced to the character of an independent nation seems to have been distinguished by some token of providential agency ... We ought to be no less persuaded that the propitious smiles of heaven cannot be expected on a nation that disregards the eternal rules of order and right, which heaven itself has ordained."
GEORGE WASHINGTON

"Whereas it is the duty of all nations to acknowledge the providence of Almighty God, to obey his will, to be grateful for his benefits, and humbly implore His protection and favor..."
GEORGE WASHINGTON

"It is the duty of nations, as well as of men, to owe their dependence upon the overruling power of God and to recognize the sublime truth announced in the Holy Scriptures and proven by all history, that those nations only are blessed whose God is the Lord."
ABRAHAM LINCOLN

"The moral principles and percepts contained in the Scriptures ought to form the basis of all our civil constitutions and laws. All the miseries and evils which men suffer from vice, crime, ambition, injustice, oppression, slavery, and war, proceed from their despising or neglecting the precepts contained in the Bible."

NOAH WEBSTER

"Lastly, our ancestors established their system of government on morality and religious sentiment. Moral habits, they believed, cannot safely be trusted on any other foundation than religious principle, nor any government be secure which is not supported by moral habits."

DANIEL WEBSTER

Alex DeTocqueville, 19th Century French political philosopher and author of Democracy in America visited America in her infancy to find the secret of her greatness. As he traveled from town to town, he talked with many people and asked many questions. He examined our young national government, our schools and centers of business, but could not find in them the reason for our strength. Not until he visited the churches of America and witnessed the pulpits of this land "aflame with righteousness" did he find the secret of our greatness. Returning to France, he summarized his findings: "America is great because America is good; and if America ever ceases to be good, America will cease to be great."

Catherine Millard in her book *Great American Statesmen and Heroes* quotes Patrick Henry from his most famous speech on March 23, 1775 which was delivered at the second Virginia Convention[2]:

"... They tell us, Sir, that we are weak; unable to cope with so formidable an adversary. But when shall we be stronger? Will it be the next week, or the next year? Will it be when we are totally disarmed, and when a British guard shall be stationed in every house? Shall we gather strength by irresolution and inaction? Shall we acquire the means of effectual resistance by lying supinely on your backs, and hugging the delusive phantom of hope, until our enemies shall have bound us hand and foot? Sir, we are not weak, if we make a proper use of the means which the God of nature hath placed in our power. Three millions of people armed in the holy cause of liberty, and in such a country as that which we possess, are invincible by any force which our enemy can send against us. Besides, sir, we shall not fight our battles alone. There is a just God who presides over the destinies of nations; and who will raise up friends to fight our battles for us. The battle, sir, is not to the strong alone; it is to the vigilant, the active, the brave. Besides, sir, we have no election. If we were base enough to desire it, it is now too late to retire from the contest. There is no retreat but in submission and slavery! Our chains are forged! Their clanking may be heard on the plains of Boston! The war is inevitable – and let it come! I repeat it, sir, let it come! It is vane, sir, to extenuate the matter. Gentlemen may cry peace, peace – but there is no peace. The war is actually begun! The next gale that sweeps from the North will bring to our ears the clash of resounding arms! Our brethren are already in the field! Why stand we here idle? What is it that gentlemen wish? What would they have? Is life so dear, or peace so sweet, as to be purchased at the price of chains and slavery? ***Forbid it, Almighty God! I know not what course others may take; but as for me, give me liberty, or give me death!***"

This was the cry that heralded the American Revolution.

May God enable us to herald a new American Revolution that will reclaim America from God defying, America hating, anti-Constitutionalists who have denigrated our nation into a cesspool of degenerate laws and licentious behavior. Almighty God has provided us with the requisite authority to Reclaim America through SINGLE ISSUE Federal Conventions.

It is apparent everywhere that we have become a very selfish, unthankful people majoring in frivolous trivia rather than substantive matters. We have failed miserably to train up successive generations in the biblical heritage we have inherited. Too many in America are deathly scared of anything religious. They are totally ignorant of the fact that the moral fabric of America was formed by Christians. The Bible has never threatened America. It has helped to build it. Consider the following: [3]

1. The American Sunday School Movement was the Churches way to pass on its heritage to future generations. The Churches mission was undergirded with the spirit of patriotism through Sunday School education. Many of America's patriots were supporters of the concept of training up the next generation through Sunday Schools. One supporter was Dr. Benjamin Rush, a signer of the Declaration of Independence and the most eminent physician in his generation. Bushrod Washington, nephew of George Washington and Vice President of the American Sunday School Union, wrote the most widely circulated book on George Washington. Another officer was John Marshall, Chief Justice of the United States Supreme Court. Pennsylvania Governor John Pollock, Vice President of the American Sunday School Union and director of the United States Mint first inscribed on our coins the motto, "In God We Trust." Francis Scott Key, who wrote *The Star Spangled Banner*, was a manager and Vice President.

2. Christians in earlier years planted many of America's colleges: Northwestern University of Chicago (founded by Methodists), University of California at Berkeley (founded by Presbyterians), Harvard University (founded in 1638 by Puritans), Yale (founded in 1701 by Christians in Connecticut), Princeton (founded in 1746 by Evangelical Christians), plus Columbia, William and Mary, and many other Christian Colleges.

3. The phrase *"In God We Trust."* appears opposite the President of the Senate and inscribed in marble behind the Speaker of the House of Representatives.

4. Above the head of the Chief Justice of the Supreme Court are *The Ten Commandments.* At each opening session the Court Crier declares: *"God save the United States and the Honorable Court."*

5. On the top of the Washington Monument are the words: *"Praise be to God."*

6. Numerous quotations from the Scripture are inscribed on the walls of The Library of Congress. One such inscription says:

"What doth the Lord require of thee, but to do justly and love mercy and walk humbly with thy God." (Micah 6:8) Another says: *"The light shineth in darkness, and the darkness comprehendeth it not."* (John 1:5)

On the Jefferson Memorial, Thomas Jefferson still speaks: *"God who gave us life gave us liberty, Can the liberties of a nation be secure when we have removed a conviction that these liberties are the gift of God? Indeed I tremble for my country when I reflect that God is just, that his justice cannot sleep forever."* Senator Robert Byrd of West Virginia cites these words of Jefferson as *"a forceful and explicit warning that to remove God from this country will destroy it."*

7. Inscribed on the Lincoln Memorial are these words: *"That this nation, under God, shall have a new birth of freedom, and that government of the people, by the people, for the people, shall not perish from the earth."* Lincoln continues: *"As was said 3000 years ago, so it still must be said, "The judgments of the Lord are true and righteous altogether."*

8. The Supreme Court in 1892 in its Church of The Holy Trinity v. United States said: *"Our laws and our institutions must necessarily be based upon and embody the teachings of The Redeemer of mankind. It is impossible that it should be otherwise; and in this sense and to this extent our civilization and our institutions are emphatically Christian . . . This is a religious people. This is historically true. From the discovery of this continent to the present hour, there is a single voice making this affirmation . . . we find everywhere a clear recognition of the same truth . . . These, and many other matters which might be noticed, add a volume of unofficial declarations to the mass of organic utterances that this is a Christian nation."*

If you are a Constitutional patriot you must understand that we have one option left for peacefully reclaiming America to its founding and God given righteous standards. That option can be found in Article V and IV, Section 4 of the United States Constitution. The Founders empowered future generations to reestablish the venerable principles left to us and our posterity through the Constitution. SINGLE ISSUE" Federal Conventions that address one Amendment at a time is the only safe way to protect the splendor of our Constitution. We can reinstate the God fearing sole America once had.

STATES AND CITIZENS CONSTITUTIONAL RIGHTS

Amendment IX

"The enumeration in the Constitution, of certain rights, shall not be construed to deny or disparage others retained by the people."

The Constitution guarantees that when a specific right is not enumerated, it is retained by the people. There are many constitutional rights, both enumerated and unenumerated, that have been stripped away because of flawed rulings by the Supreme Court and Congressional legislation:

- economic rights
- posterity rights
- free speech rights
- property rights
- Unborn Child's right to life
- father's right to a live heritage
- grandparent's right to a live heritage
- due process rights
- criminal defendants rights
- religious rights
- procreation rights

Amendment X

"The powers not delegated to the United States by the Constitution, nor prohibited by it to the States, are reserved to the States respectively, or to the people."

"SINGLE ISSUE" Federal Conventions are the only way for the States to regain States and citizen Rights that have been usurped by the Federal Government. The following is a partial list of areas in which States Rights have been denied or diminished through Federal regulations, Congressional legislation and Court decisions:

- 2nd Amendment Rights
- Environmental regulations
- Educational mandates
- Busing mandates
- Prayer in public schools and public arena
- State Constitutional powers
- State Legislative powers
- Interstate commerce
- Criminal and civil law
- Health care mandates, etc.

The States can reclaim their Constitutional Rights and powers by joining together and agreeing on selected Amendments to the Federal Constitution and advancing them under the authority reserved to the States in Article V and Article IV, Section 4.

Article V

"The Congress, whenever two thirds of both Houses shall deem it necessary, shall propose Amendments to this Constitution, or, on the Application of the Legislatures of two thirds of the several States, shall call a Convention for proposing Amendments, which, in either Case, shall be valid to all Intents and Purposes, as Part of this Constitution, when ratified by the Legislatures of three fourths of the several States, or by Conventions in three fourths thereof, as the one or the other Mode of Ratification may be proposed by the Congress; Provided that no Amendment which may be made prior to the Year One thousand eight hundred and eight shall in any Manner affect the first and fourth Clauses in the Ninth Section of the first Article; and that no State, without its Consent, shall be deprived of its equal Suffrage in the Senate."

Article IV, Section 4

"The United States shall guarantee to every State in this Union a Republican Form of Government, and shall protect each of them against Invasion; and on Application of the Legislature, or of the Executive (when the Legislature cannot be convened), against domestic Violence."

State Legislatures, not Congress, have the authority to reclaim and protect their Constitutional powers through "SINGLE ISSUE" Federal Conventions. Article IV, Section 4 grants equal authority to every State regardless of population or political influence in Congress. Implied in Article V is the "SINGLE ISSUE" intention of the Founders when they wrote ". . . or, on the Application of the Legislatures of two thirds of the several States, shall call a Convention for *proposing Amendments*. . ." The United States Congress can only propose Amendments to the Constitution. The State Legislatures alone can Call for a Convention for the purpose of amending the Constitution. The Founders gave to the States the option of Calling for a Limited Convention or an Open Convention.

State Legislators are encouraged to email their concerns, proposed Amendments and ideas to director@citizeninitiatives.org. Citizen Initiatives will be advancing "SINGLE ISSUE" Amendments that reinstate States Rights.

CHAPTER 2

SINGLE ISSUE FEDERAL CONVENTIONS

Article V, and the Convention process, were given to us by the Founding Fathers for a time such as this. The Framers anticipated that there would come a time when Congress and the Courts would not willingly address an egregious wrong suffered by the people and gave citizens, through State Legislatures, the authority to remedy the wrong without revolution.

Open vs. "SINGLE ISSUE" Federal Conventions

Some constitutional lawyers argue that Calling for a Convention through State Legislatures carries too great a risk. We intend to cover several of their major points, but first, we would like the reader to consider the following. Assume for the moment that you have $50,000 and want to invest it in a promising growth stock that you are certain will triple in value over the next five years. Before you complete the stock purchase, you wisely go to your attorney asking for his advice. I can guaranty that your attorney will not be as excited about the investment opportunity as you. He will begin his consultation by telling you the reasons why you may lose your money. Some aspects of the deal that he will be concerned about are SEC and environmental regulations, the exchange that lists the stock, the class of stock, the capital structure of the company, questionable market conditions, stock performance, lawsuits against the company, contract issues and more. The reason why he will examine the negative side of your investment opportunity is because that's what attorneys, as a profession, do. If he gave you a glowing report and confirmed your euphoria about the opportunity, he could find himself in violation of the law. If the investment went sour, he of course could lose a client and maybe find himself in the middle of a lawsuit. Attorneys by their very professional nature are negative. They strive to find what is or may be wrong with a matter. That is exactly what many Constitutional lawyers do when they advise their clients on the suitability of "SINGLE ISSUE" Federal Conventions.

Many have been trained in law school to believe "SINGLE ISSUE" Federal Conventions are not possible. Often they have not given the matter serious thought even when they have graduated from law school as Constitutional lawyers. It is the hope of this writer that the reader will use common sense and personal faith when considering how "SINGLE ISSUE" Federal Conventions can empower the people to rebuild the moral and economic foundations of America. We will never rebuild America with flawed Constitutional arguments. We must go beyond the crippling ideas of the past that have prevented the American people from protecting our Constitution and installing righteous laws. We are in a great battle for the survival of Constitutional government of the people, by the people and for the people.

We will begin by examining some of the negative arguments offered by those who oppose "SINGLE ISSUE" Federal Conventions. In the majority of cases, they will view the Convention alternative as too risky, because they do not believe a "SINGLE ISSUE" Convention is possible. Please keep in mind that there are many constitutional advocates who favor the "SINGLE ISSUE" Federal Convention strategy as proposed by CITIZEN INITIATIVES.

1st Negative Argument: The problems are so severe that the Convention method has never been used to amend the United States Constitution.

Answer: The fact that a Constitutional Convention has never been used to amend the Constitution establishes only the fact that we have never Called for a "SINGLE ISSUE" Federal Convention. Virtually, every criticism of the Convention method is based on conjecture. The problems that are considered "so severe" are based on America's transition experience when the Continental Congress agreed to call for a Continental Convention for the purpose of revising the Articles of Confederation. This was a duly authorized function of the Continental Congress and was in response to the innumerable problems the new nation was facing because the national government did not have appropriate authority under the

Articles of Confederation. The transition from the Articles of Confederation to the United States Constitution followed proper constitutional mandates and was not an usurpation of authority by the Constitutional Convention as some have claimed. It was in fact the Congress of the Confederation (created under the Articles of Confederation) that convened the Convention (which was an "Open" Convention) in Philadelphia and forwarded the new Constitution, sent to it by the Philadelphia Convention to State Conventions for ratification. If the Congress of the Confederation was afraid of an Open Convention, it could have created Amendments on its own to address the national crisis and forwarded them to the States for ratification. In such a case there would have been no need for a Convention as proposed by Alexander Hamilton. The logical conclusion we must come to is that the Congress of the Confederation wanted the collective wisdom of the Several States when addressing the needs of a dysfunctional Federal Government. They also understood that convening an Open Convention could change or disband the Articles of Confederation, even though the ostensible reason for convening a Convention was to amend the Articles of Confederation. There was no usurpation of power by the Constitutional Convention over the Congress of Confederation.

2nd Negative Argument: The United States Continental Convention was empowered only to amend the Articles of Confederation, which was the first United States Constitution in effect since Independence. The Continental Convention ignored its limits, wrote a new Constitution contradictory to and totally different from the Articles of Confederation, and stated that when nine States ratified it, it would become America's new Constitution. Thus the 1787 Constitutional Convention was the second revolution because without appropriate permission from the previous government, it revolutionized our system of government. Experts agree that there is no way to limit what a Constitutional Convention might do because it could ignore any limits and offer what it felt might be approved by a sufficient number of States. Nor would the present constitutional requirement that ¾'s of the States have to approve what came out of such a Convention be a limit. The number of States required to approve was determined by the 1787 Convention, not by the Articles of Confederation, which required that all 13 States approve any amendments. Today, a new Convention could state that its proposed Constitution is to become effective upon approval by a mere majority of the States.

Answer: This mixture of fact and fancy has been the core reason why Americans have been paralyzed in their efforts to protect and install righteous laws through "SINGLE ISSUE" Federal Conventions. There are several key points to make in response to this 2nd negative argument:

1. Since Independence, the 13 new States were suffering from a decentralized national government that was not capable of regulating commerce, raising taxes, or supporting war. While questions swirled about the ineffectiveness of the national government, other problems mounted; serious economic woes in the States, a depleted national treasury, paper money was flooding the country, extraordinary inflation, small farmers being thrown into debt prisons and their farms confiscated and sold for taxes, the threat of anarchy, and more. The political and economic climate was ripe for disaster and many wanted solutions.

2. A proposal was offered by James Madison, Jr. and John Tyler in the Virginia Assembly asking that the Continental Congress be given regulatory powers in matters of commerce. The Virginia Assembly devised a plan to invite the Several States to attend a Convention at Annapolis, MD, in September 1786, to discuss commerce problems. James Madison and Alexander Hamilton issued a report on the meeting in Annapolis, calling upon the Congress of the Confederation (created under the Articles of Confederation) to summon delegates from all the States to meet for the purpose of revising the Articles of Confederation.

Article IX, Articles of Confederation

"The United States in Congress assembled shall also be the last resort on appeal in all disputes and differences now subsisting or that hereafter may arise between two or more States concerning boundary, jurisdiction or any other causes whatever; which authority shall always be exercised in the manner following. Whenever the legislative or executive authority or lawful agent of any State in controversy with another shall present a petition to Congress stating the matter in question and praying for a hearing, notice thereof shall be given by order of Congress to the legislative or executive authority of the other State in controversy, and a day assigned for the appearance of the parties by their lawful agents, who shall then be directed to appoint by joint consent, commissioners or judges to constitute a court for hearing and determining the matter in question: but if they cannot agree, Congress shall name three persons out of each of the United States . . ."

Take notice of the fact that James Madison and Alexander Hamilton followed the instructions in Article IX. The Congress of the Confederation had the authority to settle all disputes between the States. Commerce problems between the States was a legitimate matter for Congress to address. Requesting Congress to assemble delegates for a Convention from all the States was within the authority that the Articles gave to Congress.

Article XIII, Articles of Confederation

Every State shall abide by the determination of the United States in Congress assembled, on all questions which by this confederation are submitted to them. And the Articles of this Confederation shall be inviolably observed by every State, and the Union shall be perpetual; nor shall any alteration at any time hereafter be made in any of them; unless such alteration be agreed to in a Congress of the United States, and be afterwards confirmed by the legislatures of every State.

Any alteration (amendment) to the Articles of Confederation would require unanimous ratification by the States: *". . . and be afterwards confirmed by the legislatures of every State."* Because Congress convened an Open Convention it gave the Convention authority to propose whatever alterations it desired. Early on Congress probably intended, *but not required,* the Convention to deliberate on matters of commerce only. It had the authority to require the delegates to limit discussions through an agreement that each State would be required to sign. Congress could have exercised external control by disbanding the Convention once its self imposed limits were violated. It had the final word in deciding if a Convention should be convened at all (Article IX). It did not limit the Convention. As the Convention went forward Congress undoubtedly recognized that there were irreconcilable differences between the States. Remember, any amendment to the Articles of Confederation required unanimous consent. It may have also been comforted when the Convention unanimously agreed to send a new Constitution to the States for ratification. This would explain why Congress cooperated with the Convention when it requested that the proposed Constitution be ratified by State Conventions rather than State Legislatures.

Once again, the Congress of the Confederation had the requisite authority to convene an Open or "SINGLE ISSUE" Convention. There was no mechanism in the Articles of Confederation that allowed the States to Call for and force Congress to convene a Convention. The Articles only provided for Congress to address differences between the States by scheduling hearings or by convening a Convention. THERE WAS NO USURPATION OF POWER BY THE CONGRESS OF THE CONFEDERATION OR BY THE CONVENTION.

Article II, Articles of Confederation

Each state retains its sovereignty, freedom, and independence, and every power, jurisdiction, and right, which is not by this Confederation expressly delegated to the United States, in Congress assembled.

The central reason for the many problems the nation had during Colonial years is the fact that each State was sovereign and unwilling to reconcile its differences for the betterment of the country. Rhode Island is an example of this when it refused to attend the Convention. The Congress was trying to find a way to resolve serious issues within the authority of the Articles and convened a Convention. It wisely did not limit discussions at the Convention because the delegates needed great latitude in finding resolutions to the country's predicament.

Article X, Articles of Confederation

The Committee of the States, or any nine of them, shall be authorized to execute, in the recess of Congress, such of the powers of Congress as the United States in Congress assembled, by the consent of the nine States, shall from time to time think expedient to vest them with; provided that no power be delegated to the said Committee, for the exercise of which, by the Articles of Confederation, the voice of nine States in the Congress of the United States assembled be requisite.

It was not by accident that the Constitutional Convention required nine States to ratify the new Constitution. The Articles required nine States to agree on important matters that would solve national problems.

3. There were 74 delegates appointed to the Convention, but only 55 actually attended the sessions. Rhode Island was the only State to refuse to send delegates to the Convention on the grounds that it was a conspiracy to overthrow the established government. *In fact what Rhode Island did was*

abdicate its authority, under the Articles of Confederation, by not attending the Convention. The Federal Convention refused to be held hostage by Rhode Island's absence and proceeded with its urgent business. This was providential.

4. The following points are important: A) the Federal Convention was duly assembled under the authority given to the Congress of the Confederation by the Articles of Confederation; B) the Congress called for delegates from all 13 States for the purpose of revising the Articles of Confederation; C) it was convened as an *Open* Convention, not a limited one (the Convention was not charged by Congress to restrict its deliberations to specific subject matters, even though the ostensible reason for convening it was to revise the Articles); D) all States had an equal opportunity to participate at the Convention; E) the fact that Rhode Island refused to attend did not disqualify the Convention from being duly Called and convened under Article IX and XIII of the Articles of Confederation.; F) the 12 States, that agreed to attend, recognized that there were serious problems that the Articles of Confederation could not address and something had to be done quickly. To allow one State to prevent the nation from solving its political and economic problems was unacceptable to Congress and the Convention; G) Rhode Island could have sent delegates to the Convention to argue why it was not duly convened. They could have argued against the final draft of the proposed Constitution and cast the sole dissenting vote. They did none of these things; and H) on September 15, 1787 all 12 State delegations, attending the Convention, approved the new Constitution. The new Constitution, was in fact, approved by every State that was willing to attend the Convention. The States did not usurp the authority of Congress or the Articles of Confederation. They unanimously agreed that the Articles had to be disbanded and a new Constitution be ratified to assure the survival of the new nation. After the proposed Constitution was sent to State Conventions for ratification the 12 States that attended the Convention and drafted the

Constitution ratified it (only 9 States were needed). This was not a second revolution, as sum have argued. It had the unanimous consent of all 12 States assembled and duly changed the requirement from every state to 9 states for ratification. This 9 State requirement also shows that the delegates at the Convention were willing to allow 4 States to form their own sovereign nations. Rhode Island would, 2½ years later, become the 13th State to ratify the new Constitution. It did so after the new Congress sent to the States Amendments that we now know as the Bill of Rights. Rhode Island's refusal to attend the Federal Constitutional Convention meant it abdicated its authority under the Articles of Confederation and left the Federal Convention with the full authority it needed to create a new Constitution. Rhode Island had the option of becoming an independent State without obligations under the new Constitution. The transition from the Articles of Confederation to the New Constitution was in compliance with the requirements in the Articles of Confederation.

5. As was pointed out above, the Constitutional Convention was duly formed during a time of political and economic upheaval. It was convened as an *Open* Convention. The Articles did not authorize the States to Call for an Open or "SINGLE ISSUE" Convention. The Congress of the Confederation, of course, had the power to convene either. Under our present Constitution Congress *cannot, on its own, convene a Convention.* All Congress can do is propose Amendments to the States. The States *alone* have the authority to Call for and restrict a Federal Convention. The Congress of the Confederation, on the other hand, believed it had the authority to convene a Convention (Article XIII) without all 13 States making a request. Remember, it was James Madison and Alexander Hamilton who issued a report on the meeting at Annapolis and called upon the Congress of the Confederation (created under the Articles of Confederation) to summon delegates from all the States to meet for the purpose of revising the Articles of Confederation. All 13 States did not directly initiate this Call.

CITIZEN INITIATIVES' Legislative Calls require a quorum of 17 States in order to conduct Convention business. This quorum gives the Calling States greater discretion at the Convention for making sure the Amendment is not voted down. The 34 States making Calls on Congress will undoubtedly be in agreement with the proposed Amendment, thereby giving the Calling States full control at the Convention.

1. The argument that there is no way to control a Federal Convention under our new Constitution is folly. The second paragraph of the proposed Bill or Rights reads:

   "THE Conventions of a number of the States having at the time of their adopting the Constitution, expressed a desire, in order to prevent misconstruction or abuse of its powers, that further declaratory and restrictive clauses should be added: And as extending the ground of public confidence in the Government, will best insure the beneficent ends of its institution."

   In fact, <u>the Constitutional Convention was limited in its authority by the ratifying States</u>. The States wanted their citizens protected from intrusive government and required that the new Congress, as its first order of business, send to the States restrictive Amendments to the proposed Constitution. After the Constitution was ratified and the first Congress convened, it did just that and today we have 10 Amendments, plus one ratified in 1992, that protect the civil liberties of Americans. We call it the Bill of Rights. *If Congress had refused to send the Amendments to the States, the States could have rescinded their ratifications and the nation would have remained under the Articles of Confederation. In fact, the States gave the new Constitution conditional ratifications and retained control of the direction of the Convention and our Republic.* The States alone determine the purpose, agenda and terms of a Federal Convention, not Congress. Even the Convention itself does not have final authority to control the deliberations at the Convention. When the Calling States enter into a binding contract through their Legislative Calls on Congress, the parameters of the deliberations at the Convention are predetermined. This Constitutional authority, which rests in State Legislatures and given to the States by our Founders, is the States most powerful vehicle for *RECLAIMING AMERICA through "SINGLE ISSUE" Federal Conventions.* I pray that the States will not be deceived by flawed legal and Constitutional reasoning and continue to ignore the authority they have in Article V and Article IV, Section 4 of the United States Constitution.

2. Each Legislative Call includes an option for Congress. If it sends the Amendment to the States for ratification voluntarily, without changing the wording of the Amendment, then the States are agreeing to rescind their Calls. For some of the Amendments Congress may do just that in order to avoid being forced to convene a Convention.

The Legislative Calls for each of the Amendments proposed by CITIZEN INITIATIVES will be advanced through "SINGLE ISSUE" Federal Conventions and will be limited by the terms and conditions of a 13 page Legislative Call on Congress. Each Amendment has one Legislative Call that becomes a binding contract between the Calling States.

The following table records the actual ratification votes and dates by State Delegates in State Conventions. Note that Rhode Island ultimately ratified the Constitution on May 29, 1790. This meant that all 13 States ratified the new Constitution making ratification unanimous. There is no issue of usurpation of power by the Constitutional Convention over the Congress of the Confederation or the Articles of Confederation.

Ratification of the U.S. Constitution				
	Date	State	Votes	
			Yes	No
1	December 7, 1787	Delaware	30	0
2	December 12, 1787	Pennsylvania	46	23
3	December 18, 1787	New Jersey	38	0
4	January 2, 1788	Georgia	26	0
5	January 9, 1788	Connecticut	128	40
6	February 6, 1788	Massachusetts	187	168
7	April 28, 1788	Maryland	63	11
8	May 23, 1788	South Carolina	149	73
9	June 21, 1788	New Hampshire	57	47
10	June 25, 1788	Virginia	89	79
11	July 26, 1788	New York	30	27
12	November 21, 1789	North Carolina	194	77
13	May 29, 1790	Rhode Island	34	32

The Congress of the Confederation, under the authority of the Articles of Confederation, courageously made it possible for the nation to have a balanced government that shares power between the Executive Branch, the States, the Courts and Congress. This balance has now shifted in favor of Congress and the Courts. Only the people can reclaim our States Rights and Civil Rights by amending the United States Constitution through "SINGLE ISSUE" Federal Conventions.

Private Conventions: The Convention process is used by many private organizations, Church denominations, para-church ministries and Unions. When a denomination, for example, decides that it wants to consider an amendment to its constitution, it does not convene an Open convention.   It limits the discussion to a specific issue and the vote taken deals only with the proposed amendment. In effect the denomination controls the convention by predetermining the terms, conditions and agenda at the convention. This methodology fits State Legislatures perfectly when calling for a "SINGLE ISSUE" Federal Convention through Legislative Calls.

RECLAIMING AMERICA

CHAPTER 3

INCREMENTAL LEGISLATION

Why It Has Failed for Christian Conservatives

Incremental Legislation is the strategy individuals and organizations use to seek a redress of specific grievances and issues through State Legislatures, Congress, State Courts, Federal Courts, and regulatory agencies. The assumption is that their grievances can be addressed incrementally which will eventually create new laws that conform to the advocates desires or chip away and overturn adverse Court decisions, State and Congressional legislation, regulatory rules, etc. For some issues such as Same Sex Marriage, Homosexual Rights, Equal Employment Opportunity, Feminist Rights, Abortion Rights, Minority Rights, etc. the strategy has worked well. Advocates of these issues have been passionate in their efforts to achieve their goals. For Christian Conservative groups advocating Right to Life, Traditional Marriage, School Vouchers, Balanced Federal Budget, Parental Rights, Property Rights, 2nd Amendment Rights, etc. Incremental Legislation has failed. Advocates for these kind of issues have been timid and poorly motivated for the political and legal battles required to succeed. Why has Incremental Legislation worked for some groups and not others?

Sixty years ago our nation practiced a morality that was centered in Christian virtue. Americans had a reverential fear of God and great respect for the teachings of Jesus Christ the son of the living God. There was ingrained in the people the conviction that men are made in the image of God which gives them immeasurable value. Sanctity of human life was God given. It was regarded as a natural Right that must never be violated no matter how convincing advocates of abortion argued to the contrary. It was commonly believed that there is a heaven and hell and that there are severe consequences for evil choices. Americans also believed that our laws and life styles should be based on God's righteous laws and Scriptural teachings. There have always been some who took pleasure in gratifying their flesh while ridiculing moral virtue. However, today, Christian virtue is looked upon with great distain almost everywhere (Federal Courts, Congress, State Courts, State Legislatures, the media and even among the general population). There are several reasons for this:

1. Our educational institutions, as a result of the Monkey Trial (Scope v. State of Tennessee 1926), adopted the idea that Darwinism should replace creationism in public schools. They advanced the idea that men are creatures that accidentally crawled out of a primordial ooze and eventually developed into thinking animals. "Created in the image of God" was discredited because it interfered with the new man made "science" of *evolution*. Absolute values that determine truth were replaced with situational ethics, relativism, and delusional fables and imaginations. Upon this faulty premise was developed an academic discipline "evolution" that today regards itself as the *only* factual answer to the questions of the ages. In fact, evolution is a theory not a science and makes innumerable flawed assumptions about the origins of the earth and universe. Christian doctrine, God and the Bible have been discarded as fanciful notions of the unlearned. As a consequence, our children for the last 50 years have been told that Darwin's rationale is "science" and the Biblical account of creation was unsubstantiated religion. Christian morality has been denigrated by our institutions of higher learning which permeated into our politics, courts and society. There has been a unified chorus of criticism against America's Christian heritage. At the same time Christian leaders recoiled with silence, leaving the Church and American society defenseless against anti-Christian propaganda which weakened the family, America's institutions and our Biblical values.

> "Train up a child in the way he should go and, when he is old, he will not depart from it."
>
> PROVERBS 22:6

America has lost its Christian character because the Church refused to engage her enemies by proclaiming not only the Gospel of salvation but the Gospel of righteous laws. As a result she abandoned the culture and future generations.

> "Go ye, therefore, and teach all nations, baptizing them in the name of the Father, and of the Son, and of the Holy Ghost. <u>Teaching them to observe all things whatsoever I have commanded you; and, lo, I am with you always. Even unto the end of the world. Amen."</u>
> MATTHEW 28:19,20

The Great Commission is really a two sided coin: one, "Go ye, therefore, and teach all nations, baptizing them . . ."; and two, "Teaching them to observe all things . . . ". The American Church has almost universally avoided the second part which is to ". . . teach them to observe all things . . . " Somehow the Church has convinced itself that proclaiming the first part was sufficient. The righteous laws of the land, which the Church inherited from our Founders, would somehow be protected by preaching only the first part of the Great Commission. The fact is that Christians have been locked in a battle for the minds, souls and lives of men since the first Century. The heritage we have undeservedly received brings with it a trail of blood and human suffering that was paid for by other generations of Christian men. The faith that was passed on to us came at a terrible price. How dare we presumptuously and sheepishly ignore the warfare around us by not engaging our adversaries in legal, political, legislative and judicial battles to protect and install righteous laws. The unjustified value Christians have placed on their personal possessions and comforts, which will all be burned up in the end, is the great sin of the American Church. We have left for our posterity a cesspool of unrighteous laws that our children will find impossible to reverse.

2. For decades preachers have taught that we cannot legislate morality. What a shame that these men have been allowed to mislead the Church without rebuttal. Literally every

righteous law, in America, has its roots in Christian morality (e.g. "Thou shalt not kill.", "Thou shalt not covet.", "Thou shalt not steal.", "Thou shalt not commit adultery.", etc.). What you cannot legislate is spirituality (e.g. "Thou shalt love thy neighbor."). These are acts that require volition on the part of an individual that the law cannot control. Laws (including Constitutional Amendments) can be used to codify a moral value that society wants enforced, such as, "Thou shalt not steal." They can also be used to create a new morality such as a woman's right to an abortion under the guise of reproductive privacy. In the later case the moral values enforced for generations to protect Unborn human life were Constitutionally overturned and a new morality created contrary to the will of the people. Laws can deny, protect or create new moral values in a society.

3. Virtually all laws establish some degree of morality whether righteous or unrighteous depends on the values of those promoting, legislating or adjudicating them. Much of our morality was passed on to us through English Common Law[4]. Statutes try to codify every conduct of men. Common Law uses community values and court precedents along with a great deal of Christian tradition to determine what is legal and illegal behavior. Today cunning advocates of anti-Christian teachings have nullified almost all Christian morality through statutes and Incremental Legislation while Church leaders have been asleep.

God has not been remiss in telling the Church what its duties are in society. You can find "Teaching them to observe all things..." in the rest of the Bible. For example:

> "Who will rise up for me against the evildoers? Or who will stand up for me against the workers of iniquity?... Shall the throne of iniquity have fellowship with thee, which frameth mischief by a law?"
>
> PSALM 94:16,20

The Church should have been engaged in a dual battle: one, preaching the Gospel, and two, fighting for the protection and installation of God's righteous laws in the States, Congress and Judiciary. As a result of the Churches' sins of omission, Incremental Legislation was a success, but for the adversaries of Christian morality.

4. Through cunning efforts by evolutionists, environmentalists, populists, feminists, liberals, progressives, socialists, communists, atheists, humanists and new age adherents - including beatniks, flower power people and free love advocates from the 60's, Incremental Legislation became a major force in American politics. These groups developed new ways to advance their ideologies through advocacy groups like the ACLU, Sierra Club, National Organization of Women, abortion rights groups, anti-religionists advocates, regulatory agencies and others. Today these Incremental Legislationists have succeeded in taking prayer and Bible reading out of public schools, they have forged legislation that restricts or prevents the preaching of the Gospel in public places, removed the "Ten Commandments" and nativity scene from public property, gave American women the Constitutional right, without ratification by the States, to kill her and the father's child in the womb with impunity, made white men the hated majority by minorities and woman, designed environmental laws that dramatically restrict the exercise of Constitutional Rights, especially property rights, and much more.

5. While these anti-Christian efforts were going forward, leaders in the Church and para-church organizations retreated from the battle in a similar way to that which occurred in Germany during the 30's and 40's. Instead of the Church in Germany opposing Hitler and his National Socialists, she rationalized that it was not her battle and cowardly rejected the appeals of some who wanted her help to stop the evils that were coming against the German people. The Church never came to the rescue of persecuted Jews and selected minority groups who were chosen for extermination. There is a striking similarity to the Church in

America that has refused to fight for the God given Constitutional Right to life for Unborn Children. Tax exempt status is not an allowable excuse with God. Refusing to protect and install righteous laws because the Church has been called to a higher calling will not excuse her. Deliberate disobedience of "Thou shalt not kill!" by allowing 48 million babies to perish, which are God's heritage, will echo in the halls of heaven demanding God's justice. The Word of God will be God's standard when judging our sins of omission and commission:

> "Blessed is the nation whose God is the Lord; and the people whom he hath chosen for his own inheritance."
>
> PSALM 33:13

> "Righteousness exalteth a nation, but sin is a reproach to any people."
>
> PROVERBS 14:34

> "None calleth for justice, nor any pleadeth for truth: they trust in vanity, and speak lies; they conceive mischief, and bring forth iniquity."
>
> ISAIAH 59:4

6. Because the American Church and para-church ministries refused to protect and install righteous laws through aggressive advocacy in State Legislatures, State Courts, U.S. Congress, and Judiciary her Incremental Legislative efforts have been tepid. Couple this tepidity with restrictive IRS requirements for tax exempt organizations, inhibiting doctrines that claim the Church is called to preach only the Gospel, and the claim that the Church can't get involved in political or social issues and we begin to understand why her efforts have been and remain sorrowfully ineffective.

7. Our Constitution does not condemn people of other religions. In fact, it protects their God given right to practice their religion of choice. Christian men and women from the inception of this country (starting with the Mayflower in

1620) forged the principle that one's faith was a matter of personal conviction. However, what our Christian ideals and Constitution must not allow is for non Christian groups to jettison our Christian/Judeo heritage through Incremental Legislation and Constitutional Amendments. Christians created a nation that allows for diversity, not domination or denigration of our Christian heritage and values. These very values give non-Christians the right to worship as they please in America.

Amendment I, United States Constitution

Congress shall make no law respecting an establishment of religion, or prohibiting the free exercise thereof; or abridging the freedom of speech, or of the press; or the right of the people peaceably to assemble, and to petition the Government for a redress of grievances.

The idea that Incremental Legislation can be a successful strategy to overturn decisions like Roe vs. Wade is mistaken. When the Supreme Court decides a Constitutional issue, only a Constitutional Amendment initiated by Congress or a "SINGLE ISSUE" Convention can permanently nullify the Court's decision. It is true that the Supreme Court can overturn its own decisions, but that is very unlikely. On the other hand, a favorable decision by the Supreme Court through Incremental Legislative efforts could be a disaster for the States. For example, if Roe vs. Wade was overturned, the 50 States would have to decide separately the Unborn's Right to Life. The resulting confusion could leave abortion rights in many States. The Pro Life States could enact laws that differ in degree of protection that is afforded the Unborn. It would be virtually impossible to uniformly protect the Unborn in all States. Only a Constitutional Amendment granting the Unborn "Personhood" would universally protect the Unborn in every State. For all these reasons Incremental Legislation is a flawed strategy for Christian Conservatives when dealing with God given natural Rights that must be universally and permanently protected. Such Rights are not negotiable and codifying them in the Constitution is our best way to protect the Unborn Child and our posterity. This scenario also applies to other God given rights Conservatives need to address.

Even if we win a case in the Courts or succeed to install a new law in the States or Congress, the final arbitrator is always the United States Supreme Court. Congress and the States cannot overturn Supreme Court decisions. Given the liberal and progressive tendencies of the Supreme Court over the last 50 years, it's improbable that our causes will be confirmed. Only "SINGLE ISSUE" Federal Conventions can codify our Constitutional Rights. This is not to argue that we must abandon Incremental Legislative efforts entirely, even though they usually provide only temporary victories. The battle for righteous laws must go on in local, county, State and national forums. We must elect and reelect political candidates who support our causes. Judicial judges must be CONSTITUTIONAL CONSTRUCTIONISTS so future court battles don't alter our "SINGLE ISSUE" Federal Convention victories.

Incremental Legislative efforts must also be used to help instruct each generation of the blessings it inherited and its duty to protect and propagate that heritage.

Finally the Church must abandon its self imposed inhibitions and begin in earnest to fight for righteous laws in the Courts, State legislatures and Congress.

CHAPTER 4

STATE AND NATIONAL STRATEGIES

```
┌─────────────────────────────┐
│     CITIZEN INITIATIVES      │
│      State & National        │
│        Strategies            │
└─────────────────────────────┘
```

STATE INITIATIVES	STATE INITIATIVES	CONGRESSIONAL INITIATIVES
24 Initiative States placing Legislative Calls on Ballots	Lobbying State Legislatures for Legislative Calls	Lobbying Congress Individual Amendments

STATE INITIATIVES	JUDICIAL INITIATIVES	PRESIDENTIAL INITIATIVE
Redress Petitions to State Legislators	Individual & Class Action Law Suits	Lobbying White House for Help in States & Congress

CITIZEN INITIATVES is a multi faceted political, legal and Constitutional effort to place as much pressure on State Legislators and Congress as possible. Our ultimate objective is to secure Legislative Calls from 34 States for each proposed Amendment. At the same time we will be lobbying Congress to send each Amendment to the States for ratification voluntarily. Congress may do so in order to avoid being forced into convening a "SINGLE ISSUE" Federal Convention. The States are agreeing in their Legislative Calls to rescind their Calls if Congress sends the Amendment to the States for ratification before 34 States complete their Calls. Judicial efforts are also being planned to use the Courts on behalf of each selected Amendment as seems appropriate and wise.

STATE INITIATIVES

Initiative and Referenda States

Many States allow citizens to adopt laws or amend State Constitutions through the ballot. Initiative States are States where citizens have the right to place, on the ballot, a proposed law or amendment to the State Constitution. Referenda States are States where citizens have the right to reject laws or amendments to the Constitution that the Legislatures have enacted. The Initiative process is used more frequently and is the more powerful of the two.

There is no national Initiative process for amending the United States Constitution. Amending the United States Constitution must be done through the State Legislatures and Congress.

There are 24 States that have some form of Direct or Indirect Initiative process for their citizens. Of these, 21 States allow Direct or Indirect Statutes to be proposed by the citizenry.

Direct Initiative States allow citizens to propose constitutional amendments or statutes on the election ballot without legislative approval.

Indirect Initiative States require citizens to submit the proposed constitutional amendment or statute to the Legislature, during a regular legislative session, before placing it on the election ballot. If the Legislature refuses to approve the amendment or statute, or if it alters the wording and meaning, the citizens have the right to continue with their petition drive to qualify for the ballot without Legislature approval. Some States allow the Legislature to place an alternate amendment or statute on the ballot alongside the one proposed by its citizens.

Popular Referendum States give the people the right to refer legislation enacted by the Legislature to the people to accept or reject at the ballot.

Legislative Referendum States require the Legislature or duly authorized State agency to place amendments or statutes on the ballot for the people to decide. All States, but Delaware, require constitutional amendments proposed by the Legislature to be placed on the ballot for the citizenry to decide.

States where some form of Initiative or Popular Referendum is available	Date process was adopted	Type of process		Type of Initiative process available		Type of Initiative process used to propose Constitutional amendments		Type of Initiative process used to propose States laws	
		Initiative	Popular Referendum	Const'l Amendment	Statute	Direct Amend.	Indirect Amend.	Direct Statute	Indirect Statute
Alaska	1956	X	X		X			X	
Arizona	1911	X	X	X	X	X		X	
Arkansas	1910	X	X	X	X	X		X	
California	1911/66	X	X	X	X	X		X	
Colorado	1912	X	X	X	X	X		X	
Florida	1972	X		X		X			
Idaho	1912	X	X		X			X	
Illinois	1970	X		X		X			
Kentucky	1910		X		X				
Maine	1908	X	X		X				X
Maryland	1915		X						
Massachusetts	1918	X	X	X	X		X		X
Michigan	1908	X	X	X	X	X			X

Mississippi	1914/92	X		X			X		
Missouri	1908	X	X	X	X	X		X	
Montana	1904/72	X	X	X	X	X		X	
Nebraska	1912	X	X	X	X	X		X	
Nevada	1905	X	X	X	X	X			
New Mexico	1911		X						X
No. Dakota	1914	X	X	X	X	X		X	X
Ohio	1912	X	X	X	X	X			X
Oklahoma	1907	X	X	X	X	X		X	
Oregon	1902	X	X	X	X	X		X	
So. Dakota	1898/88	X	X	X	X	X		X	
Utah	1900/17	X	X		X			X	X
Washington	1912	X	X		X			X	X
Wyoming	1968	X	X		X			X	
Totals	**27**	**24**	**24**	**18**	**21**	**16**	**2**	**16**	**7**

STATE STRATEGIES

Initiative States: Before a State Constitutional Amendment, or State Statute, can qualify for a State ballot, a percentage of the voters who voted in the previous election have to sign an Initiative petition. Each Initiative State determines the percentage that is needed to qualify for the next election ballot. Usually States require 5% to 10% of qualified voters to sign the petition. CITIZEN INITIATIVES plans to place on State ballots a Statute requiring the Legislature to make a Call on Congress to convene selected "SINGLE ISSUE" Federal Conventions when the State Legislators refuse to do so voluntarily. We will not be attempting to amend State Constitutions. We will, however, lobby Initiative State Legislatures with Redress Petitions in the hopes of convincing the Legislatures to make the Call on Congress before our State Initiative qualifies for the ballot.

Legislative States: "Redress of Grievances" petitions will be used to direct Legislative States to make a Call on Congress to convene the selected "SINGLE ISSUE" Federal Convention. Lobbying the Legislatures, in each of these Legislative States, will also be necessary. When a State Legislature is unwilling to make a Call, they will be directed to place the issue on the State ballot for the voters to decide. Many of these Legislative States want their States and citizens Rights reinstated. These facts will work in our favor in many of the 50 States.

CONGRESSIONAL STRATEGIES

Both Houses of Congress: Signed "Redress of Grievances" petitions from all 50 States will be sent to Congress directing Congress to send each proposed Amendment to State Legislatures for ratification before they are forced to convene a Convention. Congress will not want to be forced by State Legislatures to convene a Convention. As the Calls from the States begin to mount, Congress will see the writing on the wall for many of the proposed Amendments and voluntarily send the Amendment to State Legislatures for ratification. As long as Congress has not changed the wording of the proposed Amendment, and acts before 34 States make their Calls, CITIZEN INITIATIVES will work with the States to rescind their Calls for a Convention.

Presidential Efforts: The President of the United States has no constitutional role in the Convention process. However, he can exert great pressure on Congress to send the proposed Amendment to State Legislatures for ratification, before Congress is forced by the States to convene a Convention. CITIZEN INITIATIVES will be working with the Administration to secure the President's support on selected Amendments.

Individual and Class Action Lawsuits: CITIZEN INITIATIVES will consider individual and class action law suits against entities that are blocking or preventing citizens from exercising their Constitutional Rights. All of the proposed Amendments have legal elements that can provide meritorious appellate reviews.

The Constitutional Convention process is the ONLY way provided in the United States Constitution for the States, and American citizens, to correct an egregious wrong that Congress and the Courts have refused to address.

VOTING STRATEGY

The percentage of votes that are needed to win a ballot Initiative can range from 9% to 49.2% of the total vote cast. The reason for this is the fact that not all voters vote for Initiative or Referenda issues. Voter turnout in Presidential years is substantially higher than in Congressional years. The following data shows approximate voting results in Initiative and Referenda States in recent Presidential years. The number of voters who would vote for a ballot Initiative in a Congressional year is considerably lower than the results shown in the following table. This fact should fare well for CITIZEN INITIATIVES and proposed Legislative Calls for a "SINGLE ISSUE" Federal Conventions. Our strategy will be to qualify for State ballots, where necessary, in non-Presidential years.

APPROXIMATE VOTER TURNOUT
PRESIDENTIAL ELECTIONS

	Total VAP	Total REG	Turnout	% to VAP	% to REG	% of Vote to Win Initiative States*
AL	3,323,678	2,528,963	1,666,272	50.13%	65.89%	
AK	476,215?	473,648	285,560	65.46%	60.29%	11.9%
AZ	3,763,685	2,173,122	1,532,016	40.71%	70.50%	40.1%
AR	1,993,031	1,555,809	921,781	46.25%	59.25%	
CA	24,621,819	15,707,307	10,965,856	44.54%	69.81%	41.8%
CO	3,200,466	2,898,138	1,741,368	54.41%	60.09%	49.2%
CT	2,563,877	1,901,203	1,459,525	56.93%	76.77%	30.9%
DE	589,013	506,397	327,529	55.61%	64.68%	

DC	457,067	354,410	201,894	44.17%	56.97%	
FL	12,336,038	8,752,717	5,963,110	48.34%	68.13%	46.9%
GA	6,017,219	3,859,960	2,596,645	43.15%	67.27%	
HI	915,770	637,349	367,951	40.18%	57.73%	
ID	924,923	728,085	501,615	54.23%	68.90%	45.9%
IL	9,173,842	7,129,026	4,742,108	51.69%	66.52%	31.1%
IN	4,506,089	4,000,809	2,199,305	48.81%	54.97%	
IA	2,192,686	1,841,346	1,315,563	60.00%	71.45%	
KS	1,975,425	1,623,623	1,072,216	54.28%	66.04%	
KY	3,046,951	2,569,168	1,544,187	50.68%	60.10%	35.9%
LA	3,249,177	2,796,551	1,765,656	54.34%	63.14%	
ME	973,685	882,337	651,817	66.94%	73.87%	50.1%
MD	3,940,314	2,715,366	2,023,735	51.36%	74.53%	30.2%
MA	4,849,033	4,008,796	2,702,984	55.74%	67.43%	46.1%
MI	7,342,677	6,859,332	4,232,711	57.65%	61.71%	47.6%
MN	3,632,585	3,265,324	2,438,685	67.13%	74.68%	
MS	2,069,471		994,184	48.04%		?
MO	4,167,519	3,860,672	2,359,906	56.63%	61.13%	44.7%
MT	672,133?	698,260	410,997	61.15%	58.86%	46.7%
NE	1,261,021	1,085,217	697,019	55.27%	64.23%	45.8%
NV	1,486,458	898,347	608,970	40.97%	67.79%	48.7%
NH	926,224	856,519	569,071	61.44%	66.44%	
NJ	6,326,792	4,699,026	3,187,226	50.38%	67.83%	
NM	1,310,472	972,895	598,605	45.68%	61.53%	
NY	14,286,350	11,262,816	6,821,999	47.75%	60.57%	
NC	6,085,266	5,128,662	2,914,990	47.90%	56.84%	
ND	481,351	N/A	288,256	59.88%	N/A	46.2%
OH	8,464,801	7,535,188	4,701,998	55.55%	62.40%	39.5%
OK	2,558,294	2,233,602	1,234,229	48.24%	55.26%	45.6%
OR	2,574,873	1,943,699	1,533,968	59.57%	78.92%	44.7%
PA	9,358,833	7,781,997	4,913,119	52.50%	63.13%	
RI	800,497	655,107	408,783	51.07%	62.40%	40.5%
SC	3,002,371	2,157,006	1,384,253	46.11%	64.17%	

SD	552,195	471,152	316,269	57.27%	67.13%	47.3%
TN	4,290,762	3,400,487	2,076,181	48.39%	61.06%	
TX	14,965,061	12,365,235	6,407,637	42.82%	51.82%	
UT	1,514,471	1,123,238	770,754	50.89%	68.62%	44.2%
VT	461,304	427,354	294,308	63.80%	68.87%	
VA	5,340,253	4,070,581	2,739,447	51.30%	67.30%	
WA	4,380,278	3,335,714	2,487,433	56.79%	74.57%	38.3%
WV	1,405,951	1,067,822	648,124	46.10%	60.70%	
WI	3,994,919	N/A	2,598,607	65.05%	N/A	
WY	364,909	220,062	218,351	59.84%	99.22%	44.2%
Total	209,128,094	158,019,444	105,404,773	50.40%	66.70%	

*Based on voter turnout for initiatives in listed Initiative States (initiative turnout varies depending on many factors, including the type of Initiative being decided).

VAP = Voting Age Population – all persons age 18 or over

REG = Total number of registered voters

VAP data from U.S. Census Bureau. Registered voters from state election offices.

Compilation source David Leip © All Rights Reserved

Legislative States (Non-Initiative States) need approximately the same percentage of votes to win an initiative at the ballot.

In the following United States Map the dark states are those that allow initiatives or statutes to be placed on the ballot by their citizens. The white States allow only State Legislatures to place initiatives or statutes on their ballots.

CITIZEN INITIATIVES plans to concentrate its efforts in smaller more favorable States (Initiative and Legislative), where Legislative Calls will be easier to secure and where the voting population will be more favorable to proposed Amendments. Remember, only 34 States need to make a Call on Congress to convene a "SINGLE ISSUE" Federal Convention. To win at State ballots may require as little as 9% of the State vote to force the hand of State Legislators.

RECLAIMING AMERICA

CHAPTER 5

OTHER ASPECTS OF THE AMENDMENT STRATEGY

Qualifying for State Ballots in Initiative States

When State Legislatures refuse to make a Call on Congress to convene a "SINGLE ISSUE" Federal Convention, CITIZEN INITIATIVES plans to place the Legislative Call on the State ballot. Assuming a specific Legislative Call is approved by the State electorate, then the legislators will be forced to complete the Call on Congress.

CITIZEN INITIATIVES believes Legislative Calls for proposed Amendments should qualify for the ballot in 21 of 24 Initiative States. If all 19 proposed Amendments qualified for the ballot in a given State, then there would be 19 separate initiatives that we would have to qualify for at the ballot. Only 21 of the 24 Initiative States allow for Direct or Indirect Statute Initiatives. By placing the Legislative Call on the ballot in non-Presidential years the victory margin in some States, as was mentioned earlier, could be as low as 9% or registered voters.

We believe that we can win in at least 18 of the 21 Initiative States for most of our proposed Amendments. Of course, some of the 24 Initiative States will not require ballot Initiatives because State Legislators will make their Calls on Congress voluntarily. In Legislative States, we expect at least 16 Legislatures will make the Call. We will be instructing legislators about the facts regarding each proposed Amendment with special emphasis on the opportunity the States have for reclaiming their States Rights in selected "SINGLE ISSUE" Federal Conventions.

There are important advantages for us once aggressive State campaigns begin:

1) State Legislators will begin to understand that "SINGLE ISSUE" Federal Conventions are safe and empower them to become the final arbitrator for selected Constitutional issues.

2) Advertising and publicity campaigns from petition drives and ballot initiatives will greatly help in our efforts to change perceptions for many Americans.

3) State Legislators in Initiative States will not be able to reject ballot results that instruct them to Call on Congress directing Congress to convene a "SINGLE ISSUE" Federal Convention.

4) As a result of the activity and victories in some States, State Legislators from other States will be more attentive to our lobbying and "Redress of Grievances" petitions directing them to make a Call on Congress.

5) In Legislative States that refuse to make a Call voluntarily they will be directed to place the Legislative Call on the next general election ballot for the voters to decide.

6) Congress will be more attentive to our Congressional "Redress of Grievances" petitions directing them to send the proposed Amendment to State Legislatures for ratification. As we get closer to 34 States completing their Calls, Congress will want to avoid convening a Convention and likely send the Amendment to the States for ratification voluntarily;

7) The United States Supreme Court will be listening to our national campaigns and may be more agreeable to read-dressing some of its flawed decisions in past cases. As our court battles and potential Class Action law suits move forward, the Court may be nudged to revisit some of their flawed analysis in matters such as Roe vs. Wade. However, even if the Court reverses itself, it will still be necessary to amend the Constitution thus preventing the Court from revisiting the same issue in the future.

8) On some proposed Amendments the President may be willing to use his influence in Congress and State Legislatures.

CHAPTER 6

CONGRESSIONAL PREROGATIVES IN THE CONVENTION PROCESS

Congressional prerogatives: Congress has great latitude in the eventual composition of an Open Convention. It is greatly restricted by the States when a "SINGLE ISSUE" Federal Convention is being convened.

The Founding Fathers provided two ways for Americans to peacefully modify their Constitution: 1) through proposed Amendments by Congress to the States for ratification; and 2) through Calls for a Convention by State Legislatures (Congress cannot Call for or convene a Convention on its own). The Convention method is a way for the people to judge the Constitution itself.

There are several prerogatives in Article V of the Constitution that Congress retains which provides a modicum of protection from rogue elements at an Open Convention and some influence over a "SINGLE ISSUE" Convention:

1) Congress would have influence and/or control of the timing, place, composition and *maybe* length of an "Open" Convention. Congress could recommend to State Legislatures that a Convention be limited to a period of time. The States would have to confirm this through binding agreements, thereby limiting the Convention to the pre-agreed time period. Other agreements between Congress and the States are also possible in order to convert a Called for Open Convention into a limited or "SINGLE ISSUE" Convention. Congress is not likely to pursue this approach because it would be easier to find agreement with the States on the wording of a State supported Amendment than to try to limit a Called for Convention. Note, these scenarios require the States to initiate a Call for a Convention in order to secure a desired end.

2) Congress will have some influence on the selection of delegates to a Federal Convention through the State and Congressional political process.
3) Once a Convention has completed its work, Congress has the authority to send the proposed amendment(s) to either State Legislatures or State Conventions for ratification. This prerogative can prevent State Legislatures from completely controlling the ratification process.
4) Congress will have some influence on the selection of delegates to State Ratification Conventions. The composition of State delegates at State Conventions will affect the outcome of ratification votes.

Because Article V authorizes Congress to alter the Constitution through proposed Amendments, each Legislative Call for a 'SINGLE ISSUE" Federal Convention will force Congress to decide if it will send our Amendment(s) to the States, voluntarily, for ratification or be forced to convene a Convention. CITIZEN INITIATIVES will be trying to persuade Congress to send it on its own. If Congress refuses to address our grievances and refuses to send our Amendment(s) to the States for ratification, then Legislative Calls from the States for "SINGLE ISSUE" Federal Conventions will go forward.

Whatever a Federal Convention proposes to the States, it must be ratified by ¾'s of the 50 States. There is no option at a "SINGLE ISSUE" Federal Convention to change the ratification requirements. The Constitution cannot be altered in any way except for the language of the proposed Amendment in the States' Legislative Calls. It is virtually impossible for the Constitution to be tampered with through "SINGLE ISSUE" Federal Conventions because the States will have entered into an irrevocable contract between the Calling States that predetermines the terms and conditions at the Convention.

Approximately 5,000 amendments have been proposed by members of Congress over the last 220 years. Only 27 were ratified by the States. Ten of these Amendments are the Bill of Rights. Initially, there were 12 Amendments proposed to the States by our first Congress. Ten were ratified shortly after the States received them and one was ratified in 1992. The ratification process was the Founding Fathers way of making certain that no proposed amendment slips past the States without the States controlling the outcome. They never assumed their Constitution would settle all issues past, present and future. They left the door open for prudent men to resolve future conflicts through Article V and other mandates in the Constitution. When Congress and the Courts are unwilling to address egregious wrongs suffered by the people, then the people through State Legislatures have the authority to force Congress to act.

RECLAIMING AMERICA

CHAPTER 7

WE HAVE THE VOTING POWER

In States where we are required to place a Legislative Call on the State ballot knowing the composition of potential favorable voters is very important.

There are approximately 368,000 churches in the United States. 125 million church adherents belong to churches that either lean toward or have strong Conservative values. It is estimated that another 20 million Conservative voters, who do not identify with an organized religion, will be supportive with one or more of the proposed Amendments. CITIZEN INITIATIVES plans to promote its Constitutional Amendments in 250,000 of the 368,000 churches and through multi-media campaigns. Given the political climate in America today, we have an excellent opportunity to succeed in securing from State Legislatures Legislative Calls for most of our proposed Amendments.

There are three sides of the "voting power" question: 1) do we have enough votes in Initiative State ballots to force State Legislatures to make a Call on Congress; 2) do we have enough votes from legislators in Legislative States to reach the 34 States needed to force Congress' hand; and 3) will we have enough legislator or delegate votes in all States to win the ratification battle.

1. In Initiative States we have at least 2.3 conservative or leaning conservative voters for every vote needed to win (see Voting Tables in Chapter 4). To win at the ballot in Initiative and Legislative States, in non-Presidential years, as little as 11 million Conservatives would be needed out of 119 million voting adults. That represents only 9% of the voting population in the 50 States. We have far more than enough voters to win at the ballot and to force State Legislators to make a Call on Congress for "SINGLE ISSUE" Federal Conventions.

a. When we consider the results of our independent polling research[1], 66% of the general population when confronted with the issues and costs relating to abortion in America agree that they would support a "SINGLE ISSUE" Federal Convention to protect the Unborn Child. Educating the populations in the States about the loss of Constitutional and States Rights and associated losses in GDP and tax revenue will persuade many to vote in our favor for most of CITIZEN INITIATIVES' proposed Amendments.

b. For the first time in 60 years fiscal policy, and the deepening recession, complements social policy. The feverish anger of conservatives over the National and State debt will be the catalyst for advancing many additional "SINGLE ISSUE" Federal Conventions. For example, the advancement of the Balanced Federal Budget Amendment will help advance the Constitutional History Amendment, School Voucher Amendment, Legal Immigration Amendment, Free Markets Amendment, etc. This is truly a once in a *generational* lifetime opportunity for conservatives.

c. In Initiative States CITIZEN INITIATIVES expects to secure a Call from 18 of 24 States. In Legislative States we expect to secure the Call from 16 of 26 States. 34 Calling States will force Congress to convene a "SINGLE ISSUE" Federal Convention for each proposed Amendment.

2. In Legislative States we have the same positive voting percentages to win at the ballot. The problem we will face is persuading legislators to either make the Call on Congress voluntarily or place the Legislative Call on the ballot for the people to decide. We will not be able to force the issue by placing the Call on the ballot through a citizen initiative. The party affiliations and political philosophy of legislators change with each election which for State House of Representatives is usually every two years. CITIZEN

INITIATIVES plans to conduct a continual lobbying effort on State Legislators in an effort to persuade them to make the Call or place it on the ballot. Given the political and economic changes taking place in America the task of persuading legislators will not be as difficult as several years ago. This again is a once in a *generational* lifetime opportunity for conservatives.

    a.   Legislators to whom we have presented an Initiative have generally responded favorably. It is also true that many of the legislators we have talked with do not have a correct understanding of the "SINGLE ISSUE" Federal Convention process. CITIZEN INITIATIVES will be working hard to educate many of them on the issues and Convention process. Reinstating States and citizen Rights will be foremost in our efforts in appealing to them for support. Regular Legislative Seminars are planned at the Capitals of all States. Town Hall Seminars are also planned in metropolitan areas for the purpose of gaining support from local citizens.

3.   38 States must ratify each proposed Amendment. As the "SINGLE ISSUE" campaign runs its course in the States CITIZEN INITIATIVES believes 4 additional States will come forward. Their legislators will not want to be left behind to answer to their constituents for neglecting to secure their citizens' Constitutional Rights. Of course, legislators will also be reminded of States' Rights that have been taken away by Federal Courts and Congress. This political pressure on the legislators in Initiative and Legislative States will help to secure 38 ratifying votes for many of the proposed Amendments.

RECLAIMING AMERICA

POTENTIAL CONSERVATIVE VOTERS

Organization	Adherents	Organization	Adherents	Organization	Adherents
American Bapt Assoc	275000	Evangelical Free	243000	Old Order Amish	81000
Assemblies of God	2528000	Evangelical Presp	61000	Orthodox Church	1000000
Baptist Bible Fellow	1200000	Free Methodist	73000	Pentecostal Assemblies	1500000
Baptist Gen Conf	141000	Full Gospel Fellow	275000	Pentecostal Ch of God	104000
Baptist Miss	235000	General Bapt	72000	Presbyterian Ch Amer	280000
Christian Miss All	346000	Regular Bapt	102000	Progressive Natl Bapt	2500000
Christian Brethren	100000	General Conf Menon	82000	Reformed Ch Amer	296000
Christian Church	879000	Grace Gospel	60000	Religious Soc Friends	104000
Christian Reform	199000	Greek Orthodox	1955000	Reorg Ch Jesus Christ	140000
Church of God	5500000	Ind Fund Churches	62000	Roman Catholic	62018000
Church of God Prophecy	77000	Intl Church of Four Sq	238000	Romanian Orthodox	65000
Church of God And	234000	Intl Council of Community	250000	Salvation Army	471000
Church of God Cleve	753000	Intl Pentecostal	177000	Serbian Orthodox	67000
Church of Jesus Christ	4923	Jehovah's Witnesses	1040000	Seventh Day Adventist	840000
Church of Brethren	141000	Lutheran MO	2594000	Southern Bapt Conv	15729000
Church of Nazarene	627000	Mennonite Church	92000	Wesleyan Church	120000
Churches of Christ	1500000	Muslim/Islamic	67000	Other Potential Conservatives	20000000
Conservative Bapt	200000	Natl Assoc Free Will Bapt	210000		
Coptic Orthodox	180000	National Bapt Conv	3500000		
Cumberland Presp	87000	Nation Bapt Conv USA	8200000		
Evangelical Covnant	97000	Natl Miss Bapt	2500000	**Total Adherents**	142471920

In summary, CITIZEN INITIATIVS will be working tirelessly in all 50 States to secure 34 Legislative Calls for each proposed Amendment. It will also be working in State Legislatures after each "SINGLE ISSUE" Federal Convention agrees to send its proposed Amendment to the States, through Congress, for ratification. CITIZEN INITIATIVES will also be lobbying Congress to send each proposed Amendment to the States for ratification before it is forced to convene "SINGLE ISSUE" Federal Conventions.

RECLAIMING AMERICA

CHAPTER 8

PROPOSED AMENDMENTS TO THE UNITIED STATES CONSTITUTION BY CITIZEN INITIATIVES

CITIZEN INITIATIVES plans to advance 19 Amendments to the United States Constitution through "SINGLE ISSUE" Federal Conventions. The Balanced Federal Budget Amendment will spearhead our efforts and is being introduced to State Legislatures at this present time.

Active Amendments:

- **BALANCED FEDERAL BUDGET AMENDMENT**
- **LEGAL IMMIGRATION AMENDMENT**
- **FREE MARKETS AMENDMENT**
- **TRUTH IN MEDIA AMENDMENT**
- **TRADITIONAL MARRIAGE AMENDMENT**
- **ENERGY AMENDMENT**
- **SCHOOL VOUCHER AMENDMENT**
- **TRUTH IN EDUCATION AMENDMENT**
- **CONSTITUTIONAL HISTORY AMENDMENT**
- **UNBORN CHILD AMENDMENT**
- **PARENTAL RIGHTS AMENDMENT**
- **AMERICAN SOVEREIGNTY AMENDMENT**
- **PROPERTY RIGHTS AMENDMENT**

Future Amendments:

- **RESTORING THE 2ND AMENDMENT**
- **HEALTH CARE CHOICE AMENDMENT**
- **STATES RIGHTS AMENDMENT**
- **PRAYER IN AMERICA AMENDMENT**
- **TERM LIMITS AMENDMENT**
- **POLITICAL CORRECTNESS AMENDMENT**

Each of the 19 Amendments must be advanced as separate initiatives and each has a separate Legislative Call that is the binding contract between the Calling States. The text of each Legislative Call must be identical for all 50 States for each proposed Amendment. This will guarantee that the terms, conditions and agenda at the "SINGLE ISSUE" Federal Convention for each proposed Amendment are identical for each State. The Convention rules, including the quorum needed for conducting business at the Convention, are defined in the Legislative Calls for each Amendment. They have been drawn up so the Calling States control the deliberations and voting outcome at each Convention. There will be no *run away* Convention. CITIZEN INITIATIVES' primary responsibility is to facilitate the Call for "SINGLE ISSUE" Federal Conventions from the 50 State Legislatures. After 34 States complete their Calls CITIZEN INITIATIVES will organize the events and activities at the Convention. Once the Convention approves a proposed Amendment CITIZEN INITIATIVES will work in State Legislatures to secure the necessary 38 ratification votes.

Starting in Chapter 9 the text of 13 proposed Amendments are provided for your study. 9 of them have a State Legislative Call following the Amendment. The titles of 3 Amendments are included without text or Legislative Calls. The reader is encouraged to contact CITIZEN INITIATIVES with other proposed Amendments and comments: director@citizeninitiatives.org.

Each Amendment represents one Legislative Call for a "SINGLE ISSUE" Federal Convention. Each Legislative Call has 50 copies, one for each State.

CHAPTER 9

BALANCED FEDERAL BUDGET AMENDMENT

Text of proposed
BALANCED FEDERAL BUDGET AMENDMENT
ARTICLE 28 (or alternate number to be assigned by Congress)

Section 1. It is the right of citizens to enjoy a fiscally sound and debt free federal government which is foundational to a free people and must not be violated by the State.

Section 2. It is hereby mandated that the United States Congress will conduct the fiscal affairs of the United States Government according to the requirements of this Article.

Section 3. A Balanced Federal Budget consists of accurately assigning the sum of all federal receipts (which includes all tax revenues and all other sources of government income) to pay for all Federal expenditures within a given year and with the mandate not to allow expenditures to exceed revenue and income. The following exceptions apply:

1. In time of war or national emergency the United States Congress can authorize expenditures to exceed income and revenue as is required to protect the interests and security of the United States and its citizens. However, the United States Congress is required to amortize the repayment of any debt incurred over a maximum of ten years from the end of the war or national emergency. The United States Congress is prohibited from extending the repayment of the debt beyond ten years which includes the repayment of monies borrowed and any interest that may have accrued in order to service said debt. Congress can repay the debt, in full, in less than ten years, but must pay no less than $1/10^{th}$ of the original amount owed by the Government, including interest, in each

remaining year of the ten year term, unless the balance is less than $1/10^{th}$ of the original amount.

2. The United States Congress is authorized to allow expenditures to exceed revenues and income when in the collective wisdom of two thirds of the members of both Houses of the United States Congress it is necessary to do so. However, the United States Congress is required to amortize the repayment of any debt incurred over a maximum of five years from the date said debt was authorized by Congress. The United States Congress is prohibited from extending the repayment of said debt beyond five years which includes the repayment of monies borrowed and any interest that may have accrued in order to service said debt. Congress can repay the debt, in full, in less than five years, but must pay no less than $1/5^{th}$ of the original amount owed by the Government, including interest, in each remaining year of the five year term, unless the balance is less than $1/5^{th}$ of the original amount.

Section 4. The United States Congress is prohibited from taking any debt that may remain from previous year deficits and include it/them as part of a new deficit expenditure in current or future years.

Section 5. It is further prohibited for the United States Congress to extend the repayment of any and all debt incurred beyond the time lines required in this Article.

Section 6. All current debt owed by the United State Government at the time this Article is ratified, including accrued interest to service said debt, must be repaid by the United States Congress within 20 years from the date this Article is ratified by the several States. Congress can repay the current debt, in full, in less than twenty years, but must pay no less than $1/20^{th}$ of the original amount owed by the Government, including interest, in each remaining year of the 20 year term, unless the balance is less than $1/20^{th}$ of the original amount.

Section 7. To secure the rights of citizens to enjoy a fiscally sound and debt free federal government, which is foundational to a free people, it is hereby prohibited for the United States Congress to allow federal expenditures to exceed federal revenue and income, in any given year, as mandated by the requirements and allowances of this Article.

Section 8. This Article shall be immediately enforceable upon the United States Congress when ratified by three quarters of the several States.

At the time of this writing the national debt is $14.3 trillion, with unfunded liabilities exceeding $60 trillion. **THIS IS INSANITY**. There can be only one end to this train wreck and that is the destruction of American freedoms because we have become a debtor nation. For the sake of our Constitution, national security, personal liberties and posterity we must reverse these spending practices that may satisfy our immediate appetites, but leave future generations with an indebtedness they will find impossible to pay.

RECLAIMING AMERICA

AUTHORIZED CALL
BY THE ALABAMA STATE LEGISLATURE ON THE UNITED STATES CONGRESS INSTRUCTING CONGRESS TO CONVENE A FEDERAL CONVENTION TO BE TITLED THE BALANCED FEDERAL BUDGET AMENDMENT CONVENTION

THIS AUTHORIZED CALL ALSO DEFINES THE AGREEMENT THE ALABAMA STATE LEGISLATURE IS ENTERING INTO BETWEEN ITSELF AND OTHER CALLING STATES

To: **BOTH HOUSES OF UNITED STATES CONGRESS**

UNITED STATES SENATE:

President of the Senate, United States Vice President
Majority Leader Senator
Minority Leader Senator
President Pro Tempore Senator
Republican Whip Senator
Democratic Whip Senator

(Deliver this Official Call to every current leader and member of the United State Senate at Washington, DC)

HOUSE OF REPRESENTATIVE:

Speaker of the House Representative
House Majority Leader Representative
House Majority Whip Representative
House Minority Leader Representative
House Minority Whip Representative

(Deliver this Official Call to every current leader and member of the United State House of Representatives at Washington, DC)

From: **THE STATE LEGISLATURE OF THE STATE OF ALABAMA**

The Legislature of the State of Alabama hereby Calls on the United States Congress instructing Congress to convene a Federal Convention called the BALANCED FEDERAL BUDGET AMENDMENT Convention under the authority reserved to the States in Article V of the United States Constitution. Article IV, Section 4 guarantees to every State a Republican form of

Government which gives each State equal standing when Calling for a Constitutional Convention. Article V reserves to the Several States the right to Call for a Federal Constitutional Convention for the purpose of amending the United States Constitution when Congress and/or the Courts refuse to address an egregious wrong suffered by the people. The States *alone* have the authority to "limit" the agenda and authority of a Federal Convention. The States alone can Call for a "Single Issue" Convention by agreeing among themselves the purpose, terms, conditions, duration, and agenda for the Convention. Congress does not have the authority to define a "Single Issue" Convention. Congress' authority, under Article V of the United States Constitution, empowers it to convene a Convention as Called for and defined by the Several States. The Several States alone have the authority to enforce the terms and/or conditions set forth in this Agreement at the BALANCED FEDERAL BUDGET AMENDMENT Convention.

The BALANCED FEDERAL BUDGET AMENDMENT Convention will be a "Single Issue" Federal Convention as defined in this Legislative Call on the United States Congress and in this binding Agreement between the Several States. The delegates summoned to this Convention by Congress will have the authority to decide only one issue, should the BALANCED FEDERAL BUDGET AMENDMENT, as herein written, be sent to Congress with instructions to send the Amendment back to the Several States for ratification? The delegates at the BALANCED FEDERAL BUDGET AMENDMENT Convention will have no authority to change the wording of the proposed Amendment, neither are they authorized to deliberate on or discuss any other subject matter or issue at the Convention. The purpose, terms and/or conditions that will govern the agenda and affairs of the BALANCED FEDERAL BUDGET AMENDMENT Convention are as follows:

THE PURPOSE OF THE CONVENTION

The *only* purpose for convening the BALANCED FEDERAL BUDGET AMENDMENT Convention is for the State Delegations, representing the Several States, to decide if the BALANCED FEDERAL BUDGET AMENDMENT, as herein written, should be sent to the United States Congress with instructions for Congress to send the Amendment to the Several States for ratification? Absolutely no other business is authorized at this Convention.

CONVENTION RULES OF ORDER

The "Convention Rules of Order" that all Delegates and State Delegations are required to follow as a condition of participating at the BALANCED FEDERAL BUDGET AMENDMENT Convention are described in this Legislative Call on Congress. From time to time, in order to facilitate Convention business, the Convention Chairman may require the Convention to follow "Robert's Rules of

Order" when a specific Rule of Order is not defined in this Legislative Call. The Delegates and State Delegations are required to honor the Convention Chairman's instructions when applying Convention Rules of Order and/or Roberts Rules of Order.

BALANCED FEDERAL BUDGET AMENDMENT COMMITTEE

The BALANCED FEDERAL BUDGET AMENDMENT Committee is the citizens group that founded the BALANCED FEDERAL BUDGET AMENDMENT Initiative. This Committee will be responsible for pre-Convention planning and organization. The Chairman and Vice Chairman of the BALANCED FEDERAL BUDGET AMENDMENT Committee will be Ex-Officio (without voting rights) members of the Convention. They can be called upon by the Convention Chairman to clarify the BALANCED FEDERAL BUDGET AMENDMENT legislative strategy for the Delegates, provide progress reports in the States and also be available for questions and answers from Delegates at the Convention. They will be subject to the terms and/or conditions of this Legislative Call and Agreement between the States.

If they are also appointed as Delegates by their State Legislatures, then they will be entitled to voting privileges as Delegates at the Convention. The Chairman of the BALANCED FEDERAL BUDGET AMENDMENT Committee is R. C. "Kacprowicz" Casper.

If the Convention votes in favor of the Amendment, the BALANCED FEDERAL BUDGET AMENDMENT Committee will be responsible for post-convention planning and organization during the ratification process.

FUNDING THE CONVENTION AND STATE DELEGATIONS

The State Legislatures that send Delegates to the BALANCED FEDERAL BUDGET AMENDMENT Convention shall be responsible for providing monies necessary for their State Delegations to participate at the Convention. The amounts each State Delegation will require will be decided by each State Legislature. Other expenses or costs necessary to fund the Convention are to be shared by the Calling States equally. From time to time the Convention Chairman will notify the State Delegations what monies will be necessary to carry on the business of the Convention.

FUNDING FOR "PRE AND POST-CONVENTION PLANNING AND ORGANIZATION"

Each State Legislature making a Call on Congress to convene the BALANCED FEDERAL BUDGET AMENDMENT Convention will be asked to share expenses for "pre-Convention planning" and "pre-Convention organization". If the Convention votes to send the BALANCED FEDERAL BUDGET AMENDMENT to Congress to be ratified by the States, then the BALANCED FEDERAL BUDGET AMENDMENT Committee will ask the Calling States to help fund post-convention planning and organization to cover expenses for the ratification process.

DELEGATES SUMMONED BY CONGRESS

Congress has the authority, under Article V, to summon Delegates from the Several States to the BALANCED FEDERAL BUDGET AMENDMENT Convention. Congress is hereby directed to summon to the Convention the appropriate number of Delegates that each State is entitled to immediately after two thirds of the States complete their Call directing Congress to convene the BALANCED FEDERAL BUDGET AMENDMENT Convention. The number of Delegates to be summoned to the Convention should be equal to the number of members each State has in the House of Representatives and in the Senate of the United States Congress.

DELEGATES AND STATE DELEGATIONS

Only State Delegates summoned by Congress to the BALANCED FEDERAL BUDGET AMENDMENT Convention and appointed by their State Legislatures to form State Delegations to represent their respective States are authorized to attend and speak at the BALANCED FEDERAL BUDGET AMENDMENT Convention. Each State Legislature has the responsibility to select, from within its State, individual Delegates who will represent its State at the Convention. The number of Delegates selected by a State Legislature can be no greater than the number of Delegates summoned by Congress from its State. Each State Delegation must select a Delegate from within its delegation to be its Spokesman at the Convention. Only a Delegation's Spokesman will be recognized by the Convention Chairman.

THE PRE-CONVENTION "ACTING CONVENTION CHAIRMAN" AND "ASSISTANT ACTING CONVENTION CHAIRMAN"

The Chairman and Vice Chairman of the BALANCED FEDERAL BUDGET AMENDMENT Committee will have exclusive authority to complete all pre-convention planning and organization for the BALANCED FEDERAL BUDGET AMENDMENT Convention. They will perform their duties under the titles "Acting Convention Chairman" and "Assistant Acting Convention Chairman" respectfully. They will also be available to State Legislatures to assist with their Legislative Calls and pre-Convention planning.

The Chairman and Vice Chairman of the BALANCED FEDERAL BUDGET AMENDMENT Committee will also be responsible for post-convention planning and organization if the Convention votes to send the BALANCED FEDERAL BUDGET AMENDMENT to Congress to be ratified by the States.

VOTING BY DELEGATES IN STATE DELEGATIONS

It is recommended that a simple majority of the Delegates within each State Delegation be required to decide a State Delegation's vote at the Convention. A quorum within each State Delegation will consist of one Delegate. The business of the Convention and voting will not be delayed if a State Delegation does not cast a vote during a roll call.

QUORUM REQUIRED FOR CONDUCTING BUSINESS AND VOTING AT THE CONVENTION

Each State Delegation will have one vote on all matters that are to be decided by the Convention. A simple majority vote by the State Delegations at the Convention is required to decide the outcome of all business brought before the Convention for a vote, including whether or not the BALANCED FEDERAL BUDGET AMENDMENT, as herein written, should be sent to the Several States, via Congress, for ratification. A quorum at the Convention for the purpose of conducting business and voting will consist of 17 State Delegations.

CLOSED DELIBERATIONS AT THE CONVENTION

The BALANCED FEDERAL BUDGET AMENDMENT Convention will be closed to all media and news groups. Only delegates appointed by their State Legislatures and the Chairman and Vice Chairman of the BALANCED FEDERAL BUDGET AMENDMENT Committee will be authorized to enter and speak at the Convention. No visitors, reporters, government officials, professionals or inquirers, of any kind, will be permitted to enter the Convention facilities. Unauthorized visitors will be escorted by the Sergeant of Arms out of the Convention. After the vote by the State Delegations is taken to determine if the BALANCED FEDERAL BUDGET AMENDMENT will be sent to the Several States, via Congress, for ratification, the Chairman of the Convention will call a special press conference to announce the Convention's decision. Within 30 days from the special press conference the Chairman will make available to the public the records kept by the Convention during its proceedings.

STATE LEGISLATURES NOT AUTHORIZING THIS CALL FOR THE BALANCED FEDERAL BUDGET AMENDMENT CONVENTION

State Legislatures that did not authorize this Call for the BALANCED FEDERAL BUDGET AMENDMENT Convention and yet agree to send delegates representing their State agree to follow the terms and/or conditions set forth in this Agreement and Legislative Call. They need to pay particular attention to the "Convention's Rules of Order" described in this Agreement and the prohibitions in the section titled "Prohibitions for Delegates, State Delegations and/or Convention Officials at the Convention". These non-calling States must notify the "Acting Convention Chairman" before the Convention convenes of their intention to attend the Convention so accommodations can be completed for their Delegations. In order to receive Convention Passes, all Delegates attending the Convention, will be required to sign an agreement promising to abide by the terms and/or conditions in this Legislative Call and Agreement.

NO WEAPONS ALLOWED AT THE CONVENTION

Delegates and BALANCED FEDERAL BUDGET AMENDMENT Committee officials will not be allowed to bring into the BALANCED FEDERAL BUDGET AMENDMENT Convention any weapons or objects that can be construed as weapons.

PRESENTING ARGUMENTS AT THE CONVENTION BY STATE DELEGATIONS

Each State Delegation will be allotted a maximum of 60 minutes for presenting its argument(s) at the Convention for or against sending the BALANCED FEDERAL BUDGET AMENDMENT to the United States Congress with instruction for Congress to send the Amendment to the Several States for ratification. Only Delegates who have been officially selected by their State Legislatures and Ex-Officio members of the Convention are authorized to speak before the Convention. Each State Delegation can use one or more of its Delegates to present its position(s). However, the total time allotted for each State Delegation is 60 minutes, which includes any time that is necessary to replace one Delegate with another. The Chairman of the BALANCED FEDERAL BUDGET AMENDMENT Committee will also be limited to 60 minutes during his speaking segment. Speakers cannot reserve portions of their time to another time or day. Speakers must complete their arguments in the 60 minute segment assigned to them.

The order each State Delegation will follow when presenting their position(s) will be according to when each State completed its Legislative Call on Congress, or when it notified the "Acting Convention Chairman" that it intends to attend the Convention even though it may not complete a Legislative Call on Congress. The State Delegation presentations will be scheduled in the following manner: the first State making a Call on Congress will go first; the first State notifying the "Acting Convention Chairman" that it plans to attend will go second. The second State making a Call on Congress will go third; then the second State notifying the "Acting Convention Chairman" will go fourth, and so forth until all States wanting to present their positions have had an opportunity to do so. The Convention Chairman can rearrange the schedule if any conflicts arise at the Convention. The last speaker to be scheduled at the Convention for a 60 minute segment will be the Chairman of the BALANCED FEDERAL BUDGET AMENDMENT Committee.

DUTIES OF THE "ACTING CONVENTION CHAIRMAN"

The duties of the "Acting Convention Chairman include:

1) organize a pre-Convention support group for assisting Calling States with their Legislative Calls and non-calling States with their intentions to attend the Convention
2) set up an BALANCED FEDERAL BUDGET AMENDMENT Committee checking account
3) use generally accepted accounting principles when keeping records of all receipts and expenditures
4) provide financial reports and minutes of pre-convention activities as requested by States that are funding pre-convention operations
5) keep minutes of all business meetings of the BALANCED FEDERAL BUDGET AMENDMENT Committee
6) determine the budget that will be needed for pre-convention planning and organizing and notify each State Legislature of its share of the expenses
7) assist the Calling States and Attending States with their pre-convention planning
8) assist the Calling States with their Legislative Calls on Congress
9) after the BALANCED FEDERAL BUDGET AMENDMENT Convention has been convened call the Convention to order
10) invite nominations from the State Delegations present at the Convention to fill the "Convention Chairman's" position (the maximum number of nominees permitted is five and only one nominee from any one State Delegation is permitted)
11) take a roll call from the State Delegations for the nominee(s)
12) declare the winner based on the nominee who has received the most votes (a plurality of State Delegations). Each State Delegation will have one vote
13) officiate the installation of the "Convention Chairman" at the Convention by having the Chairman place his/her right hand on the Bible while repeating the following oath

"I solemnly promise to officiate the office of Convention Chairman for the BALANCED FEDERAL BUDGET AMENDMENT Convention according to the terms and/or conditions set forth in the Legislative Calls from the Several States to the best of my ability, so help me God".

In the event the "Acting Convention Chairman" is nominated and elected to the Convention Chairman position, the "Assistant Acting Convention Chairman" will conduct the installation ceremony for the Convention Chairman.

ELECTION, AUTHORITY AND DUTIES OF CONVENTION OFFICIALS

CONVENTION CHAIRMAN: - The "Convention Chairman" is the senior official at the BALANCED FEDERAL BUDGET AMENDMENT Convention. He/she will have the requisite authority to oversee all activities at the Convention, including the nomination and election of all officials. The Convention Chairman's duties include:

1) organize and oversee all business and activities at the Convention
2) organize and officiate all nominations, elections and installations of officials at the Convention (this will be the Convention Chairman's first order of business)
3) organize and officiate all nominations, elections and installations of official positions that may become vacant at the Convention
4) oversee the enforcement of all Convention Rules
5) oversee the enforcement of the terms and/or conditions (herein described) of this Call and Agreement by the States
6) oversee the investigation of alleged and/or actual violations of this Agreement as defined in the section titled "Violating this Agreement"
7) bring before the Convention all matters that require a vote
8) bring before the Convention the financial needs of the Convention and time lines for when these monies are needed
9) cut off motions or discussions by State Delegations before the Convention if and when it seems appropriate
10) recognize the Spokesman within a State Delegation for the purpose of addressing a matter of importance to the Spokesman's Delegation (the Convention Chairman will have full authority to determine if a matter brought before the Convention by the Spokesman is appropriate for further discussion and/or if a decision by the Convention is necessary)
11) keep the business of the Convention moving forward expeditiously, cutting off all motions and discussions when it appears one or more Delegates are trying to hinder, delay or stop the work of the Convention
12) keep the business of the Convention focused on one objective which is, should the Convention send the BALANCED FEDERAL BUDGET AMENDMENT to Congress instructing Congress to send it to the Several States for ratification?

13) instruct Convention Officials (Assistant Convention Chairman, Secretary, Financial Officer, Executive Administrator, Sergeant at Arms, and Deputies) on their duties at the Convention
14) officiate and remedy any and all problems that may develop at the Convention
15) oversee the design and production of "Official" Convention Badges for the Sergeant at Arms and Deputies
16) notify all State Legislatures of the decision the Convention made as to whether or not the BALANCED FEDERAL BUDGET AMENDMENT should be sent to Congress instructing Congress to send it to the States for ratification?
17) if the State Delegations voted to send the Amendment to the States for ratification, include the Convention's recommendation to the United States Congress as to whether it should be ratified by State Conventions or State Legislatures
18) declare the BALANCED FEDERAL BUDGET AMENDMENT Convention closed after the State Delegations have decided if the BALANCED FEDERAL BUDGET AMENDMENT should be sent to Congress instructing Congress to send it to the States for ratification?
19) arrange a Special News Conference to announce the decision by the BALANCED FEDERAL BUDGET AMENDMENT Convention
20) make available the proceedings of the Convention to the public 30 days after the Convention is closed

The first order of business for the "Convention Chairman" will be to open the Convention to nominations from State Delegations present for each of the following Convention Officials; one Assistant Convention Chairman, one Secretary, one Financial Officer, one Executive Administrator, one Sergeant at Arms and ten Deputies (the maximum number of nominees permitted for each Convention Official position is five. Only one nominee for each Convention Official position is permitted from any one State Delegation. The nominee with a plurality of votes from the State Delegations will be the winner). The Convention Chairman" can call for nominations for more than 10 Deputies if and when circumstances warrant.

ASSISTANT CONVENTION CHAIRMAN
The "Assistant Convention Chairman" duties include:

1) be amenable to the "Convention Chairman"
2) provide assistance to the "Convention Chairman" in all matters pertaining to the business of the Convention
3) monitor activities at the Convention and report to the "Convention Chairman" violations or possible violations of the terms and/or conditions of this Legislative Call and Agreement

perform the duties of the "Convention Chairman" when called upon by the Chairman or when the Chairman is unable to perform the duties of his/her office

4) the "Assistant Convention Chairman" will take the following oath, administered by the Convention Chairman, while placing his/her right hand on the Bible

"I solemnly promise to officiate the office of Assistant Convention Chairman for the BALANCED FEDERAL BUDGET AMENDMENT Convention according to the terms and/or conditions set forth in the Legislative Calls from the Several States to the best of my ability, so help me God".

SECRETARY
The "Secretary's" duties include:

1) keep official minutes of all proceedings at the Convention
2) monitor activities at the Convention and report to the Convention Chairman violations or possible violations of Convention Rules and of the terms and/or conditions of this Legislative Call and Agreement
3) make available to the "Convention Chairman", upon request, the official minutes of the Convention
4) be amenable to the "Convention Chairman" and "Assistant Convention Chairman"
5) in the absence of the "Convention Chairman" and the "Assistant Convention Chairman" due to death or a disablement that prevents them from performing the duties of their offices at the Convention, the Secretary shall call the Convention to order for the purpose of nominating and electing a new "Convention Chairman" and "Assistant Convention Chairman". In this capacity the Secretary will assume the duties and authority of the "Convention Chairman". If the Secretary is unable to perform the duties described herein, then they will fall to the Financial Officer.
6) the "Secretary" will take the following oath while placing his/her right hand on the Bible

"I solemnly promise to officiate the office of Secretary for the BALANCED FEDERAL BUDGET AMENDMENT Convention according to the terms and/or conditions set forth in the Legislative Calls from the Several States to the best of my ability, so help me God".

FINANCIAL OFFICER
The "Financial Officer's" duties include:

1) keep detailed accounting records of all financial matters at the Convention using generally accepted accounting principles
2) be amenable to the "Convention Chairman" and "Assistant Convention Chairman"
3) monitor activities at the Convention and report to the Convention Chairman violations or possible violations of the terms and/or conditions of this Legislative Call and Agreement
4) set up a checking account in the name of the BALANCED FEDERAL BUDGET AMENDMENT Convention requiring any two of the following three officers when signing a check or making withdrawals – Convention Chairman, Assistant Convention Chairman, Financial Officer
5) make available to the "Convention Chairman", upon request, all financial records at the Convention
6) provide to the Convention Chairman the financial needs of the Convention and the time lines as to when these monies are needed
7) in the absence of a "Convention Chairman", "Assistant Convention Chairman", and "Secretary" due to death or a disablement that prevents them from performing the duties of their offices at the Convention, the Financial Officer shall call the Convention to order for the purpose of nominating and electing a new "Convention Chairman", "Assistant Convention Chairman", and "Secretary". In this capacity the Financial Officer will assume the duties and authority of the "Convention Chairman"
8) the "Financial Officer" will take the following oath while placing his/her right hand on the Bible

"I solemnly promise to officiate the office of Financial Officer for the BALANCED FEDERAL BUDGET AMENDMENT Convention according to generally accepted accounting principles and according to the terms and/or conditions set forth in the Legislative Calls from the Several States to the best of my ability, so help me God".

EXECUTIVE ADMINISTRATOR
The "Executive Administrator's" duties include:

1) facilitate all Convention business as directed by the Convention Chairman
2) be amenable to the Convention Chairman and Assistant Convention Chairman
3) monitor activities at the Convention and report to the Convention Chairman violations or possible violations of the terms and/or conditions of this Legislative Call and Agreement
4) keep detailed reports of all administrative activities at the Convention
5) make available to the "Convention Chairman" upon request all administrative records and/or reports at the Convention

6) the "Executive Administrator" will take the following oath while placing his/her right hand on the Bible

"I solemnly promise to officiate the office of Executive Administrator for the BALANCED FEDERAL BUDGET AMENDMENT Convention according to the terms and/or conditions set forth in the Legislative Calls from the Several States to the best of my ability, so help me God".

SERGEANT AT ARMS
The "Sergeant at Arms'" duties include:

1) be amenable to the Convention Chairman and Assistant Convention Chairman
2) monitor all activities at the Convention and report to the Convention Chairman violations or possible violations of the terms and/or conditions of this Legislative Call and Agreement
3) maintain order at the Convention
4) enforce all remedies for violations of this Legislative Call and Agreement as directed by the Convention Chairman
5) organize and direct the activities of all Deputies at the Convention
6) oversee, train and manage all Deputies at the Convention
7) the "Sergeant at Arms" will take the following oath while placing his/her right hand on the Bible

"I solemnly promise to officiate the office of Sergeant at Arms for the BALANCED FEDERAL BUDGET AMENDMENT Convention according to the terms and/or conditions set forth in the Legislative Calls from the Several States to the best of my ability, so help me God".

DEPUTIES
The "Deputies'" duties include:

1) be amenable to the Convention Chairman, Assistant Convention Chairman and Sergeant at Arms
2) monitor all activities at the Convention and report to the Sergeant at Arms violations or possible violations of the terms and/or conditions of this Legislative Call and Agreement
3) maintain order at the Convention as directed by the Sergeant at Arms
4) enforce all remedies for violations of this Legislative Call and Agreement as directed by the Convention Chairman and/or the Sergeant at Arms
5) "Deputies" will take the following oath while placing his/her right hand on the Bible

"I solemnly promise to officiate the office of Deputy for the BALANCED FEDERAL BUDGET AMENDMENT Convention according to the terms and/or conditions set forth in the Legislative Calls from the Several States to the best of my ability, so help me God".

CHALLENGING THE QUALIFICATIONS OF CONVENTION OFFICIALS

A State Delegation can challenge the qualifications of any Convention Official at the BALANCED FEDERAL BUDGET AMENDMENT Convention by bringing its allegation(s), during a business session, to the Convention floor. The Convention Chairman will consider the allegation(s) and determine if it merits further investigation. If the Chairman decides that the allegation(s) merits further investigation, he/she will direct the Sergeant at Arms to conduct the necessary inquiry. He/she will then follow the instructions outlined in the section "Violating this Agreement" for proscribing a remedy or remedies.

The "Convention Chairman" can also reject a challenge to the qualifications of any Convention Official if he/she concludes that the Delegate making the allegation(s) is trying to disrupt and/or delay Convention business. If after following the instructions outlined in "Violating this Agreement" the Delegate is found to have made a false accusation against a Convention Official, the Delegate's State Delegation will be charged with a violation of the terms and/or conditions of this Call and Agreement.

PROHIBITIONS FOR STATE DELEGATES, STATE DELEGATIONS AND CONVENTION OFFICIALS AT THE CONVENTION

State Delegates, State Delegations and Convention Officials are prohibited from violating any of the following Convention prohibitions:

1. State Delegates, State Delegations and Convention Officials are prohibited, at the Convention, from introducing, discussing, voting on, or sending to the States for consideration and/or ratification any amendment to the United States Constitution other than the BALANCED FEDERAL BUDGET AMENDMENT, as herein written
2. State Delegates, State Delegations and Convention Officials are prohibited from altering or changing, in any way (which includes the wording, spelling, punctuation, or paragraph sections), the BALANCED FEDERAL BUDGET AMENDMENT from the written form shown in the section titled **"The full text of the BALANCED FEDERAL BUDGET AMENDMENT"**
3. State Delegates, State Delegations and Convention Officials are prohibited, at the Convention, from introducing, discussing, voting on,

or sending to the States for consideration and/or ratification any alternate form of government for the United States of America

4. State Delegates, State Delegations and Convention Officials are prohibited, at the Convention, from introducing, discussing, voting on, or sending to the States for consideration and/or ratification any alternate constitution or governing document for the United States of America

5. State Delegates, State Delegations and Convention Officials are prohibited, at the Convention, from introducing, discussing, voting on, or sending to the States for consideration and/or ratification any changes, of any kind, to the existing Constitution of the United States of America other than the BALANCED FEDERAL BUDGET AMENDMENT

6. State Delegates, State Delegations and Convention Officials are prohibited, at the Convention, from introducing, discussing, voting on, or sending to the States for consideration any changes, of any kind, to this binding Agreement between the States Calling for the BALANCED FEDERAL BUDGET AMENDMENT Convention

7. State Delegates, State Delegations and Convention Officials are prohibited, at the Convention, from introducing, discussing, voting on, or sending to the States for consideration and/or ratification any subject matter, issue or topic (of any kind) other than the proposed BALANCED FEDERAL BUDGET AMENDMENT in its written form shown in the section titled "The full text of the BALANCED FEDERAL BUDGET AMENDMENT"

THE DATE, TIME, DURATION AND PLACE OF
THE BALANCED FEDERAL BUDGET AMENDMENT CONVENTION.

The United States Congress will be responsible for determining and announcing to the Several States the date, time, and place that the BALANCED FEDERAL BUDGET AMENDMENT Convention is to convene immediately after two thirds of the States, under the authority given to the States in Article V of the United States Constitution, have completed their Calls on Congress to convene the BALANCED FEDERAL BUDGET AMENDMENT Convention. The Convention is expected to complete its business by the 180th day after convening. The Convention Chairman can extend the duration of the BALANCED FEDERAL BUDGET AMENDMENT Convention for one additional 180 day period. The maximum number of days the Convention is authorized to be in session are 360 days. If the Convention has not decided if the BALANCED FEDERAL BUDGET AMENDMENT should be sent to Congress with instructions to send the Amendment to the Several States for ratification by the end of 360 days, then the Call for the BALANCED FEDERAL BUDGET AMENDMENT Convention, which was approved by the Several States under the authority granted in Article V of the United States

Constitution and this agreement, will be automatically withdrawn by the Calling States and the Convention will automatically terminate at 5:00 P.M. Eastern Standard Time on the 360th day after convening. Termination of the BALANCED FEDERAL BUDGET AMENDMENT Convention will automatically occur on the 360th day after convening the Convention, without requiring a formal notice by the States to the Convention, nor by the States to the United States Congress, nor by the Convention to the States, nor by the Convention to the United States Congress, although it is recommended that the Convention notify the United States Congress and the State Legislatures of its termination as a courtesy.

Under no circumstance(s) are the Delegates at the BALANCED FEDERAL BUDGET AMENDMENT Convention authorized to re-convene a new or different Convention, no matter what their purpose or intent. The official Legislative Call and authority granted by the Several States and the subsequent convening of the BALANCED FEDERAL BUDGET AMENDMENT Convention by Congress will be automatically invalidated and the Convention will be abolished at 5:00 P.M. Eastern Standard Time on the 360th day after the convening of the BALANCED FEDERAL BUDGET AMENDMENT Convention.

VIOLATING THIS AGREEMENT

The Convention Chairman (or in the absence of the Convention Chairman the Assistant Convention Chairman) will handle allegations of a violation(s) or actual violation(s) of the terms and/or conditions of this binding Agreement between the Several States, by any one or more Delegate(s) and/or Convention Official(s), as follows:

1. When an alleged violation has been presented to the Convention Chairman, and if the Chairman decides that the allegation(s) merits further investigation, he/she will instruct the Sergeant at Arms to conduct the necessary inquiry.

2. After the inquiry has been completed, and assuming the Convention Chairman concludes that the evidence does not substantiate further review by the Convention, the allegation(s) will be dismissed by the Chairman and the Convention will go forward with its business.

3. If however, after the inquiry has been completed, the Convention Chairman concludes that the evidence does substantiate further review by the Convention, the Chairman will present the allegation(s) and findings of the inquiry to the Convention for a discussion and vote. If a majority of the State Delegations (one vote per State Delegation) decide that no violation of the terms and/or conditions of this Legislative Call and Agreement has occurred, then the Chairman will

declare that the alleged violation(s) of the terms and/or conditions of this Legislative Call and Agreement is/are dismissed. The Convention will then go forward with its business.

4. If however, after the inquiry has been completed, the Convention Chairman concludes that the evidence does substantiate further review by the Convention, the Chairman will present the allegation(s) and findings of the inquiry to the Convention for a discussion and vote. If a majority of the State Delegations (one vote per State Delegation) decide that one or more violation(s) of the terms and/or conditions of this Legislative Call and Agreement has/have occurred, then the Chairman will declare to the Convention that the Delegate(s) responsible for the violation(s), and their State Delegation(s), has/have been charged with "Violating this Agreement". The Convention will then go forward with its business.

5. If a State Delegation is charged with two violations of the terms and/or conditions of this Legislative Call and Agreement, the Convention Chairman will declare to the Convention that the State Delegation charged with violating this Agreement a second time has no further standing or authority at the Convention. The Chairman will notify the charged State Delegation that its entire delegation of Delegates must leave the Convention immediately and they will not be allowed back into the Convention. The Chairman will instruct the Sergeant at Arms that he should escort the charged State Delegation out of the Convention. The Convention Chairman will then notify the State Legislature that sent the charged State Delegation of the actions that the Convention has taken and inform them that they can send a replacement State Delegation to the Convention as long as they do not disrupt the proceedings of the Convention. None of the original Delegates who were charged by the Convention will be allowed back into the Convention as part of a replacement delegation.

6. The Convention Chairman will not allow unreasonable delays in the proceedings of the Convention due to disruptive Delegates or State Delegations. He/she will move the business of the Convention forward expeditiously.

THE FULL TEXT OF THE BALANCED FEDERAL BUDGET AMENDMENT

The full text of the BALANCED FEDERAL BUDGET AMENDMENT to be submitted to the Several States by the United States Congress for ratification shall read as follows:

BALANCED FEDERAL BUDGET AMENDMENT
ARTICLE 28 (or alternate number to be assigned by Congress)

Section 1. It is the right of citizens to enjoy a fiscally sound and debt free federal government which is foundational to a free people and must not be violated by the State.

Section 2. It is hereby mandated that the United States Congress will conduct the fiscal affairs of the United States Government according to the requirements of this Article.

Section 3. A Balanced Federal Budget consists of accurately assigning the sum of all federal receipts (which includes all tax revenues and all other sources of government income) to pay for all Federal expenditures within a given year and with the mandate not to allow expenditures to exceed revenue and income. The following exceptions apply:

1. In time of war or national emergency the United States Congress can authorize expenditures to exceed income and revenue as is required to protect the interests and security of the United States and its citizens. However, the United States Congress is required to amortize the repayment of any debt incurred over a maximum of ten years from the end of the war or national emergency. The United States Congress is prohibited from extending the repayment of the debt beyond ten years which includes the repayment of monies borrowed and any interest that may have accrued in order to service said debt. Congress can repay the debt, in full, in less than ten years, but must pay no less than $1/10^{th}$ of the original amount owed by the Government, including interest, in each remaining year of the ten year term, unless the balance is less than $1/10^{th}$ of the original amount.

2. The United States Congress is authorized to allow expenditures to exceed revenues and income when in the collective wisdom of two thirds of the members of both Houses of the United States Congress it is necessary to do so. However, the United States Congress is required to amortize the repayment of any debt incurred over a maximum of five years from the date said debt was authorized by Congress. The United States Congress is prohibited from extending the repayment of said debt beyond five years which includes the repayment of monies borrowed and any interest that may have accrued in order to service said debt. Congress can repay the debt, in full, in less than five years, but must pay no less than $1/5^{th}$ of the original amount owed by the Government, including interest, in each remaining year of the five year term, unless the balance is less than $1/5^{th}$ of the original amount.

Section 4. The United States Congress is prohibited from taking any debt that may remain from previous year deficits and include it/them as part of a new deficit expenditure in current or future years.

Section 5. It is further prohibited for the United States Congress to extend the repayment of any and all debt incurred beyond the time lines required in this Article.

Section 6. All current debt owed by the United State Government at the time this Article is ratified, including accrued interest to service said debt, must be repaid by the United States Congress within 20 years from the date this Article is ratified by the several States. Congress can repay the current debt, in full, in less than twenty years, but must pay no less than $1/20^{th}$ of the original amount owed by the Government, including interest, in each remaining year of the 20 year term, unless the balance is less than $1/20^{th}$ of the original amount.

Section 7. To secure the rights of citizens to enjoy a fiscally sound and debt free federal government, which is foundational to a free people, it is hereby prohibited for the United States Congress to allow federal expenditures to exceed federal revenue and income, in any given year, as mandated by the requirements and allowances of this Article.

Section 8. This Article shall be immediately enforceable upon the United States Congress when ratified by three quarters of the several States.

RATIFICATION OF THE "BALANCED FEDERAL BUDGET AMENDMENT"

Under the requirements of Article V of the United States Constitution and also under Article IV, Section 4 which guarantees to every State a Republican form of Government, the BALANCED FEDERAL BUDGET AMENDMENT will become a ratified Amendment to the United States Constitution when three quarters of the Several States complete their ratifications of the Amendment.

"CONGRESSIONAL" OPTION

If the United States Congress voluntarily sends the BALANCED FEDERAL BUDGET AMENDMENT to the Several States for ratification without making any changes, of any kind (which includes the wording, spelling, punctuation and paragraph sections) in the proposed Amendment as herein written, and before two thirds of the States complete their Call for Congress to convene the BALANCED FEDERAL BUDGET AMENDMENT Convention, then the

Legislature of the State of Alabama will withdraw its Call for the BALANCED FEDERAL BUDGET AMENDMENT Convention.

OFFICIAL AGREEMENT BY THE ALABAMA STATE LEGISLATURE BETWEEN ITSELF AND THE CALLING STATES

The Legislature of the State of Alabama enters into this binding Agreement with every other State Legislature that likewise agrees to the terms and/or conditions of this Legislative Call and Agreement as set forth herein. This is an irrevocable contract, during the term of this Agreement, between the State of Alabama and each and every State that signs this Agreement and completes its Call on the United States Congress directing Congress to convene a Federal Convention titled the BALANCED FEDERAL BUDGET AMENDMENT Convention. The Legislature of the State of Alabama agrees that it, and its delegates who are selected to attend the Convention, will abide by the purpose, terms, conditions, agenda, and "Convention Rules of Order" as explained in this Agreement.

The Legislature of the State of Alabama enters into this Agreement with every other State Legislature that likewise agrees to the terms and/or conditions of this Agreement and Legislative Call as set forth herein, understanding that the BALANCED FEDERAL BUDGET AMENDMENT Convention, by definition herein explained, is a "SINGLE ISSUE" Federal Convention and that the Convention will have no authority, under this Call and Agreement between the States, to review and/or consider any other subject matter, issue, or topic during its sessions other than business matters relating to the question, should the BALANCED FEDERAL BUDGET AMENDMENT, as herein written, be sent by the Convention to the United States Congress instructing Congress to send the Amendment to the Several States for ratification? The Legislature of the State of Alabama irrevocably declares by signing this Agreement that any subject matter, issue or topic (other than the BALANCED FEDERAL BUDGET AMENDMENT) that delegates might try to present to the Convention and subsequently to the States for review and/or ratification will be immediately, upon introduction at the Convention, unauthorized, invalid and automatically rejected by the Legislature of the State of Alabama, and the Legislature of the State of Alabama irrevocably declares that it will not review and/or consider for ratification any such subject matter, issue or topic, no matter how presented to it by the Convention. Only the BALANCED FEDERAL BUDGET AMENDMENT, as herein written, will be considered by the Legislature of the State of Alabama for ratification.

The Legislature of the State of Alabama also irrevocably declares that under no circumstance(s) will it consider for review and/or ratification any amendment to the United States Constitution, submitted to it by the BALANCED FEDERAL BUDGET AMENDMENT Convention other than the BALANCED FEDERAL BUDGET AMENDMENT as herein written.

The Legislature of the State of Alabama further irrevocably declares that under no circumstance(s) will it consider for review and/or ratification any modified form of the BALANCED FEDERAL BUDGET AMENDMENT submitted to it by the BALANCED FEDERAL BUDGET AMENDMENT Convention that would change, alter, or replace, in any way (which includes the wording, spelling, punctuation, or paragraph sections), the BALANCED FEDERAL BUDGET AMENDMENT from its written form herein.

The Legislature of the State of Alabama further irrevocably declares that under no circumstance(s) will it consider for review and/or ratification any proposal, of any kind, sent to it by the BALANCED FEDERAL BUDGET AMENDMENT Convention that would change, replace, or alter the United States Constitution other than the BALANCED FEDERAL BUDGET AMENDMENT as herein written.

The Legislature of the State of Alabama further irrevocably declares that under no circumstance(s) will it consider for review any proposal, of any kind, sent to it by the BALANCED FEDERAL BUDGET AMENDMENT Convention that would change, replace, or alter, in any way (which includes the wording, spelling, punctuation and section paragraphs), this Official Legislative Call for the BALANCED FEDERAL BUDGET AMENDMENT Convention and the terms and/or conditions of this Agreement between the States as herein written.

Under the authority reserved to the State of Alabama in Article V of the United States Constitution and also under Article IV, Section 4 which guarantees to every State a Republican form of Government, the Legislature of the State of Alabama hereby approves this Legislative Call on the United States Congress directing Congress to convene the BALANCED FEDERAL BUDGET AMENDMENT Convention and binds itself with each and every State that likewise approves this identical Legislative Call according the terms and/or conditions set forth in this Agreement.

OFFICIAL CALL BY THE STATE OF ALABAMA ON THE UNITED STATES CONGRESS DIRECTING CONGRESS TO CONVENE THE BALANCED FEDERAL BUDGET AMENDMENT CONVENTION

The Legislature of the State of Alabama hereby Calls on the United States Congress directing Congress to convene a Federal Convention to be titled the BALANCED FEDERAL BUDGET AMENDMENT Convention. The Convention is to be convened immediately after two thirds of the Several States have completed their Calls for the BALANCED FEDERAL BUDGET AMENDMENT Convention.

The State of Alabama is authorized to make this Call for the BALANCED FEDERAL BUDGET AMENDMENT Convention under the authority reserved to the States in Article V of the United States Constitution and under Article IV, Section 4 which guarantees to every State a Republican form of Government. Both Articles give to each State an equal standing when calling for a Constitutional Convention. Article V and Article IV, Section 4 reserves to the Several States the right to Call for a Federal Convention for the purpose of amending the United States Constitution when Congress and/or the Courts refuse to address an egregious wrong suffered by the people.

Submitted to Both Houses of the United States Congress on this date
_____, _____ by the Legislature of the State of Alabama.

State of Alabama Seal:

Authorized Signatures with titles:

_____Title_____

_____Title_____

_____Title_____

_____Title_____

_____Title_____

RECLAIMING AMERICA

CHAPTER 10

LEGAL IMMIGRATION AMENDMENT

Text of proposed
LEGAL IMMIGRATION AMENDMENT
ARTICLE 28 (or alternate number to be assigned by Congress)

Section 1. America's Immigration experience is unique among nations and revered by the American people. It is the right of citizens to receive from America's Immigration policies protection from immigrants entering the United States illegally and from temporary visitors overstaying their visas and other entry permits.

Section 2. Legal immigrants applying for and eventually being approved for citizenship in the United States from all countries shall not exceed 150,000 a year. The total number of immigrants who can be granted citizenship in the United States from any individual country shall not exceed 5,000 a year.

Section 3. The United States Congress shall determine the qualifications of individual applicants who are applying for citizenship. Congress shall also determine which countries of origin are authorized to send immigrants to the United States.

Section 4. The United States Congress is authorized to grant citizenship through amnesty to persons who are in the United States illegally when: one, two thirds of both Houses of the United States Congress agree that such amnesty should be granted and; two, the maximum number of individuals who are in the United States illegally and who would be granted citizenship through amnesty in a given year must not exceed 50,000.

Section 5. All illegal immigrants, including those who have over stayed their visas or other entry permits, must be returned to their countries of origin within six months from the date this Article is ratified by the States. Individuals who have been returned to their countries of origin can apply for citizenship or temporary entry permits through proper United States immigration authorities.

Section 6. Individuals who are born in the United States to parents who are in the United States illegally shall not be granted citizenship. Citizenship shall be automatically granted to persons born in the United States when one or both of their parents are legal citizens.

Section 7. To secure the rights of citizens the provisions of this Article shall govern immigration policies for the United States of America. The provisions of this Article are enforceable within the United States which shall include the Several States, the District of Columbia, and the Commonwealth of Puerto Rico, the Commonwealth of the Northern Mariana Islands and the territories and possessions of the United States.

Section 8. Congress shall have the power to enforce by appropriate legislation, the provisions of the Article.

When the government refuses to protect America's boarders and allows nearly 30 million illegal immigrants to enter the country, it becomes the duty of the American people to install laws that will protect their heritage, values, voting franchise and Constitutional history by imposing on the government mandates for an orderly immigration policy. When our politicians grant blanket amnesty to illegal immigrants for the purpose of gaining another voting bloc, they steal from the American people their treasured voting franchise which is guaranteed in the Constitution. With each illegal immigrant who is granted amnesty one American citizen loses the power to influence elections. In effect, the sovereignty of America is denigrated with each illegal immigrant who is given amnesty. The Legal Immigration Amendment will protect the American people from dishonest politicians and bring sanity to our immigration policies.

AUTHORIZED CALL
BY THE ALABAMA STATE LEGISLATURE
ON THE UNITED STATES CONGRESS INSTRUCTING
CONGRESS TO CONVENE A FEDERAL CONVENTION TO BE
TITLED THE LEGAL IMMIGRATION AMENDMENT
CONVENTION

THIS AUTHORIZED CALL ALSO DEFINES THE AGREEMENT
THE ALABAMA STATE LEGISLATURE IS ENTERING INTO
BETWEEN ITSELF AND OTHER CALLING STATES

To: **BOTH HOUSES OF UNITED STATES CONGRESS**

UNITED STATES SENATE:

President of the Senate, United States Vice President
Majority Leader Senator
Minority Leader Senator
President Pro Tempore Senator
Republican Whip Senator
Democratic Whip Senator

(Deliver this Official Call to every current leader and member of the United State Senate at Washington, DC)

HOUSE OF REPRESENTATIVE:

Speaker of the House Representative
House Majority Leader Representative
House Majority Whip Representative
House Minority Leader Representative
House Minority Whip Representative

(Deliver this Official Call to every current leader and member of the United State House of Representatives at Washington, DC)

From: **THE STATE LEGISLATURE OF THE STATE OF ALABAMA**

The Legislature of the State of Alabama hereby Calls on the United States Congress instructing Congress to convene a Federal Convention called the LEGAL IMMIGRATION AMENDMENT Convention under the authority reserved to the States in Article V of the United States Constitution. Article IV, Section 4 guarantees to every State a Republican form of Government which gives each State equal standing when Calling for a Constitutional Convention. Article V reserves to the Several States the right to Call for a Federal Constitutional Convention for the purpose of amending the United States Constitution when Congress and/or the Courts refuse to address an egregious wrong suffered by the people. The States *alone* have the authority to "limit" the agenda and authority of a Federal Convention. The States alone can Call for a "Single Issue" Convention by agreeing among themselves the purpose, terms, conditions, duration, and agenda for the Convention. Congress does not have the authority to define a "Single Issue" Convention. Congress' authority, under Article V of the United States Constitution, empowers it to convene a Convention as Called for and defined by the Several States. The Several States alone have the authority to enforce the terms and/or conditions set forth in this Agreement at the LEGAL IMMIGRATION AMENDMENT Convention.

The LEGAL IMMIGRATION AMENDMENT Convention will be a "Single Issue" Federal Convention as defined in this Legislative Call on the United States Congress and in this binding Agreement between the Several States. The delegates summoned to this Convention by Congress will have the authority to decide only one issue, should the LEGAL IMMIGRATION AMENDMENT, as herein written, be sent to Congress with instructions to send the Amendment back to the Several States for ratification? The delegates at the LEGAL IMMIGRATION AMENDMENT Convention will have no authority to change the wording of the proposed Amendment, neither are they authorized to deliberate on or discuss any other subject matter or issue at the Convention. The purpose, terms and/or conditions that will govern the agenda and affairs of the LEGAL IMMIGRATION AMENDMENT Convention are as follows:

THE PURPOSE OF THE CONVENTION

The *only* purpose for convening the LEGAL IMMIGRATION AMENDMENT Convention is for the State Delegations, representing the Several States, to decide if the LEGAL IMMIGRATION AMENDMENT, as herein written, should be sent to the United States Congress with instructions for Congress to send the Amendment to the Several States for ratification? Absolutely no other business is authorized at this Convention.

CONVENTION RULES OF ORDER

The "Convention Rules of Order" that all Delegates and State Delegations are required to follow as a condition of participating at the LEGAL IMMIGRATION AMENDMENT Convention are described in this Legislative Call on Congress. From time to time, in order to facilitate Convention business, the Convention Chairman may require the Convention to follow "Robert's Rules of Order" when a specific Rule of Order is not defined in this Legislative Call. The Delegates and State Delegations are required to honor the Convention

Chairman's instructions when applying Convention Rules of Order and/or Roberts Rules of Order.

LEGAL IMMIGRATION AMENDMENT COMMITTEE

The LEGAL IMMIGRATION AMENDMENT Committee is the citizens group that founded the LEGAL IMMIGRATION AMENDMENT Initiative. This Committee will be responsible for pre-Convention planning and organization. The Chairman and Vice Chairman of the LEGAL IMMIGRATION AMENDMENT Committee will be Ex-Officio (without voting rights) members of the Convention. They can be called upon by the Convention Chairman to clarify the LEGAL IMMIGRATION AMENDMENT legislative strategy for the Delegates, provide progress reports in the States and also be available for questions and answers from Delegates at the Convention. They will be subject to the terms and/or conditions of this Legislative Call and Agreement between the States.

If they are also appointed as Delegates by their State Legislatures, then they will be entitled to voting privileges as Delegates at the Convention. The Chairman of the LEGAL IMMIGRATION AMENDMENT Committee is R. C. "Kacprowicz" Casper.

If the Convention votes in favor of the Amendment, the LEGAL IMMIGRATION AMENDMENT Committee will be responsible for post-convention planning and organization during the ratification process.

FUNDING THE CONVENTION AND STATE DELEGATIONS

The State Legislatures that send Delegates to the LEGAL IMMIGRATION AMENDMENT Convention shall be responsible for providing monies necessary for their State Delegations to participate at the Convention. The amounts each State Delegation will require will be decided by each State Legislature. Other expenses or costs necessary to fund the Convention are to be shared by the Calling States equally. From time to time the Convention Chairman will notify the State Delegations what monies will be necessary to carry on the business of the Convention.

FUNDING FOR "PRE AND POST-CONVENTION PLANNING AND ORGANIZATION"

Each State Legislature making a Call on Congress to convene the LEGAL IMMIGRATION AMENDMENT Convention will be asked to share expenses for "pre-Convention planning" and "pre-Convention organization". If the Convention votes to send the LEGAL IMMIGRATION AMENDMENT to Congress to be ratified by the States, then the LEGAL IMMIGRATION AMENDMENT Committee will ask the Calling States to help fund post-convention planning and organization to cover expenses for the ratification process.

DELEGATES SUMMONED BY CONGRESS

Congress has the authority, under Article V, to summon Delegates from the Several States to the LEGAL IMMIGRATION AMENDMENT Convention. Congress is hereby directed to summon to the Convention the appropriate number of Delegates that each State is entitled to immediately after two thirds of the States complete their Call directing Congress to convene the LEGAL IMMIGRATION AMENDMENT Convention. The number of Delegates to be summoned to the Convention should be equal to the number of members each State has in the House of Representatives and in the Senate of the United States Congress.

DELEGATES AND STATE DELEGATIONS

Only State Delegates summoned by Congress to the LEGAL IMMIGRATION AMENDMENT Convention and appointed by their State Legislatures to form State Delegations to represent their respective States are authorized to attend and speak at the LEGAL IMMIGRATION AMENDMENT Convention. Each State Legislature has the responsibility to select, from within its State, individual Delegates who will represent its State at the Convention. The number of Delegates selected by a State Legislature can be no greater than the number of Delegates summoned by Congress from its State. Each State Delegation must select a Delegate from within its delegation to be its Spokesman at the Convention. Only a Delegation's Spokesman will be recognized by the Convention Chairman.

THE PRE-CONVENTION "ACTING CONVENTION CHAIRMAN" AND "ASSISTANT ACTING CONVENTION CHAIRMAN"

The Chairman and Vice Chairman of the LEGAL IMMIGRATION AMENDMENT Committee will have exclusive authority to complete all pre-convention planning and organization for the LEGAL IMMIGRATION AMENDMENT Convention. They will perform their duties under the titles "Acting Convention Chairman" and "Assistant Acting Convention Chairman" respectfully. They will also be available to State Legislatures to assist with their Legislative Calls and pre-Convention planning.

The Chairman and Vice Chairman of the LEGAL IMMIGRATION AMENDMENT Committee will also be responsible for post-convention planning and organization if the Convention votes to send the LEGAL IMMIGRATION AMENDMENT to Congress to be ratified by the States.

VOTING BY DELEGATES IN STATE DELEGATIONS

It is recommended that a simple majority of the Delegates within each State Delegation be required to decide a State Delegation's vote at the Convention. A quorum within each State Delegation will consist of one Delegate. The business of the Convention and voting will not be delayed if a State Delegation does not cast a vote during a roll call.

QUORUM REQUIRED FOR CONDUCTING BUSINESS AND VOTING AT THE CONVENTION

Each State Delegation will have one vote on all matters that are to be decided by the Convention. A simple majority vote by the State Delegations at the Convention is required to decide the outcome of all business brought before the Convention for a vote, including whether or not the LEGAL IMMIGRATION AMENDMENT, as herein written, should be sent to the Several States, via Congress, for ratification. A quorum at the Convention for the purpose of conducting business and voting will consist of 17 State Delegations.

CLOSED DELIBERATIONS AT THE CONVENTION

The LEGAL IMMIGRATION AMENDMENT Convention will be closed to all media and news groups. Only delegates appointed by their State Legislatures and the Chairman and Vice Chairman of the LEGAL IMMIGRATION AMENDMENT Committee will be authorized to enter and speak at the Convention. No visitors, reporters, government officials, professionals or inquirers, of any kind, will be permitted to enter the Convention facilities. Unauthorized visitors will be escorted by the Sergeant of Arms out of the Convention. After the vote by the State Delegations is taken to determine if the LEGAL IMMIGRATION AMENDMENT will be sent to the Several States, via Congress, for ratification, the Chairman of the Convention will call a special press conference to announce the Convention's decision. Within 30 days from the special press conference the Chairman will make available to the public the records kept by the Convention during its proceedings.

STATE LEGISLATURES NOT AUTHORIZING THIS CALL FOR THE LEGAL IMMIGRATION AMENDMENT CONVENTION

State Legislatures that did not authorize this Call for the LEGAL IMMIGRATION AMENDMENT Convention and yet agree to send delegates representing their State agree to follow the terms and/or conditions set forth in this Agreement and Legislative Call. They need to pay particular attention to the "Convention's Rules of Order" described in this Agreement and the prohibitions in the section titled "Prohibitions for Delegates, State Delegations and/or Convention Officials at the Convention". These non-calling States must notify the "Acting Convention Chairman" before the Convention convenes of

their intention to attend the Convention so accommodations can be completed for their Delegations. In order to receive Convention Passes, all Delegates attending the Convention, will be required to sign an agreement promising to abide by the terms and/or conditions in this Legislative Call and Agreement.

NO WEAPONS ALLOWED AT THE CONVENTION

Delegates and LEGAL IMMIGRATION AMENDMENT Committee officials will not be allowed to bring into the LEGAL IMMIGRATION AMENDMENT Convention any weapons or objects that can be construed as weapons.

PRESENTING ARGUMENTS AT THE CONVENTION BY STATE DELEGATIONS

Each State Delegation will be allotted a maximum of 60 minutes for presenting its argument(s) at the Convention for or against sending the LEGAL IMMIGRATION AMENDMENT to the United States Congress with instruction for Congress to send the Amendment to the Several States for ratification. Only Delegates who have been officially selected by their State Legislatures and Ex-Officio members of the Convention are authorized to speak before the Convention. Each State Delegation can use one or more of its Delegates to present its position(s). However, the total time allotted for each State Delegation is 60 minutes, which includes any time that is necessary to replace one Delegate with another. The Chairman of the LEGAL IMMIGRATION AMENDMENT Committee will also be limited to 60 minutes during his speaking segment. Speakers cannot reserve portions of their time to another time or day. Speakers must complete their arguments in the 60 minute segment assigned to them.

The order each State Delegation will follow when presenting their position(s) will be according to when each State completed its Legislative Call on Congress, or when it notified the "Acting Convention Chairman" that it intends to attend the Convention even though it may not complete a Legislative Call on Congress. The State Delegation presentations will be scheduled in the following manner: the first State making a Call on Congress will go first; the first State notifying the "Acting Convention Chairman" that it plans to attend will go second. The second State making a Call on Congress will go third; then the second State notifying the "Acting Convention Chairman" will go fourth, and so forth until all States wanting to present their positions have had an opportunity to do so. The Convention Chairman can rearrange the schedule if any conflicts arise at the Convention. The last speaker to be scheduled at the Convention for a 60 minute segment will be the Chairman of the LEGAL IMMIGRATION AMENDMENT Committee.

DUTIES OF THE "ACTING CONVENTION CHAIRMAN"

The duties of the "Acting Convention Chairman include:

1. organize a pre-Convention support group for assisting Calling States with their Legislative Calls and non-calling States with their intentions to attend the Convention
2. set up an LEGAL IMMIGRATION AMENDMENT Committee checking account
2. use generally accepted accounting principles when keeping records of all receipts and expenditures
3. provide financial reports and minutes of pre-convention activities as requested by States that are funding pre-convention operations
4. keep minutes of all business meetings of the LEGAL IMMIGRATION AMENDMENT Committee
5. determine the budget that will be needed for pre-convention planning and organizing and notify each State Legislature of its share of the expenses
6. assist the Calling States and Attending States with their pre-convention planning
7. assist the Calling States with their Legislative Calls on Congress
8. after the LEGAL IMMIGRATION AMENDMENT Convention has been convened call the Convention to order
9. invite nominations from the State Delegations present at the Convention to fill the "Convention Chairman's" position (the maximum number of nominees permitted is five and only one nominee from any one State Delegation is permitted)
10. take a roll call from the State Delegations for the nominee(s)
11. declare the winner based on the nominee who has received the most votes (a plurality of State Delegations). Each State Delegation will have one vote
12. officiate the installation of the "Convention Chairman" at the Convention by having the Chairman place his/her right hand on the Bible while repeating the following oath

"I solemnly promise to officiate the office of Convention Chairman for the LEGAL IMMIGRATION AMENDMENT Convention according to the terms and/or conditions set forth in the Legislative Calls from the Several States to the best of my ability, so help me God".

In the event the "Acting Convention Chairman" is nominated and elected to the Convention Chairman position, the "Assistant Acting Convention Chairman" will conduct the installation ceremony for the Convention Chairman.

ELECTION, AUTHORITY AND DUTIES OF CONVENTION OFFICIALS

CONVENTION CHAIRMAN: - The "Convention Chairman" is the senior official at the LEGAL IMMIGRATION AMENDMENT Convention. He/she will have the requisite authority to oversee all activities at the Convention, including the nomination and election of all officials. The Convention Chairman's duties include:

1. organize and oversee all business and activities at the Convention
2. organize and officiate all nominations, elections and installations of officials at the Convention (this will be the Convention Chairman's first order of business)
3. organize and officiate all nominations, elections and installations of official positions that may become vacant at the Convention
4. oversee the enforcement of all Convention Rules
5. oversee the enforcement of the terms and/or conditions (herein described) of this Call and Agreement by the States
6. oversee the investigation of alleged and/or actual violations of this Agreement as defined in the section titled "Violating this Agreement"
7. bring before the Convention all matters that require a vote
8. bring before the Convention the financial needs of the Convention and time lines for when these monies are needed
9. cut off motions or discussions by State Delegations before the Convention if and when it seems appropriate
10. recognize the Spokesman within a State Delegation for the purpose of addressing a matter of importance to the Spokesman's Delegation (the Convention Chairman will have full authority to determine if a matter brought before the Convention by the Spokesman is appropriate for further discussion and/or if a decision by the Convention is necessary)
11. keep the business of the Convention moving forward expeditiously, cutting off all motions and discussions when it appears one or more Delegates are trying to hinder, delay or stop the work of the Convention
12. keep the business of the Convention focused on one objective which is, should the Convention send the LEGAL IMMIGRATION AMENDMENT to Congress instructing Congress to send it to the Several States for ratification?
13. instruct Convention Officials (Assistant Convention Chairman, Secretary, Financial Officer, Executive Administrator, Sergeant at Arms, and Deputies) on their duties at the Convention
14. officiate and remedy any and all problems that may develop at the Convention
15. oversee the design and production of "Official" Convention Badges for the Sergeant at Arms and Deputies
16. notify all State Legislatures of the decision the Convention made as to whether or not the LEGAL IMMIGRATION AMENDMENT should be sent to Congress instructing Congress to send it to the States for ratification?

17. if the State Delegations voted to send the Amendment to the States for ratification, include the Convention's recommendation to the United States Congress as to whether it should be ratified by State Conventions or State Legislatures
18. declare the LEGAL IMMIGRATION AMENDMENT Convention closed after the State Delegations have decided if the LEGAL IMMIGRATION AMENDMENT should be sent to Congress instructing Congress to send it to the States for ratification?
19. arrange a Special News Conference to announce the decision by the LEGAL IMMIGRATION AMENDMENT Convention
20. make available the proceedings of the Convention to the public 30 days after the Convention is closed

The first order of business for the "Convention Chairman" will be to open the Convention to nominations from State Delegations present for each of the following Convention Officials; one Assistant Convention Chairman, one Secretary, one Financial Officer, one Executive Administrator, one Sergeant at Arms and ten Deputies (the maximum number of nominees permitted for each Convention Official position is five. Only one nominee for each Convention Official position is permitted from any one State Delegation. The nominee with a plurality of votes from the State Delegations will be the winner). The "Convention Chairman" can call for nominations for more than 10 Deputies if and when circumstances warrant.

ASSISTANT CONVENTION CHAIRMAN
The "Assistant Convention Chairman" duties include:

1. be amenable to the "Convention Chairman"
2. provide assistance to the "Convention Chairman" in all matters pertaining to the business of the Convention
3. monitor activities at the Convention and report to the "Convention Chairman" violations or possible violations of the terms and/or conditions of this Legislative Call and Agreement
4. perform the duties of the "Convention Chairman" when called upon by the Chairman or when the Chairman is unable to perform the duties of his/her office
5. the "Assistant Convention Chairman" will take the following oath, administered by the Convention Chairman, while placing his/her right hand on the Bible

"I solemnly promise to officiate the office of Assistant Convention Chairman for the LEGAL IMMIGRATION AMENDMENT Convention according to the terms and/or conditions set forth in the Legislative Calls from the Several States to the best of my ability, so help me God".

SECRETARY - The "Secretary's" duties include:

1. keep official minutes of all proceedings at the Convention
2. monitor activities at the Convention and report to the Convention Chairman violations or possible violations of Convention Rules and of the terms and/or conditions of this Legislative Call and Agreement
3. make available to the "Convention Chairman", upon request, the official minutes of the Convention
4. be amenable to the "Convention Chairman" and "Assistant Convention Chairman"
5. in the absence of the "Convention Chairman" and the "Assistant Convention Chairman" due to death or a disablement that prevents them from performing the duties of their offices at the Convention, the Secretary shall call the Convention to order for the purpose of nominating and electing a new "Convention Chairman" and "Assistant Convention Chairman". In this capacity the Secretary will assume the duties and authority of the "Convention Chairman". If the Secretary is unable to perform the duties described herein, then they will fall to the Financial Officer.
6. the "Secretary" will take the following oath while placing his/her right hand on the Bible

   "I solemnly promise to officiate the office of Secretary for the LEGAL IMMIGRATION AMENDMENT Convention according to the terms and/or conditions set forth in the Legislative Calls from the Several States to the best of my ability, so help me God".

FINANCIAL OFFICER - The "Financial Officer's" duties include:

1. keep detailed accounting records of all financial matters at the Convention using generally accepted accounting principles
2. be amenable to the "Convention Chairman" and "Assistant Convention Chairman"
3. monitor activities at the Convention and report to the Convention Chairman violations or possible violations of the terms and/or conditions of this Legislative Call and Agreement
4. set up a checking account in the name of the LEGAL IMMIGRATION AMENDMENT Convention requiring any two of the following three officers when signing a check or making withdrawals – Convention Chairman, Assistant Convention Chairman, Financial Officer
5. make available to the "Convention Chairman", upon request, all financial records at the Convention
6. provide to the Convention Chairman the financial needs of the Convention and the time lines as to when these monies are needed

7. in the absence of a "Convention Chairman", "Assistant Convention Chairman", and "Secretary" due to death or a disablement that prevents them from performing the duties of their offices at the Convention, the Financial Officer shall call the Convention to order for the purpose of nominating and electing a new "Convention Chairman", "Assistant Convention Chairman", and "Secretary". In this capacity the Financial Officer will assume the duties and authority of the "Convention Chairman"

8. the "Financial Officer" will take the following oath while placing his/her right hand on the Bible

"I solemnly promise to officiate the office of Financial Officer for the LEGAL IMMIGRATION AMENDMENT Convention according to generally accepted accounting principles and according to the terms and/or conditions set forth in the Legislative Calls from the Several States to the best of my ability, so help me God".

EXECUTIVE ADMINISTRATOR

The "Executive Administrator's" duties include:

1. facilitate all Convention business as directed by the Convention Chairman
2. be amenable to the Convention Chairman and Assistant Convention Chairman
3. monitor activities at the Convention and report to the Convention Chairman violations or possible violations of the terms and/or conditions of this Legislative Call and Agreement
4. keep detailed reports of all administrative activities at the Convention
5. make available to the "Convention Chairman" upon request all administrative records and/or reports at the Convention
6. the "Executive Administrator" will take the following oath while placing his/her right hand on the Bible

"I solemnly promise to officiate the office of Executive Administrator for the LEGAL IMMIGRATION AMENDMENT Convention according to the terms and/or conditions set forth in the Legislative Calls from the Several States to the best of my ability, so help me God".

SERGEANT AT ARMS – The "Sergeant at Arms'" duties include:

1. be amenable to the Convention Chairman and Assistant Convention Chairman monitor all activities at the Convention and report to the

Convention Chairman violations or possible violations of the terms and/or conditions of this Legislative Call and Agreement
2. maintain order at the Convention
3. enforce all remedies for violations of this Legislative Call and Agreement as directed by the Convention Chairman
4. organize and direct the activities of all Deputies at the Convention
5. oversee, train and manage all Deputies at the Convention
6. the "Sergeant at Arms" will take the following oath while placing his/her right hand on the Bible

"I solemnly promise to officiate the office of Sergeant at Arms for the LEGAL IMMIGRATION AMENDMENT Convention according to the terms and/or conditions set forth in the Legislative Calls from the Several States to the best of my ability, so help me God".

DEPUTIES – The "Deputies'" duties include:

1. be amenable to the Convention Chairman, Assistant Convention Chairman and Sergeant at Arms
2. monitor all activities at the Convention and report to the Sergeant at Arms violations or possible violations of the terms and/or conditions of this Legislative Call and Agreement
3. maintain order at the Convention as directed by the Sergeant at Arms
4. enforce all remedies for violations of this Legislative Call and Agreement as directed by the Convention Chairman and/or the Sergeant at Arms
5. "Deputies" will take the following oath while placing his/her right hand on the Bible

"I solemnly promise to officiate the office of Deputy for the LEGAL IMMIGRATION AMENDMENT Convention according to the terms and/or conditions set forth in the Legislative Calls from the Several States to the best of my ability, so help me God".

CHALLENGING THE QUALIFICATIONS OF
CONVENTION OFFICIALS

A State Delegation can challenge the qualifications of any Convention Official at the LEGAL IMMIGRATION AMENDMENT Convention by bringing its allegation(s), during a business session, to the Convention floor. The Convention Chairman will consider the allegation(s) and determine if it merits further investigation. If the Chairman decides that the allegation(s) merits further investigation, he/she will direct the Sergeant at Arms to conduct the necessary inquiry. He/she will then follow the instructions outlined in the section "Violating this Agreement" for proscribing a remedy or remedies.

The "Convention Chairman" can also reject a challenge to the qualifications of any Convention Official if he/she concludes that the Delegate making the allegation(s) is trying to disrupt and/or delay Convention business. If after following the instructions outlined in "Violating this Agreement" the Delegate is found to have made a false accusation against a Convention Official, the Delegate's State Delegation will be charged with a violation of the terms and/or conditions of this Call and Agreement.

PROHIBITIONS FOR STATE DELEGATES, STATE DELEGATIONS AND CONVENTION OFFICIALS AT THE CONVENTION

State Delegates, State Delegations and Convention Officials are prohibited from violating any of the following Convention prohibitions:

1. State Delegates, State Delegations and Convention Officials are prohibited, at the Convention, from introducing, discussing, voting on, or sending to the States for consideration and/or ratification any amendment to the United States Constitution other than the LEGAL IMMIGRATION AMENDMENT, as herein written
2. State Delegates, State Delegations and Convention Officials are prohibited from altering or changing, in any way (which includes the wording, spelling, punctuation, or paragraph sections), the LEGAL IMMIGRATION AMENDMENT from the written form shown in the section titled "The full text of the LEGAL IMMIGRATION AMENDMENT"
3. State Delegates, State Delegations and Convention Officials are prohibited, at the Convention, from introducing, discussing, voting on, or sending to the States for consideration and/or ratification any alternate form of government for the United States of America
4. State Delegates, State Delegations and Convention Officials are prohibited, at the Convention, from introducing, discussing, voting on, or sending to the States for consideration and/or ratification any alternate constitution or governing document for the United States of America
5. State Delegates, State Delegations and Convention Officials are prohibited, at the Convention, from introducing, discussing, voting on, or sending to the States for consideration and/or ratification any changes, of any kind, to the existing Constitution of the United States of America other than the LEGAL IMMIGRATION AMENDMENT
6. State Delegates, State Delegations and Convention Officials are prohibited, at the Convention, from introducing, discussing, voting on, or sending to the States for consideration any changes, of any kind, to this binding Agreement between the States Calling for the LEGAL IMMIGRATION AMENDMENT Convention

7. State Delegates, State Delegations and Convention Officials are prohibited, at the Convention, from introducing, discussing, voting on, or sending to the States for consideration and/or ratification any subject matter, issue or topic (of any kind) other than the proposed LEGAL IMMIGRATION AMENDMENT in its written form shown in the section titled "The full text of the LEGAL IMMIGRATION AMENDMENT"

THE DATE, TIME, DURATION AND PLACE OF THE LEGAL IMMIGRATION AMENDMENT CONVENTION.

The United States Congress will be responsible for determining and announcing to the Several States the date, time, and place that the LEGAL IMMIGRATION AMENDMENT Convention is to convene immediately after two thirds of the States, under the authority given to the States in Article V of the United States Constitution, have completed their Calls on Congress to convene the LEGAL IMMIGRATION AMENDMENT Convention. The Convention is expected to complete its business by the 180th day after convening. The Convention Chairman can extend the duration of the LEGAL IMMIGRATION AMENDMENT Convention for one additional 180 day period. The maximum number of days the Convention is authorized to be in session are 360 days. If the Convention has not decided if the LEGAL IMMIGRATION AMENDMENT should be sent to Congress with instructions to send the Amendment to the Several States for ratification by the end of 360 days, then the Call for the LEGAL IMMIGRATION AMENDMENT Convention, which was approved by the Several States under the authority granted in Article V of the United States Constitution and this agreement, will be automatically withdrawn by the Calling States and the Convention will automatically terminate at 5:00 P.M. Eastern Standard Time on the 360th day after convening. Termination of the LEGAL IMMIGRATION AMENDMENT Convention will automatically occur on the 360th day after convening the Convention, without requiring a formal notice by the States to the Convention, nor by the States to the United States Congress, nor by the Convention to the States, nor by the Convention to the United States Congress, although it is recommended that the Convention notify the United States Congress and the State Legislatures of its termination as a courtesy.

Under no circumstance(s) are the Delegates at the LEGAL IMMIGRATION AMENDMENT Convention authorized to re-convene a new or different Convention, no matter what their purpose or intent. The official Legislative Call and authority granted by the Several States and the subsequent convening of the LEGAL IMMIGRATION AMENDMENT Convention by Congress will be automatically invalidated and the Convention will be abolished at 5:00 P.M. Eastern Standard Time on the 360th day after the convening of the LEGAL IMMIGRATION AMENDMENT Convention.

VIOLATING THIS AGREEMENT

The Convention Chairman (or in the absence of the Convention Chairman the Assistant Convention Chairman) will handle allegations of a violation(s) or actual violation(s) of the terms and/or conditions of this binding Agreement between the Several States, by any one or more Delegate(s) and/or Convention Official(s), as follows:

1. When an alleged violation has been presented to the Convention Chairman, and if the Chairman decides that the allegation(s) merits further investigation, he/she will instruct the Sergeant at Arms to conduct the necessary inquiry.

2. After the inquiry has been completed, and assuming the Convention Chairman concludes that the evidence does not substantiate further review by the Convention, the allegation(s) will be dismissed by the Chairman and the Convention will go forward with its business.

3. If however, after the inquiry has been completed, the Convention Chairman concludes that the evidence does substantiate further review by the Convention, the Chairman will present the allegation(s) and findings of the inquiry to the Convention for a discussion and vote. If a majority of the State Delegations (one vote per State Delegation) decide that no violation of the terms and/or conditions of this Legislative Call and Agreement has occurred, then the Chairman will declare that the alleged violation(s) of the terms and/or conditions of this Legislative Call and Agreement is/are dismissed. The Convention will then go forward with its business.

4. If however, after the inquiry has been completed, the Convention Chairman concludes that the evidence does substantiate further review by the Convention, the Chairman will present the allegation(s) and findings of the inquiry to the Convention for a discussion and vote. If a majority of the State Delegations (one vote per State Delegation) decide that one or more violation(s) of the terms and/or conditions of this Legislative Call and Agreement has/have occurred, then the Chairman will declare to the Convention that the Delegate(s) responsible for the violation(s), and their State Delegation(s), has/have been charged with "Violating this Agreement". The Convention will then go forward with its business.

5. If a State Delegation is charged with two violations of the terms and/or conditions of this Legislative Call and Agreement, the Convention Chairman will declare to the Convention that the State Delegation charged with violating this Agreement a second time has no further

standing or authority at the Convention. The Chairman will notify the charged State Delegation that its entire delegation of Delegates must leave the Convention immediately and they will not be allowed back into the Convention. The Chairman will instruct the Sergeant at Arms that he should escort the charged State Delegation out of the Convention. The Convention Chairman will then notify the State Legislature that sent the charged State Delegation of the actions that the Convention has taken and inform them that they can send a replacement State Delegation to the Convention as long as they do not disrupt the proceedings of the Convention. None of the original Delegates who were charged by the Convention will be allowed back into the Convention as part of a replacement delegation.

6. The Convention Chairman will not allow unreasonable delays in the proceedings of the Convention due to disruptive Delegates or State Delegations. He/she will move the business of the Convention forward expeditiously.

THE FULL TEXT OF THE LEGAL IMMIGRATION AMENDMENT

The full text of the LEGAL IMMIGRATION AMENDMENT to be submitted to the Several States by the United States Congress for ratification shall read as follows:

LEGAL IMMIGRATION AMENDMENT
ARTICLE 28 (or alternate number to be assigned by Congress)

Section 1. America's Immigration experience is unique among nations and revered by the American people. It is the right of citizens to receive from America's Immigration policies protection from immigrants entering the United States illegally and from temporary visitors overstaying their visas and other entry permits.

Section 2. Legal immigrants applying for and eventually being approved for citizenship in the United States from all countries shall not exceed 150,000 a year. The total number of immigrants that can be granted citizenship in the United States from any individual country shall not exceed 5,000 a year.

Section 3. The United States Congress shall determine the qualifications of individual applicants who are applying for citizenship. Congress shall also determine which countries of origin are authorized to send immigrants to the United States.

Section 4. The United States Congress is authorized to grant citizenship through amnesty to persons who are in the United States illegally when: one, two thirds of both Houses of the United States Congress agree that such amnesty should be granted and; two, the maximum number of individuals who are in the United States illegally and who would be granted citizenship through amnesty in a given year must not exceed 50,000.

Section 5. All illegal immigrants, including those who have over stayed their visas or other entry permits, must be returned to their countries of origin within six months from the date this Article is ratified by the States. Individuals who have been returned to their countries of origin can apply for citizenship or temporary entry permits through proper United States immigration authorities.

Section 6. Individuals who are born in the United States to parents who are in the United States illegally shall not be granted citizenship. Citizenship shall be automatically granted to persons born in the United States when at least one parent is a legal citizen.

Section 7. To secure the rights of citizens the provisions of this Article shall govern immigration policies for the United States of America. The provisions of this Article are enforceable within the United States which shall include the Several States, the District of Columbia, and the Commonwealth of Puerto Rico, the Commonwealth of the Northern Mariana Islands and the territories and possessions of the United States.

Section 8. Congress shall have the power to enforce by appropriate legislation, the provisions of the Article.

RATIFICATION OF THE "LEGAL IMMIGRATION AMENDMENT"

Under the requirements of Article V of the United States Constitution and also under Article IV, Section 4 which guarantees to every State a Republican form of Government, the LEGAL IMMIGRATION AMENDMENT will become a ratified Amendment to the United States Constitution when three quarters of the Several States complete their ratifications of the Amendment.

"CONGRESSIONAL" OPTION

If the United States Congress voluntarily sends the LEGAL IMMIGRATION AMENDMENT to the Several States for ratification without making any changes, of any kind (which includes the wording, spelling, punctuation and paragraph sections) in the proposed Amendment as herein written, and before two thirds of the States complete their Call for Congress to convene the LEGAL IMMIGRATION AMENDMENT Convention, then the Legislature of the State of Alabama will withdraw its Call for the LEGAL IMMIGRATION AMENDMENT Convention.

OFFICIAL AGREEMENT BY THE ALABAMA STATE LEGISLATURE BETWEEN ITSELF AND THE CALLING STATES

The Legislature of the State of Alabama enters into this binding Agreement with every other State Legislature that likewise agrees to the terms and/or conditions of this Legislative Call and Agreement as set forth herein. This is an irrevocable contract, during the term of this Agreement, between the State of Alabama and each and every State that signs this Agreement and completes its Call on the United States Congress directing Congress to convene a Federal Convention titled the LEGAL IMMIGRATION AMENDMENT Convention. The Legislature of the State of Alabama agrees that it, and its delegates who are selected to attend the Convention, will abide by the purpose, terms, conditions, agenda, and "Convention Rules of Order" as explained in this Agreement.

The Legislature of the State of Alabama enters into this Agreement with every other State Legislature that likewise agrees to the terms and/or conditions of this Agreement and Legislative Call as set forth herein, understanding that the LEGAL IMMIGRATION AMENDMENT Convention, by definition herein explained, is a "SINGLE ISSUE" Federal Convention and that the Convention will have no authority, under this Call and Agreement between the States, to review and/or consider any other subject matter, issue, or topic during its sessions other than business matters relating to the question, should the LEGAL IMMIGRATION AMENDMENT, as herein written, be sent by the Convention to the United States Congress instructing Congress to send the Amendment to the Several States for ratification? The Legislature of the State of Alabama irrevocably declares by signing this Agreement that any subject matter, issue or topic (other than the LEGAL IMMIGRATION AMENDMENT) that delegates might try to present to the Convention and subsequently to the States for review and/or ratification will be immediately, upon introduction at the Convention, unauthorized, invalid and automatically rejected by the Legislature of the State of Alabama, and the Legislature of the State of Alabama irrevocably declares that it will not review and/or consider for ratification any such subject matter, issue or topic, no matter how presented to it by the Convention. Only the LEGAL IMMIGRATION AMENDMENT, as herein written, will be considered by the Legislature of the State of Alabama for ratification.

The Legislature of the State of Alabama also irrevocably declares that under no circumstance(s) will it consider for review and/or ratification any amendment to the United States Constitution, submitted to it by the LEGAL IMMIGRATION AMENDMENT Convention other than the LEGAL IMMIGRATION AMENDMENT as herein written.

The Legislature of the State of Alabama further irrevocably declares that under no circumstance(s) will it consider for review and/or ratification any modified form of the LEGAL IMMIGRATION AMENDMENT submitted to it by the LEGAL IMMIGRATION AMENDMENT Convention that would change, alter, or replace, in any way (which includes the wording, spelling, punctuation, or paragraph sections), the LEGAL IMMIGRATION AMENDMENT from its written form herein.

The Legislature of the State of Alabama further irrevocably declares that under no circumstance(s) will it consider for review and/or ratification any proposal, of any kind, sent to it by the LEGAL IMMIGRATION AMENDMENT Convention that would change, replace, or alter the United States Constitution other than the LEGAL IMMIGRATION AMENDMENT as herein written.

The Legislature of the State of Alabama further irrevocably declares that under no circumstance(s) will it consider for review any proposal, of any kind, sent to it by the LEGAL IMMIGRATION AMENDMENT Convention that would change, replace, or alter, in any way (which includes the wording, spelling, punctuation and section paragraphs), this Official Legislative Call for the LEGAL IMMIGRATION AMENDMENT Convention and the terms and/or conditions of this Agreement between the States as herein written.

Under the authority reserved to the State of Alabama in Article V of the United States Constitution and also under Article IV, Section 4 which guarantees to every State a Republican form of Government, the Legislature of the State of Alabama hereby approves this Legislative Call on the United States Congress directing Congress to convene the LEGAL IMMIGRATION AMENDMENT Convention and binds itself with each and every State that likewise approves this identical Legislative Call according the terms and/or conditions set forth in this Agreement.

OFFICIAL CALL BY THE STATE OF ALABAMA ON THE UNITED STATES CONGRESS DIRECTING CONGRESS TO CONVENE THE LEGAL IMMIGRATION AMENDMENT CONVENTION

The Legislature of the State of Alabama hereby Calls on the United States Congress directing Congress to convene a Federal Convention to be titled the LEGAL IMMIGRATION AMENDMENT Convention. The Convention is to be convened immediately after two thirds of the Several States have completed their Calls for the LEGAL IMMIGRATION AMENDMENT Convention.

The State of Alabama is authorized to make this Call for the LEGAL IMMIGRATION AMENDMENT Convention under the authority reserved to the States in Article V of the United States Constitution and under Article IV, Section 4 which guarantees to every State a Republican form of Government. Both Articles give to each State an equal standing when calling for a

RECLAIMING AMERICA

Constitutional Convention. Article V and Article IV, Section 4 reserves to the Several States the right to Call for a Federal Convention for the purpose of amending the United

States Constitution when Congress and/or the Courts refuse to address an egregious wrong suffered by the people.

Submitted to Both Houses of the United States Congress on this date _____, _____ by the Legislature of the State of Alabama.

State of Alabama Seal:

Authorized Signatures with titles:

_____Title_____

_____Title_____

_____Title_____

_____Title_____

_____Title_____

_____Title_____

CHAPTER 11

TRADITIONAL MARRIAGE AMENDMENT

Text of proposed
TRADITIONAL MARRIAGE AMENDMENT
ARTICLE 28 (or alternate number to be assigned by Congress)

Section 1. Traditional Marriage consists of one man and one woman united together in matrimony and who have taken marital vows to and before each other and before a licensed official who is duly appointed to this ministration by the State.

Section 2. No alternative marriage or union between two or more individuals, no matter how structured or organized, shall be legally recognized as a valid Traditional Marriage by any jurisdiction or State.

Section 3. To secure the rights of citizens including those individuals united together in Traditional Marriages, it is hereby prohibited for any jurisdiction or State to recognize any alternative marriage as a legal marriage or legal union. It is further prohibited for any jurisdiction or State to bestow on individuals living in alternative marriages any of the rights and entitlements given to individuals in Traditional Marriages. This Article shall be enforceable in the United States which shall include the Several States, the District of Columbia, and the Commonwealth of Puerto Rico, the Commonwealth of the Northern Mariana Islands and the territories and possessions of the United States.

Section 4. Congress shall have the power to enforce by appropriate legislation, the provisions of the Article.

The American people must protect the one institution that God has ordained for the protection and reproduction of the human race. One man and one woman performing their natural roles in a Traditional Marriage provides social stability morally, spiritually and financially. Deliberate falsehoods by those who argue that alternative marriages should be recognized by government as legitimate institutions denigrates the moral quality of our society and perpetuates ideas that undermine the only institution that can protect us.

1. Over 50 million marriages have wound up in divorce. Marriage is the bedrock institution given to us by God for our safety and wellbeing. Christian values and morality are passed on to successive generations through strong Christian marriages.

   According to Jennifer Baker of the *Forest Institute of Professional Psychology* in Springfield, Missouri the divorce rate in America is 50% for first marriages, 67% for second marriages, and 74% of third marriages.

   Consider the following consequences of divorce:

   a. As a consequence of divorce alternative marriages between men and men and women and women became more palatable.
   b. Another consequence has been the near total disregard for human life whereby American women can kill with impunity her unwanted Unborn Child, America's posterity and the father's heritage. There has been a dramatic uptick in the abortion rate as the number of divorces increased.
   c. Men no longer see themselves as the protector, provider and sacrificer of their wives and children. Because they no longer have a respected role in American society, they are trained up to believe their personal desires are all that matter. Masculinity, accountability and male authority are no longer honored qualities for men. With this degenerate view of manhood comes terrible consequences:

      i. In 1990 36% of America's children lived apart from their biological fathers. In 2000 that percentage is estimated at 50%. In the black community over 70% of children either don't know their fathers or live apart from them.

ii. It is estimated that only 50% of the children born during the 1970-84 "baby bust" period will still live with both of their natural parents by age 17—a staggering drop from nearly 80 percent before 1970.

iii. As a direct consequence of divorce and feminist ideologies boys have fallen behind girls in academics, earnings capacity, and workplace achievement. The reasons for this are many including indoctrination by feminists that women are either better than or equal to men, the problematic combination of testosterone and adolescents in boys that inhibits his structured learning capabilities in school, and the minority status our government has given women (which gives women great advantages in schools, pro-fessions, workplace rules, government grants, SBA loans, contracts, employee privileges, etc.).

iv. Masculinity is primarily a learned character trait. Consider this scenario: when a baby girl is born, she attaches to her mother and after being weaned she continues to identify with her mother's gender characteristics. There is no need for her to change her gender identity. However, when a boy is born the experience is not only different, but it is also traumatic. Early on he attaches to his mother and after being weaned he begins to realize that his gender is different. When his father is present, he begins to acquire masculine characteristics that will shape him for the rest of his life. The identify change from his mother's gender to masculine character traits is a traumatic transition that only boys experience. If there is no father in the home the boy has no role model to help him learn how to be a man.

v. Divorce damages the masculinity of men because it deprives boys of *the* essential male role model in his home – his father. Couple this with a society that aggressively promotes feminist ideology which demands further empowerment of women over men and the man sheepishly withdraws from his traditional role of provider, protector and sacrificer of his wife and children. Masculinity must be taught by the mother and reinforced by the father. Our culture does neither.

vi. 1 million men are felonized every year primarily because Christian morality is not taught to them as children. Instead of being taught that they have an honored place of leadership and responsibility in the home and workplace, they are denigrated with propaganda that tells them they are "male Chauvinist pigs". The male image in the media is usually one of presenting men as buffoons, especially in commercials and entertainment. The woman is shown as a voluptuous genius.

vii. Approximately 30 million American men are felons today. A fact that defames and emasculates men and God's intended role for them. The impact of felonizing 30 million men (30% of our adult male population) means that he is continually marginalized under the laws that give women minority status. His felony record prevents him from securing the best jobs, it hurts his credit, it prevents him from advancing his education, it prevents him from being awarded many government contracts, he is forever looked upon by law enforcement and prosecutors suspiciously which greatly increasing the recidivism rate among felons.

There is no greater value than to be made in the image of God. Men and women are God's crowning achievement in creation. As He continues to work out His purposes for our families and society, we will experience greater safety and blessings within traditional marriages. Divorce produces a gender imbalance that removes the protections that all in the family need. The ultimate consequence of divorce is the loss of our gender excellences and God's intended best for us.

AUTHORIZED CALL
BY THE GEORGIA STATE LEGISLATURE
ON THE UNITED STATES CONGRESS INSTRUCTING
CONGRESS TO CONVENE A FEDERAL CONVENTION TO BE
TITLED THE TRADITIONAL MARRIAGE AMENDMENT
CONVENTION

THIS AUTHORIZED CALL ALSO DEFINES THE AGREEMENT
THE GEORGIA STATE LEGISLATURE IS ENTERING INTO
BETWEEN ITSELF AND OTHER CALLING STATES

To: **BOTH HOUSES OF UNITED STATES CONGRESS**

UNITED STATES SENATE:

President of the Senate, United States Vice President
Majority Leader Senator
Minority Leader Senator
President Pro Tempore Senator
Republican Whip Senator
Democratic Whip Senator

(Deliver this Official Call to every current leader and member of the United
State Senate at Washington, DC)

HOUSE OF REPRESENTATIVE:

Speaker of the House Representative
House Majority Leader Representative
House Majority Whip Representative
House Minority Leader Representative
House Minority Whip Representative

(Deliver this Official Call to every current leader and member of the United
State House of Representatives at Washington, DC)

From: **THE STATE LEGISLATURE OF THE STATE OF GEORGIA**

The Legislature of the State of GEORGIA hereby Calls on the United States
Congress instructing Congress to convene a Federal Convention called the
TRADITIONAL MARRIAGE AMENDMENT Convention under the authority
reserved to the States in Article V of the United States Constitution. Article IV,
Section 4 guarantees to every State a Republican form of Government which

gives each State equal standing when Calling for a Constitutional Convention. Article V reserves to the Several States the right to Call for a Federal Constitutional Convention for the purpose of amending the United States Constitution when Congress and/or the Courts refuse to address an egregious wrong suffered by the people. The States *alone* have the authority to "limit" the agenda and authority of a Federal Convention. The States alone can Call for a "Single Issue" Convention by agreeing among themselves the purpose, terms, conditions, duration, and agenda for the Convention. Congress does not have the authority to define a "Single Issue" Convention. Congress' authority, under Article V of the United States Constitution, empowers it to convene a Convention as Called for and defined by the Several States. The Several States alone have the authority to enforce the terms and/or conditions set forth in this Agreement at the TRADITIONAL MARRIAGE AMENDMENT Convention.

The TRADITIONAL MARRIAGE AMENDMENT Convention will be a "Single Issue" Federal Convention as defined in this Legislative Call on the United States Congress and in this binding Agreement between the Several States. The delegates summoned to this Convention by Congress will have the authority to decide only one issue, should the TRADITIONAL MARRIAGE AMENDMENT, as herein written, be sent to Congress with instructions to send the Amendment back to the Several States for ratification? The delegates at the TRADITIONAL MARRIAGE AMENDMENT Convention will have no authority to change the wording of the proposed Amendment, neither are they authorized to deliberate on or discuss any other subject matter or issue at the Convention. The purpose, terms and/or conditions that will govern the agenda and affairs of the TRADITIONAL MARRIAGE AMENDMENT Convention are as follows:

THE PURPOSE OF THE CONVENTION

The *only* purpose for convening the TRADITIONAL MARRIAGE AMENDMENT Convention is for the State Delegations, representing the Several States, to decide if the TRADITIONAL MARRIAGE AMENDMENT, as herein written, should be sent to the United States Congress with instructions for Congress to send the Amendment to the Several States for ratification? Absolutely no other business is authorized at this Convention.

CONVENTION RULES OF ORDER

The "Convention Rules of Order" that all Delegates and State Delegations are required to follow as a condition of participating at the TRADITIONAL MARRIAGE AMENDMENT Convention are described in this Legislative Call on Congress. From time to time, in order to facilitate Convention business, the Convention Chairman may require the Convention to follow "Robert's Rules of Order" when a specific Rule of Order is not defined in this Legislative Call. The

Delegates and State Delegations are required to honor the Convention Chairman's instructions when applying Convention Rules of Order and/or Roberts Rules of Order.

TRADITIONAL MARRIAGE AMENDMENT COMMITTEE

The TRADITIONAL MARRIAGE AMENDMENT Committee is the citizens group that founded the TRADITIONAL MARRIAGE AMENDMENT Initiative. This Committee will be responsible for pre-Convention planning and organization. The Chairman and Vice Chairman of the TRADITIONAL MARRIAGE AMENDMENT Committee will be Ex-Officio (without voting rights) members of the Convention. They can be called upon by the Convention Chairman to clarify the TRADITIONAL MARRIAGE AMENDMENT legislative strategy for the Delegates, provide progress reports in the States and also be available for questions and answers from Delegates at the Convention. They will be subject to the terms and/or conditions of this Legislative Call and Agreement between the States.

If they are also appointed as Delegates by their State Legislatures, then they will be entitled to voting privileges as Delegates at the Convention. The Chairman of the TRADITIONAL MARRIAGE AMENDMENT Committee is R. C. "Kacprowicz" Casper.

If the Convention votes in favor of the Amendment, the TRADITIONAL MARRIAGE AMENDMENT Committee will be responsible for post-convention planning and organization during the ratification process.

FUNDING THE CONVENTION AND STATE DELEGATIONS

The State Legislatures that send Delegates to the TRADITIONAL MARRIAGE AMENDMENT Convention shall be responsible for providing monies necessary for their State Delegations to participate at the Convention. The amounts each State Delegation will require will be decided by each State Legislature. Other expenses or costs necessary to fund the Convention are to be shared by the Calling States equally. From time to time the Convention Chairman will notify the State Delegations what monies will be necessary to carry on the business of the Convention.

FUNDING FOR "PRE AND POST-CONVENTION PLANNING AND ORGANIZATION"

Each State Legislature making a Call on Congress to convene the TRADITIONAL MARRIAGE AMENDMENT Convention will be asked to share expenses for "pre-Convention planning" and "pre-Convention organization". If the Convention votes to send the TRADITIONAL MARRIAGE AMENDMENT to Congress to be ratified by the States, then the

TRADITIONAL MARRIAGE AMENDMENT Committee will ask the Calling States to help fund post-convention planning and organization to cover expenses for the ratification process.

DELEGATES SUMMONED BY CONGRESS

Congress has the authority, under Article V, to summon Delegates from the Several States to the TRADITIONAL MARRIAGE AMENDMENT Convention. Congress is hereby directed to summon to the Convention the appropriate number of Delegates that each State is entitled to immediately after two thirds of the States complete their Call directing Congress to convene the TRADITIONAL MARRIAGE AMENDMENT Convention. The number of Delegates to be summoned to the Convention should be equal to the number of members each State has in the House of Representatives and in the Senate of the United States Congress.

DELEGATES AND STATE DELEGATIONS

Only State Delegates summoned by Congress to the TRADITIONAL MARRIAGE AMENDMENT Convention and appointed by their State Legislatures to form State Delegations to represent their respective States are authorized to attend and speak at the TRADITIONAL MARRIAGE AMENDMENT Convention. Each State Legislature has the responsibility to select, from within its State, individual Delegates who will represent its State at the Convention. The number of Delegates selected by a State Legislature can be no greater than the number of Delegates summoned by Congress from its State. Each State Delegation must select a Delegate from within its delegation to be its Spokesman at the Convention. Only a Delegation's Spokesman will be recognized by the Convention Chairman.

THE PRE-CONVENTION "ACTING CONVENTION CHAIRMAN" AND "ASSISTANT ACTING CONVENTION CHAIRMAN"

The Chairman and Vice Chairman of the TRADITIONAL MARRIAGE AMENDMENT Committee will have exclusive authority to complete all pre-convention planning and organization for the TRADITIONAL MARRIAGE AMENDMENT Convention. They will perform their duties under the titles "Acting Convention Chairman" and "Assistant Acting Convention Chairman" respectfully. They will also be available to State Legislatures to assist with their Legislative Calls and pre-Convention planning.

The Chairman and Vice Chairman of the TRADITIONAL MARRIAGE AMENDMENT Committee will also be responsible for post-convention planning and organization if the Convention votes to send the TRADITIONAL MARRIAGE AMENDMENT to Congress to be ratified by the States.

VOTING BY DELEGATES IN STATE DELEGATIONS

It is recommended that a simple majority of the Delegates within each State Delegation be required to decide a State Delegation's vote at the Convention. A quorum within each State Delegation will consist of one Delegate. The business of the Convention and voting will not be delayed if a State Delegation does not cast a vote during a roll call.

QUORUM REQUIRED FOR CONDUCTING BUSINESS AND VOTING AT THE CONVENTION

Each State Delegation will have one vote on all matters that are to be decided by the Convention. A simple majority vote by the State Delegations at the Convention is required to decide the outcome of all business brought before the Convention for a vote, including whether or not the TRADITIONAL MARRIAGE AMENDMENT, as herein written, should be sent to the Several States, via Congress, for ratification. A quorum at the Convention for the purpose of conducting business and voting will consist of 17 State Delegations.

CLOSED DELIBERATIONS AT THE CONVENTION

The TRADITIONAL MARRIAGE AMENDMENT Convention will be closed to all media and news groups. Only delegates appointed by their State Legislatures and the Chairman and Vice Chairman of the TRADITIONAL MARRIAGE AMENDMENT Committee will be authorized to enter and speak at the Convention. No visitors, reporters, government officials, professionals or inquirers, of any kind, will be permitted to enter the Convention facilities. Unauthorized visitors will be escorted by the Sergeant of Arms out of the Convention. After the vote by the State Delegations is taken to determine if the TRADITIONAL MARRIAGE AMENDMENT will be sent to the Several States, via Congress, for ratification, the Chairman of the Convention will call a special press conference to announce the Convention's decision. Within 30 days from the special press conference the Chairman will make available to the public the records kept by the Convention during its proceedings.

STATE LEGISLATURES NOT AUTHORIZING THIS CALL FOR THE TRADITIONAL MARRIAGE AMENDMENT CONVENTION

State Legislatures that did not authorize this Call for the TRADITIONAL MARRIAGE AMENDMENT Convention and yet agree to send delegates representing their State agree to follow the terms and/or conditions set forth in this Agreement and Legislative Call. They need to pay particular attention to the "Convention's Rules of Order" described in this Agreement and the prohibitions in the section titled "Prohibitions for Delegates, State Delegations and/or Convention Officials at the Convention". These non-calling States must notify the "Acting Convention Chairman" before the Convention convenes of

their intention to attend the Convention so accommodations can be completed for their Delegations. In order to receive Convention Passes, all Delegates attending the Convention, will be required to sign an agreement promising to abide by the terms and/or conditions in this Legislative Call and Agreement.

NO WEAPONS ALLOWED AT THE CONVENTION

Delegates and TRADITIONAL MARRIAGE AMENDMENT Committee officials will not be allowed to bring into the TRADITIONAL MARRIAGE AMENDMENT Convention any weapons or objects that can be construed as weapons.

PRESENTING ARGUMENTS AT THE CONVENTION
BY STATE DELEGATIONS

Each State Delegation will be allotted a maximum of 60 minutes for presenting its argument(s) at the Convention for or against sending the TRADITIONAL MARRIAGE AMENDMENT to the United States Congress with instruction for Congress to send the Amendment to the Several States for ratification. Only Delegates who have been officially selected by their State Legislatures and Ex-Officio members of the Convention are authorized to speak before the Convention. Each State Delegation can use one or more of its Delegates to present its position(s). However, the total time allotted for each State Delegation is 60 minutes, which includes any time that is necessary to replace one Delegate with another. The Chairman of the TRADITIONAL MARRIAGE AMENDMENT Committee will also be limited to 60 minutes during his speaking segment. Speakers cannot reserve portions of their time to another time or day. Speakers must complete their arguments in the 60 minute segment assigned to them.

The order each State Delegation will follow when presenting their position(s) will be according to when each State completed its Legislative Call on Congress, or when it notified the "Acting Convention Chairman" that it intends to attend the Convention even though it may not complete a Legislative Call on Congress. The State Delegation presentations will be scheduled in the following manner: the first State making a Call on Congress will go first; the first State notifying the "Acting Convention Chairman" that it plans to attend will go second. The second State making a Call on Congress will go third; then the second State notifying the "Acting Convention Chairman" will go fourth, and so forth until all States wanting to present their positions have had an opportunity to do so. The Convention Chairman can rearrange the schedule if any conflicts arise at the Convention. The last speaker to be scheduled at the Convention for a 60 minute segment will be the Chairman of the TRADITIONAL MARRIAGE AMENDMENT Committee.

DUTIES OF THE "ACTING CONVENTION CHAIRMAN"

The duties of the "Acting Convention Chairman include:

1. organize a pre-Convention support group for assisting Calling States with their Legislative Calls and non-calling States with their intentions to attend the Convention
2. set up an TRADITIONAL MARRIAGE AMENDMENT Committee checking account use generally accepted accounting principles when keeping records of all receipts and expenditures
3. provide financial reports and minutes of pre-convention activities as requested by States that are funding pre-convention operations
4. keep minutes of all business meetings of the TRADITIONAL MARRIAGE AMENDMENT Committee
5. determine the budget that will be needed for pre-convention planning and organizing and notify each State Legislature of its share of the expenses
6. assist the Calling States and Attending States with their pre-convention planning
7. assist the Calling States with their Legislative Calls on Congress
8. after the TRADITIONAL MARRIAGE AMENDMENT Convention has been convened call the Convention to order
9. invite nominations from the State Delegations present at the Convention to fill the "Convention Chairman's" position (the maximum number of nominees permitted is five and only one nominee from any one State Delegation is permitted)
10. take a roll call from the State Delegations for the nominee(s)
11. declare the winner based on the nominee who has received the most votes (a plurality of State Delegations). Each State Delegation will have one vote
12. officiate the installation of the "Convention Chairman" at the Convention by having the Chairman place his/her right hand on the Bible while repeating the following oath

    "I solemnly promise to officiate the office of Convention Chairman for the TRADITIONAL MARRIAGE AMENDMENT Convention according to the terms and/or conditions set forth in the Legislative Calls from the Several States to the best of my ability, so help me God".

    In the event the "Acting Convention Chairman" is nominated and elected to the Convention Chairman position, the "Assistant Acting Convention Chairman" will conduct the installation ceremony for the Convention Chairman.

RECLAIMING AMERICA

ELECTION, AUTHORITY AND DUTIES OF CONVENTION OFFICIALS

CONVENTION CHAIRMAN: - The "Convention Chairman" is the senior official at the TRADITIONAL MARRIAGE AMENDMENT Convention. He/she will have the requisite authority to oversee all activities at the Convention, including the nomination and election of all officials. The Convention Chairman's duties include:

1. organize and oversee all business and activities at the Convention
2. organize and officiate all nominations, elections and installations of officials at the Convention (this will be the Convention Chairman's first order of business)
3. organize and officiate all nominations, elections and installations of official positions that may become vacant at the Convention
4. oversee the enforcement of all Convention Rules
5. oversee the enforcement of the terms and/or conditions (herein described) of this Call and Agreement by the States
6. oversee the investigation of alleged and/or actual violations of this Agreement as defined in the section titled "Violating this Agreement"
7. bring before the Convention all matters that require a vote
8. bring before the Convention the financial needs of the Convention and time lines for when these monies are needed
9. cut off motions or discussions by State Delegations before the Convention if and when it seems appropriate
10. recognize the Spokesman within a State Delegation for the purpose of addressing a matter of importance to the Spokesman's Delegation (the Convention Chairman will have full authority to determine if a matter brought before the Convention by the Spokesman is appropriate for further discussion and/or if a decision by the Convention is necessary)
11. keep the business of the Convention moving forward expeditiously, cutting off all motions and discussions when it appears one or more Delegates are trying to hinder, delay or stop the work of the Convention
12. keep the business of the Convention focused on one objective which is, should the Convention send the TRADITIONAL MARRIAGE AMENDMENT to Congress instructing Congress to send it to the Several States for ratification?
13. instruct Convention Officials (Assistant Convention Chairman, Secretary, Financial Officer, Executive Administrator, Sergeant at Arms, and Deputies) on their duties at the Convention
14. officiate and remedy any and all problems that may develop at the Convention
15. oversee the design and production of "Official" Convention Badges for the Sergeant at Arms and Deputies

16. notify all State Legislatures of the decision the Convention made as to whether or not the TRADITIONAL MARRIAGE AMENDMENT should be sent to Congress instructing Congress to send it to the States for ratification?
17. if the State Delegations voted to send the Amendment to the States for ratification, include the Convention's recommendation to the United States Congress as to whether it should be ratified by State Conventions or State Legislatures
18. declare the TRADITIONAL MARRIAGE AMENDMENT Convention closed after the State Delegations have decided if the TRADITIONAL MARRIAGE AMENDMENT should be sent to Congress instructing Congress to send it to the States for ratification?
19. arrange a Special News Conference to announce the decision by the TRADITIONAL MARRIAGE AMENDMENT Convention
20. make available the proceedings of the Convention to the public 30 days after the Convention is closed

The first order of business for the "Convention Chairman" will be to open the Convention to nominations from State Delegations present for each of the following Convention Officials; one Assistant Convention Chairman, one Secretary, one Financial Officer, one Executive Administrator, one Sergeant at Arms and ten Deputies (the maximum number of nominees permitted for each Convention Official position is five. Only one nominee for each Convention Official position is permitted from any one State Delegation. The nominee with a plurality of votes from the State Delegations will be the winner). The "Convention Chairman" can call for nominations for more than 10 Deputies if and when circumstances warrant.

ASSISTANT CONVENTION CHAIRMAN
The "Assistant Convention Chairman" duties include:

1. be amenable to the "Convention Chairman"
2. provide assistance to the "Convention Chairman" in all matters pertaining to the business of the Convention
3. monitor activities at the Convention and report to the "Convention Chairman" violations or possible violations of the terms and/or conditions of this Legislative Call and Agreement
4. perform the duties of the "Convention Chairman" when called upon by the Chairman or when the Chairman is unable to perform the duties of his/her office
5. the "Assistant Convention Chairman" will take the following oath, administered by the Convention Chairman, while placing his/her right hand on the Bible

"I solemnly promise to officiate the office of Assistant Convention Chairman for the TRADITIONAL MARRIAGE AMENDMENT Convention according to the terms and/or conditions set forth in the Legislative Calls from the Several States to the best of my ability, so help me God".

SECRETARY - The "Secretary's" duties include:

1. keep official minutes of all proceedings at the Convention
2. monitor activities at the Convention and report to the Convention Chairman violations or possible violations of Convention Rules and of the terms and/or conditions of this Legislative Call and Agreement
3. make available to the "Convention Chairman", upon request, the official minutes of the Convention
4. be amenable to the "Convention Chairman" and "Assistant Convention Chairman"
5. in the absence of the "Convention Chairman" and the "Assistant Convention Chairman" due to death or a disablement that prevents them from performing the duties of their offices at the Convention, the Secretary shall call the Convention to order for the purpose of nominating and electing a new "Convention Chairman" and "Assistant Convention Chairman". In this capacity the Secretary will assume the duties and authority of the "Convention Chairman". If the Secretary is unable to perform the duties described herein, then they will fall to the Financial Officer.
6. the "Secretary" will take the following oath while placing his/her right hand on the Bible

"I solemnly promise to officiate the office of Secretary for the TRADITIONAL MARRIAGE AMENDMENT Convention according to the terms and/or conditions set forth in the Legislative Calls from the Several States to the best of my ability, so help me God".

FINANCIAL OFFICER - The "Financial Officer's" duties include:

1. keep detailed accounting records of all financial matters at the Convention using generally accepted accounting principles
2. be amenable to the "Convention Chairman" and "Assistant Convention Chairman"
3. monitor activities at the Convention and report to the Convention Chairman violations or possible violations of the terms and/or conditions of this Legislative Call and Agreement

4. set up a checking account in the name of the TRADITIONAL MARRIAGE AMENDMENT Convention requiring any two of the following three officers when signing a check or making withdrawals – Convention Chairman, Assistant Convention Chairman, Financial Officer
5. make available to the "Convention Chairman", upon request, all financial records at the Convention
6. provide to the Convention Chairman the financial needs of the Convention and the time lines as to when these monies are needed
7. in the absence of a "Convention Chairman", "Assistant Convention Chairman", and "Secretary" due to death or a disablement that prevents them from performing the duties of their offices at the Convention, the Financial Officer shall call the Convention to order for the purpose of nominating and electing a new "Convention Chairman", "Assistant Convention Chairman", and "Secretary". In this capacity the Financial Officer will assume the duties and authority of the "Convention Chairman"
8. the "Financial Officer" will take the following oath while placing his/her right hand on the Bible

"I solemnly promise to officiate the office of Financial Officer for the TRADITIONAL MARRIAGE AMENDMENT Convention according to generally accepted accounting principles and according to the terms and/or conditions set forth in the Legislative Calls from the Several States to the best of my ability, so help me God".

EXECUTIVE ADMINISTRATOR
The "Executive Administrator's" duties include:

1. facilitate all Convention business as directed by the Convention Chairman
2. be amenable to the Convention Chairman and Assistant Convention Chairman
3. monitor activities at the Convention and report to the Convention Chairman violations or possible violations of the terms and/or conditions of this Legislative Call and Agreement
4. keep detailed reports of all administrative activities at the Convention
5. make available to the "Convention Chairman" upon request all administrative records and/or reports at the Convention
6. the "Executive Administrator" will take the following oath while placing his/her right hand on the Bible

"I solemnly promise to officiate the office of Executive Administrator for the TRADITIONAL MARRIAGE AMENDMENT Convention according to the terms and/or conditions set forth in the Legislative

Calls from the Several States to the best of my ability, so help me God".

SERGEANT AT ARMS
The "Sergeant at Arms'" duties include:

1. be amenable to the Convention Chairman and Assistant Convention Chairman
2. monitor all activities at the Convention and report to the Convention Chairman violations or possible violations of the terms and/or conditions of this Legislative Call and Agreement
3. maintain order at the Convention
4. enforce all remedies for violations of this Legislative Call and Agreement as directed by the Convention Chairman
5. organize and direct the activities of all Deputies at the Convention
6. oversee, train and manage all Deputies at the Convention
7. the "Sergeant at Arms" will take the following oath while placing his/her right hand on the Bible

"I solemnly promise to officiate the office of Sergeant at Arms for the TRADITIONAL MARRIAGE AMENDMENT Convention according to the terms and/or conditions set forth in the Legislative Calls from the Several States to the best of my ability, so help me God".

DEPUTIES – The "Deputies'" duties include:

1. be amenable to the Convention Chairman, Assistant Convention Chairman and Sergeant at Arms
2. monitor all activities at the Convention and report to the Sergeant at Arms violations or possible violations of the terms and/or conditions of this Legislative Call and Agreement
3. maintain order at the Convention as directed by the Sergeant at Arms
4. enforce all remedies for violations of this Legislative Call and Agreement as directed by the Convention Chairman and/or the Sergeant at Arms
5. "Deputies" will take the following oath while placing his/her right hand on the Bible

"I solemnly promise to officiate the office of Deputy for the TRADITIONAL MARRIAGE AMENDMENT Convention according to the terms and/or conditions set forth in the Legislative Calls from the Several States to the best of my ability, so help me God".

CHALLENGING THE QUALIFICATIONS OF CONVENTION OFFICIALS

A State Delegation can challenge the qualifications of any Convention Official at the TRADITIONAL MARRIAGE AMENDMENT Convention by bringing its allegation(s), during a business session, to the Convention floor. The Convention Chairman will consider the allegation(s) and determine if it merits further investigation. If the Chairman decides that the allegation(s) merits further investigation, he/she will direct the Sergeant at Arms to conduct the necessary inquiry. He/she will then follow the instructions outlined in the section "Violating this Agreement" for proscribing a remedy or remedies.

The "Convention Chairman" can also reject a challenge to the qualifications of any Convention Official if he/she concludes that the Delegate making the allegation(s) is trying to disrupt and/or delay Convention business. If after following the instructions outlined in "Violating this Agreement" the Delegate is found to have made a false accusation against a Convention Official, the Delegate's State Delegation will be charged with a violation of the terms and/or conditions of this Call and Agreement.

PROHIBITIONS FOR STATE DELEGATES, STATE DELEGATIONS AND CONVENTION OFFICIALS AT THE CONVENTION

State Delegates, State Delegations and Convention Officials are prohibited from violating any of the following Convention prohibitions:

1. State Delegates, State Delegations and Convention Officials are prohibited, at the Convention, from introducing, discussing, voting on, or sending to the States for consideration and/or ratification any amendment to the United States Constitution other than the TRADITIONAL MARRIAGE AMENDMENT, as herein written
2. State Delegates, State Delegations and Convention Officials are prohibited from altering or changing, in any way (which includes the wording, spelling, punctuation, or paragraph sections), the TRADITIONAL MARRIAGE AMENDMENT from the written form shown in the section titled "The full text of the TRADITIONAL MARRIAGE AMENDMENT"
3. State Delegates, State Delegations and Convention Officials are prohibited, at the Convention, from introducing, discussing, voting on, or sending to the States for consideration and/or ratification any alternate form of government for the United States of America
4. State Delegates, State Delegations and Convention Officials are prohibited, at the Convention, from introducing, discussing, voting on, or sending to the States for consideration and/or ratification any alternate constitution or governing document for the United States of America State Delegates, State Delegations and Convention Officials are prohibited, at the Convention, from introducing, discussing, voting on, or sending to the States for consideration and/or ratification any

changes, of any kind, to the existing Constitution of the United States of America other than the TRADITIONAL MARRIAGE AMENDMENT

5. State Delegates, State Delegations and Convention Officials are prohibited, at the Convention, from introducing, discussing, voting on, or sending to the States for consideration any changes, of any kind, to this binding Agreement between the States Calling for the TRADITIONAL MARRIAGE AMENDMENT Convention

6. State Delegates, State Delegations and Convention Officials are prohibited, at the Convention, from introducing, discussing, voting on, or sending to the States for consideration and/or ratification any subject matter, issue or topic (of any kind)

7. other than the proposed TRADITIONAL MARRIAGE AMENDMENT in its written form shown in the section titled **"The full text of the TRADITIONAL MARRIAGE AMENDMENT"**

THE DATE, TIME, DURATION AND PLACE OF THE TRADITIONAL MARRIAGE AMENDMENT CONVENTION.

The United States Congress will be responsible for determining and announcing to the Several States the date, time, and place that the TRADITIONAL MARRIAGE AMENDMENT Convention is to convene immediately after two thirds of the States, under the authority given to the States in Article V of the United States Constitution, have completed their Calls on Congress to convene the TRADITIONAL MARRIAGE AMENDMENT Convention. The Convention is expected to complete its business by the 180th day after convening. The Convention Chairman can extend the duration of the TRADITIONAL MARRIAGE AMENDMENT Convention for one additional 180 day period. The maximum number of days the Convention is authorized to be in session are 360 days. If the Convention has not decided if the TRADITIONAL MARRIAGE AMENDMENT should be sent to Congress with instructions to send the Amendment to the Several States for ratification by the end of 360 days, then the Call for the TRADITIONAL MARRIAGE AMENDMENT Convention, which was approved by the Several States under the authority granted in Article V of the United States Constitution and this agreement, will be automatically withdrawn by the Calling States and the Convention will automatically terminate at 5:00 P.M. Eastern Standard Time on the 360th day after convening. Termination of the TRADITIONAL MARRIAGE AMENDMENT Convention will automatically occur on the 360th day after convening the Convention, without requiring a formal notice by the States to the Convention, nor by the States to the United States Congress, nor by the Convention to the States, nor by the Convention to the United States Congress, although it is recommended that the Convention notify the United States Congress and the State Legislatures of its termination as a courtesy.

Under no circumstance(s) are the Delegates at the TRADITIONAL MARRIAGE AMENDMENT Convention authorized to re-convene a new or different Convention, no matter what their purpose or intent. The official Legislative Call and authority granted by the Several States and the subsequent convening of the TRADITIONAL MARRIAGE AMENDMENT Convention by Congress will be automatically invalidated and the Convention will be abolished at 5:00 P.M. Eastern Standard Time on the 360th day after the convening of the TRADITIONAL MARRIAGE AMENDMENT Convention.

VIOLATING THIS AGREEMENT

The Convention Chairman (or in the absence of the Convention Chairman the Assistant Convention Chairman) will handle allegations of a violation(s) or actual violation(s) of the terms and/or conditions of this binding Agreement between the Several States, by any one or more Delegate(s) and/or Convention Official(s), as follows:

1. When an alleged violation has been presented to the Convention Chairman, and if the Chairman decides that the allegation(s) merits further investigation, he/she will instruct the Sergeant at Arms to conduct the necessary inquiry.

2. After the inquiry has been completed, and assuming the Convention Chairman concludes that the evidence does not substantiate further review by the Convention, the allegation(s) will be dismissed by the Chairman and the Convention will go forward with its business.

3. If however, after the inquiry has been completed, the Convention Chairman concludes that the evidence does substantiate further review by the Convention, the Chairman will present the allegation(s) and findings of the inquiry to the Convention for a discussion and vote. If a majority of the State Delegations (one vote per State Delegation) decide that no violation of the terms and/or conditions of this Legislative Call and Agreement has occurred, then the Chairman will declare that the alleged violation(s) of the terms and/or conditions of this Legislative Call and Agreement is/are dismissed. The Convention will then go forward with its business.

4. If however, after the inquiry has been completed, the Convention Chairman concludes that the evidence does substantiate further review by the Convention, the Chairman will present the allegation(s) and findings of the inquiry to the Convention for a discussion and vote. If a majority of the State Delegations (one vote per State Delegation) decide that one or more violation(s) of the terms and/or conditions of this Legislative Call and Agreement has/have occurred, then the Chairman will declare to the Convention that the Delegate(s)

responsible for the violation(s), and their State Delegation(s), has/have been charged with "Violating this Agreement". The Convention will then go forward with its business.

5. If a State Delegation is charged with two violations of the terms and/or conditions of this Legislative Call and Agreement, the Convention Chairman will declare to the Convention that the State Delegation charged with violating this Agreement a second time has no further standing or authority at the Convention. The Chairman will notify the charged State Delegation that its entire delegation of Delegates must leave the Convention immediately and they will not be allowed back into the Convention. The Chairman will instruct the Sergeant at Arms that he should escort the charged State Delegation out of the Convention. The Convention Chairman will then notify the State Legislature that sent the charged State Delegation of the actions that the Convention has taken and inform them that they can send a replacement State Delegation to the Convention as long as they do not disrupt the proceedings of the Convention. None of the original Delegates who were charged by the Convention will be allowed back into the Convention as part of a replacement delegation.

6. The Convention Chairman will not allow unreasonable delays in the proceedings of the Convention due to disruptive Delegates or State Delegations. He/she will move the business of the Convention forward expeditiously.

THE FULL TEXT OF THE TRADITIONAL MARRIAGE AMENDMENT

The full text of the TRADITIONAL MARRIAGE AMENDMENT to be submitted to the Several States by the United States Congress for ratification shall read as follows:

TRADITIONAL MARRIAGE AMENDMENT
ARTICLE 28 (or alternate number to be assigned by Congress)

Section 1. Traditional Marriage consists of one man and one woman united together in matrimony and who have taken marital vows to and before each other and before a licensed official who is duly appointed to this ministration by the State.

Section 2. No alternative marriage or union between two or more individuals, no matter how structured or organized, shall be legally recognized as a valid Traditional Marriage by any jurisdiction or State.

Section 3. To secure the rights of citizens including those individuals united together in Traditional Marriages, it is hereby prohibited for any jurisdiction or State to recognize any alternative marriage as a legal marriage or legal union. It is further prohibited for any jurisdiction or State to bestow on individuals living in alternative marriages any of the rights and entitlements given to individuals in Traditional Marriages. This Article shall be enforceable in the United States which shall include the Several States, the District of Columbia, and the Commonwealth of Puerto Rico, the Commonwealth of the Northern Mariana Islands and the territories and possessions of the United States.

Section 4. Congress shall have the power to enforce by appropriate legislation, the provisions of the Article.

RATIFICATION OF THE "TRADITIONAL MARRIAGE AMENDMENT"

Under the requirements of Article V of the United States Constitution and also under Article IV, Section 4 which guarantees to every State a Republican form of Government, the TRADITIONAL MARRIAGE AMENDMENT will become a ratified Amendment to the United States Constitution when three quarters of the Several States complete their ratifications of the Amendment.

"CONGRESSIONAL" OPTION

If the United States Congress voluntarily sends the TRADITIONAL MARRIAGE AMENDMENT to the Several States for ratification without making any changes, of any kind (which includes the wording, spelling, punctuation and paragraph sections) in the proposed Amendment as herein written, and before two thirds of the States complete their Call for Congress to convene the TRADITIONAL MARRIAGE AMENDMENT Convention, then the Legislature of the State of GEORGIA will withdraw its Call for the TRADITIONAL MARRIAGE AMENDMENT Convention.

OFFICIAL AGREEMENT BY THE GEORGIA STATE LEGISLATURE BETWEEN ITSELF AND THE CALLING STATES

The Legislature of the State of GEORGIA enters into this binding Agreement with every other State Legislature that likewise agrees to the terms and/or conditions of this Legislative Call and Agreement as set forth herein. This is an irrevocable contract, during the term of this Agreement, between the State of

GEORGIA and each and every State that signs this Agreement and completes its Call on the United States Congress directing Congress to convene a Federal Convention titled the TRADITIONAL MARRIAGE AMENDMENT Convention. The Legislature of the State of GEORGIA agrees that it, and its delegates who are selected to attend the Convention, will abide by the purpose, terms, conditions, agenda, and "Convention Rules of Order" as explained in this Agreement.

The Legislature of the State of GEORGIA enters into this Agreement with every other State Legislature that likewise agrees to the terms and/or conditions of this Agreement and Legislative Call as set forth herein, understanding that the TRADITIONAL MARRIAGE AMENDMENT Convention, by definition herein explained, is a "SINGLE ISSUE" Federal Convention and that the Convention will have no authority, under this Call and Agreement between the States, to review and/or consider any other subject matter, issue, or topic during its sessions other than business matters relating to the question, should the TRADITIONAL MARRIAGE AMENDMENT, as herein written, be sent by the Convention to the United States Congress instructing Congress to send the Amendment to the Several States for ratification? The Legislature of the State of GEORGIA irrevocably declares by signing this Agreement that any subject matter, issue or topic (other than the TRADITIONAL MARRIAGE AMENDMENT) that delegates might try to present to the Convention and subsequently to the States for review and/or ratification will be immediately, upon introduction at the Convention, unauthorized, invalid and automatically rejected by the Legislature of the State of GEORGIA, and the Legislature of the State of GEORGIA irrevocably declares that it will not review and/or consider for ratification any such subject matter, issue or topic, no matter how presented to it by the Convention. Only the TRADITIONAL MARRIAGE AMENDMENT, as herein written, will be considered by the Legislature of the State of GEORGIA for ratification.

The Legislature of the State of GEORGIA also irrevocably declares that under no circumstance(s) will it consider for review and/or ratification any amendment to the United States Constitution, submitted to it by the TRADITIONAL MARRIAGE AMENDMENT Convention other than the TRADITIONAL MARRIAGE AMENDMENT as herein written.

The Legislature of the State of GEORGIA further irrevocably declares that under no circumstance(s) will it consider for review and/or ratification any modified form of the TRADITIONAL MARRIAGE AMENDMENT submitted to it by the TRADITIONAL MARRIAGE AMENDMENT Convention that would change, alter, or replace, in any way (which includes the wording, spelling, punctuation, or paragraph sections), the TRADITIONAL MARRIAGE AMENDMENT from its written form herein.

The Legislature of the State of GEORGIA further irrevocably declares that under no circumstance(s) will it consider for review and/or ratification any proposal, of any kind, sent to it by the TRADITIONAL MARRIAGE AMENDMENT Convention that would change, replace, or alter the United

States Constitution other than the TRADITIONAL MARRIAGE AMENDMENT as herein written.

The Legislature of the State of GEORGIA further irrevocably declares that under no circumstance(s) will it consider for review any proposal, of any kind, sent to it by the TRADITIONAL MARRIAGE AMENDMENT Convention that would change, replace, or alter, in any way (which includes the wording, spelling, punctuation and section paragraphs), this Official Legislative Call for the TRADITIONAL MARRIAGE AMENDMENT Convention and the terms and/or conditions of this Agreement between the States as herein written.

Under the authority reserved to the State of GEORGIA in Article V of the United States Constitution and also under Article IV, Section 4 which guarantees to every State a Republican form of Government, the Legislature of the State of GEORGIA hereby approves this Legislative Call on the United States Congress directing Congress to convene the TRADITIONAL MARRIAGE AMENDMENT Convention and binds itself with each and every State that likewise approves this identical Legislative Call according the terms and/or conditions set forth in this Agreement.

OFFICIAL CALL BY THE STATE OF GEORGIA ON THE UNITED STATES CONGRESS DIRECTING CONGRESS TO CONVENE THE TRADITIONAL MARRIAGE AMENDMENT CONVENTION

The Legislature of the State of GEORGIA hereby Calls on the United States Congress directing Congress to convene a Federal Convention to be titled the TRADITIONAL MARRIAGE AMENDMENT Convention. The Convention is to be convened immediately after two thirds of the Several States have completed their Calls for the TRADITIONAL MARRIAGE AMENDMENT Convention.

The State of GEORGIA is authorized to make this Call for the TRADITIONAL MARRIAGE AMENDMENT Convention under the authority reserved to the States in Article V of the United States Constitution and under Article IV, Section 4 which guarantees to every State a Republican form of Government. Both Articles give to each State an equal standing when calling for a Constitutional Convention. Article V and Article IV, Section 4 reserves to the Several States the right to Call for a Federal Convention for the purpose of amending the United States Constitution when Congress and/or the Courts refuse to address an egregious wrong suffered by the people.

Submitted to Both Houses of the United States Congress on this date _____, _____ by the Legislature of the State of GEORGIA.

RECLAIMING AMERICA

State of GEORGIA Seal:

Authorized Signatures with titles:

_____Title_____

_____Title_____

_____Title_____

_____Title_____

_____Title_____

CHAPTER 12

SCHOOL VOUCHER AMENDMENT

Text of proposed
SCHOOL VOUCHER AMENDMENT
ARTICLE 28 (or alternate number to be assigned by Congress)

Section 1. It is the right of every citizen to train up their children according to their conscience, faith and capabilities without interference from the State. The rights of parents and legal guardians to choose how their children will be educated are foundational to a free people.

Section 2. School Vouchers consist of mandatory payments by the treasuries of Local, State and Federal authorities for student costs at private schools. Mandatory payments for student costs include tuition and related educational expenses.

Section 3. Private Schools can be pre-elementary, elementary, secondary, and higher education institutions.

Section 4. Private Schools that receive Local, State or Federal monies to pay for their students tuition and expenses are required to teach their students appropriate grade level academic subjects, good morals, good values, respect for the rights of others and respect for America's unique Christian/Judeo heritage and Constitutional history. Private Schools are also required to teach their students civic responsibilities in Local, State and National communities, except at the pre-elementary level.

Section 5. Private Schools have the authority to discipline students which includes reasonable corporal punishment in elementary schools for the purpose of correcting wrong behavior.

Section 6. School Vouchers are initiated at the election of parents or legal guardians on behalf of their dependent children. For the purposes of this Article, dependent children are children up to the age of 21 and still dependent on their parents or legal guardians while attending school. School Vouchers can be used to fund a student's private education at an elementary, secondary or higher education school when government funding is already authorized for the same or comparable education at a public or government school.

Section 7. School Vouchers must be paid to private schools in an amount equal to the sum of the amounts Local, State and/or Federal authorities are authorized to pay for the education of the same or similar student at a public or government school.

Section 8. Local, State and Federal authorities are prohibited from imposing on any private school certification requirements that exceed the academic requirements for public or government schools. Local, State and Federal authorities are prohibited from imposing laws, regulations or rules on private schools that are designed to inhibit the freedom of choice parents and legal guardians have when deciding to send their children to private schools. Local, State and Federal authorities are also prohibited from interfering in the academic instruction, moral and religious teaching, discipline and curriculum of private schools.

Section 9. This Article does not prevent Local, State and Federal authorities from enforcing reasonable laws that are for the protection and welfare of the American people.

Section 10. To secure the rights of parents, legal guardians and their dependent children, it is hereby prohibited to deny a student, who is a citizen of the United States the right to a private school education or deprive said student the appropriate funding for such education when the same or comparable funding is available at a public or government school. The provisions of this Article are enforceable within the United States which shall include the Several States, the District of Columbia, the Commonwealth of Puerto Rico, the Commonwealth of the Northern Mariana Islands and the territories and possessions of the United States.

Section 11. Congress shall have the power to enforce by appropriate legislation, the provisions of the Article.

American parents and legal guardians have a God given and Constitutional Right to teach their children according to their conscience, faith and capabilities. It is a violation of their Constitutional rights to be forced to send their children to schools that intentionally teach a curriculum that defies their values and personal convictions. School Vouchers will allow all parents and legal guardians to send their children to private schools that complement their family's values.

RECLAIMING AMERICA

AUTHORIZED CALL
BY THE NORTH CAROLINA STATE LEGISLATURE ON THE UNITED STATES CONGRESS INSTRUCTING CONGRESS TO CONVENE A FEDERAL CONVENTION TO BE TITLED THE SCHOOL VOUCHER AMENDMENT CONVENTION

THIS AUTHORIZED CALL ALSO DEFINES THE AGREEMENT THE NORTH CAROLINA STATE LEGISLATURE IS ENTERING INTO BETWEEN ITSELF AND OTHER CALLING STATES

To: **BOTH HOUSES OF UNITED STATES CONGRESS**

UNITED STATES SENATE:

President of the Senate, United States Vice President
Majority Leader Senator
Minority Leader Senator
President Pro Tempore Senator
Republican Whip Senator
Democratic Whip Senator

(Deliver this Official Call to every current leader and member of the United State Senate at Washington, DC)

HOUSE OF REPRESENTATIVE:

Speaker of the House Representative
House Majority Leader Representative
House Majority Whip Representative
House Minority Leader Representative
House Minority Whip Representative

(Deliver this Official Call to every current leader and member of the United State House of Representatives at Washington, DC)

From: **THE STATE LEGISLATURE OF THE STATE OF NORTH CAROLINA**

The Legislature of the State of NORTH CAROLINA hereby Calls on the United States Congress instructing Congress to convene a Federal Convention called the SCHOOL VOUCHER AMENDMENT Convention under the authority reserved to the States in Article V of the United States Constitution. Article IV,

- 155 -

Section 4 guarantees to every State a Republican form of Government which gives each State equal standing when Calling for a Constitutional Convention. Article V reserves to the Several States the right to Call for a Federal Constitutional Convention for the purpose of amending the United States Constitution when Congress and/or the Courts refuse to address an egregious wrong suffered by the people. The States *alone* have the authority to "limit" the agenda and authority of a Federal Convention. The States alone can Call for a "Single Issue" Convention by agreeing among themselves the purpose, terms, conditions, duration, and agenda for the Convention. Congress does not have the authority to define a "Single Issue" Convention. Congress' authority, under Article V of the United States Constitution, empowers it to convene a Convention as Called for and defined by the Several States. The Several States alone have the authority to enforce the terms and/or conditions set forth in this Agreement at the SCHOOL VOUCHER AMENDMENT Convention.

The SCHOOL VOUCHER AMENDMENT Convention will be a "Single Issue" Federal Convention as defined in this Legislative Call on the United States Congress and in this binding Agreement between the Several States. The delegates summoned to this Convention by Congress will have the authority to decide only one issue, should the SCHOOL VOUCHER AMENDMENT, as herein written, be sent to Congress with instructions to send the Amendment back to the Several States for ratification? The delegates at the SCHOOL VOUCHER AMENDMENT Convention will have no authority to change the wording of the proposed Amendment, neither are they authorized to deliberate on or discuss any other subject matter or issue at the Convention. The purpose, terms and/or conditions that will govern the agenda and affairs of the SCHOOL VOUCHER AMENDMENT Convention are as follows:

THE PURPOSE OF THE CONVENTION

The *only* purpose for convening the SCHOOL VOUCHER AMENDMENT Convention is for the State Delegations, representing the Several States, to decide if the SCHOOL VOUCHER AMENDMENT, as herein written, should be sent to the United States Congress with instructions for Congress to send the Amendment to the Several States for ratification? Absolutely no other business is authorized at this Convention.

CONVENTION RULES OF ORDER

The "Convention Rules of Order" that all Delegates and State Delegations are required to follow as a condition of participating at the SCHOOL VOUCHER AMENDMENT Convention are described in this Legislative Call on Congress. From time to time, in order to facilitate Convention business, the Convention Chairman may require the Convention to follow "Robert's Rules of Order" when a specific Rule of Order is not defined in this Legislative Call. The

Delegates and State Delegations are required to honor the Convention Chairman's instructions when applying Convention Rules of Order and/or Roberts Rules of Order.

SCHOOL VOUCHER AMENDMENT COMMITTEE

The SCHOOL VOUCHER AMENDMENT Committee is the citizens group that founded the SCHOOL VOUCHER AMENDMENT Initiative. This Committee will be responsible for pre-Convention planning and organization. The Chairman and Vice Chairman of the SCHOOL VOUCHER AMENDMENT Committee will be Ex-Officio (without voting rights) members of the Convention. They can be called upon by the Convention Chairman to clarify the SCHOOL VOUCHER AMENDMENT legislative strategy for the Delegates, provide progress reports in the States and also be available for questions and answers from Delegates at the Convention. They will be subject to the terms and/or conditions of this Legislative Call and Agreement between the States.

If they are also appointed as Delegates by their State Legislatures, then they will be entitled to voting privileges as Delegates at the Convention. The Chairman of the SCHOOL VOUCHER AMENDMENT Committee is R. C. "Kacprowicz" Casper.

If the Convention votes in favor of the Amendment, the SCHOOL VOUCHER AMENDMENT Committee will be responsible for post-convention planning and organization during the ratification process.

FUNDING THE CONVENTION AND STATE DELEGATIONS

The State Legislatures that send Delegates to the SCHOOL VOUCHER AMENDMENT Convention shall be responsible for providing monies necessary for their State Delegations to participate at the Convention. The amounts each State Delegation will require will be decided by each State Legislature. Other expenses or costs necessary to fund the Convention are to be shared by the Calling States equally. From time to time the Convention Chairman will notify the State Delegations what monies will be necessary to carry on the business of the Convention.

FUNDING FOR "PRE AND POST-CONVENTION PLANNING AND ORGANIZATION"

Each State Legislature making a Call on Congress to convene the SCHOOL VOUCHER AMENDMENT Convention will be asked to share expenses for "pre-Convention planning" and "pre-Convention organization". If the Convention votes to send the SCHOOL VOUCHER AMENDMENT to Congress to be ratified by the States, then the SCHOOL VOUCHER AMENDMENT Committee will ask the Calling States to help fund post-convention planning and organization to cover expenses for the ratification process.

DELEGATES SUMMONED BY CONGRESS

Congress has the authority, under Article V, to summon Delegates from the Several States to the SCHOOL VOUCHER AMENDMENT Convention. Congress is hereby directed to summon to the Convention the appropriate number of Delegates that each State is entitled to immediately after two thirds of the States complete their Call directing Congress to convene the SCHOOL VOUCHER AMENDMENT Convention. The number of Delegates to be summoned to the Convention should be equal to the number of members each State has in the House of Representatives and in the Senate of the United States Congress.

DELEGATES AND STATE DELEGATIONS

Only State Delegates summoned by Congress to the SCHOOL VOUCHER AMENDMENT Convention and appointed by their State Legislatures to form State Delegations to represent their respective States are authorized to attend and speak at the SCHOOL VOUCHER AMENDMENT Convention. Each State Legislature has the responsibility to select, from within its State, individual Delegates who will represent its State at the Convention. The number of Delegates selected by a State Legislature can be no greater than the number of Delegates summoned by Congress from its State. Each State Delegation must select a Delegate from within its delegation to be its Spokesman at the Convention. Only a Delegation's Spokesman will be recognized by the Convention Chairman.

THE PRE-CONVENTION "ACTING CONVENTION CHAIRMAN" AND "ASSISTANT ACTING CONVENTION CHAIRMAN"

The Chairman and Vice Chairman of the SCHOOL VOUCHER AMENDMENT Committee will have exclusive authority to complete all pre-convention planning and organization for the SCHOOL VOUCHER AMENDMENT Convention. They will perform their duties under the titles "Acting Convention Chairman" and "Assistant Acting Convention Chairman" respectfully. They will also be available to State Legislatures to assist with their Legislative Calls and pre-Convention planning.

The Chairman and Vice Chairman of the SCHOOL VOUCHER AMENDMENT Committee will also be responsible for post-convention planning and organization if the Convention votes to send the SCHOOL VOUCHER AMENDMENT to Congress to be ratified by the States.

VOTING BY DELEGATES IN STATE DELEGATIONS

It is recommended that a simple majority of the Delegates within each State Delegation be required to decide a State Delegation's vote at the Convention. A quorum within each State Delegation will consist of one Delegate. The business of the Convention and voting will not be delayed if a State Delegation does not cast a vote during a roll call.

QUORUM REQUIRED FOR CONDUCTING BUSINESS AND VOTING AT THE CONVENTION

Each State Delegation will have one vote on all matters that are to be decided by the Convention. A simple majority vote by the State Delegations at the Convention is required to decide the outcome of all business brought before the Convention for a vote, including whether or not the SCHOOL VOUCHER AMENDMENT, as herein written, should be sent to the Several States, via Congress, for ratification. A quorum at the Convention for the purpose of conducting business and voting will consist of 17 State Delegations.

CLOSED DELIBERATIONS AT THE CONVENTION

The SCHOOL VOUCHER AMENDMENT Convention will be closed to all media and news groups. Only delegates appointed by their State Legislatures and the Chairman and Vice Chairman of the SCHOOL VOUCHER AMENDMENT Committee will be authorized to enter and speak at the Convention. No visitors, reporters, government officials, professionals or inquirers, of any kind, will be permitted to enter the Convention facilities. Unauthorized visitors will be escorted by the Sergeant of Arms out of the Convention. After the vote by the State Delegations is taken to determine if the SCHOOL VOUCHER AMENDMENT will be sent to the Several States, via Congress, for ratification, the Chairman of the Convention will call a special press conference to announce the Convention's decision. Within 30 days from the special press conference the Chairman will make available to the public the records kept by the Convention during its proceedings.

STATE LEGISLATURES NOT AUTHORIZING THIS CALL FOR THE SCHOOL VOUCHER AMENDMENT CONVENTION

State Legislatures that did not authorize this Call for the SCHOOL VOUCHER AMENDMENT Convention and yet agree to send delegates representing their State agree to follow the terms and/or conditions set forth in this Agreement and Legislative Call. They need to pay particular attention to the "Convention's Rules of Order" described in this Agreement and the prohibitions in the section titled "Prohibitions for Delegates, State Delegations and/or Convention Officials at the Convention". These non-calling States must notify the "Acting Convention Chairman" before the Convention convenes of their intention to attend the Convention so accommodations can be completed for their Delegations. In order to receive Convention Passes, all Delegates attending the Convention, will be required to sign an agreement promising to abide by the terms and/or conditions in this Legislative Call and Agreement.

NO WEAPONS ALLOWED AT THE CONVENTION

Delegates and SCHOOL VOUCHER AMENDMENT Committee officials will not be allowed to bring into the SCHOOL VOUCHER AMENDMENT Convention any weapons or objects that can be construed as weapons.

PRESENTING ARGUMENTS AT THE CONVENTION
BY STATE DELEGATIONS

Each State Delegation will be allotted a maximum of 60 minutes for presenting its argument(s) at the Convention for or against sending the SCHOOL VOUCHER AMENDMENT to the United States Congress with instruction for Congress to send the Amendment to the Several States for ratification. Only Delegates who have been officially selected by their State Legislatures and Ex-Officio members of the Convention are authorized to speak before the Convention. Each State Delegation can use one or more of its Delegates to present its position(s). However, the total time allotted for each State Delegation is 60 minutes, which includes any time that is necessary to replace one Delegate with another. The Chairman of the SCHOOL VOUCHER AMENDMENT Committee will also be limited to 60 minutes during his speaking segment. Speakers cannot reserve portions of their time to another time or day. Speakers must complete their arguments in the 60 minute segment assigned to them.

The order each State Delegation will follow when presenting their position(s) will be according to when each State completed its Legislative Call on Congress, or when it notified the "Acting Convention Chairman" that it intends to attend the Convention even though it may not complete a Legislative Call on Congress. The State Delegation presentations will be scheduled in the following manner: the first State making a Call on Congress will go first; the first State notifying the "Acting Convention Chairman" that it plans to attend will go second. The second State making a Call on Congress will go third; then the second State notifying the "Acting Convention Chairman" will go fourth, and so forth until all States wanting to present their positions have had an opportunity to do so. The Convention Chairman can rearrange the schedule if any conflicts arise at the Convention. The last speaker to be scheduled at the Convention for a 60 minute segment will be the Chairman of the SCHOOL VOUCHER AMENDMENT Committee.

DUTIES OF THE "ACTING CONVENTION CHAIRMAN"

The duties of the "Acting Convention Chairman include:

1. organize a pre-Convention support group for assisting Calling States with their Legislative Calls and non-calling States with their intentions to attend the Convention
2. set up an SCHOOL VOUCHER AMENDMENT Committee checking account use generally accepted accounting principles when keeping records of all receipts and expenditures
3. provide financial reports and minutes of pre-convention activities as requested by States that are funding pre-convention operations
4. keep minutes of all business meetings of the SCHOOL VOUCHER AMENDMENT Committee
5. determine the budget that will be needed for pre-convention planning and organizing and notify each State Legislature of its share of the expenses
6. assist the Calling States and Attending States with their pre-convention planning
7. assist the Calling States with their Legislative Calls on Congress
8. after the SCHOOL VOUCHER AMENDMENT Convention has been convened call the Convention to order
9. invite nominations from the State Delegations present at the Convention to fill the "Convention Chairman's" position (the maximum number of nominees permitted is five and only one nominee from any one State Delegation is permitted)
10. take a roll call from the State Delegations for the nominee(s)
11. declare the winner based on the nominee who has received the most votes (a plurality of State Delegations). Each State Delegation will have one vote
12. officiate the installation of the "Convention Chairman" at the Convention by having the Chairman place his/her right hand on the Bible while repeating the following oath

"I solemnly promise to officiate the office of Convention Chairman for the SCHOOL VOUCHER AMENDMENT Convention according to the terms and/or conditions set forth in the Legislative Calls from the Several States to the best of my ability, so help me God".

In the event the "Acting Convention Chairman" is nominated and elected to the Convention Chairman position, the "Assistant Acting Convention Chairman" will conduct the installation ceremony for the Convention Chairman.

ELECTION, AUTHORITY AND DUTIES OF CONVENTION OFFICIALS

CONVENTION CHAIRMAN - The "Convention Chairman" is the senior official at the SCHOOL VOUCHER AMENDMENT Convention. He/she will have the requisite authority to oversee all activities at the Convention, including the nomination and election of all officials. The Convention Chairman's duties include:

1. organize and oversee all business and activities at the Convention
2. organize and officiate all nominations, elections and installations of officials at the Convention (this will be the Convention Chairman's first order of business)
3. organize and officiate all nominations, elections and installations of official positions that may become vacant at the Convention
4. oversee the enforcement of all Convention Rules
5. oversee the enforcement of the terms and/or conditions (herein described) of this Call and Agreement by the States
6. oversee the investigation of alleged and/or actual violations of this Agreement as defined in the section titled "Violating this Agreement"
7. bring before the Convention all matters that require a vote
8. bring before the Convention the financial needs of the Convention and time lines for when these monies are needed
9. cut off motions or discussions by State Delegations before the Convention if and when it seems appropriate
10. recognize the Spokesman within a State Delegation for the purpose of addressing a matter of importance to the Spokesman's Delegation (the Convention Chairman will have full authority to determine if a matter brought before the Convention by the Spokesman is appropriate for further discussion and/or if a decision by the Convention is necessary)
11. keep the business of the Convention moving forward expeditiously, cutting off all motions and discussions when it appears one or more Delegates are trying to hinder, delay or stop the work of the Convention
12. keep the business of the Convention focused on one objective which is, should the Convention send the SCHOOL VOUCHER AMENDMENT to Congress instructing Congress to send it to the Several States for ratification?
13. instruct Convention Officials (Assistant Convention Chairman, Secretary, Financial Officer, Executive Administrator, Sergeant at Arms, and Deputies) on their duties at the Convention
14. officiate and remedy any and all problems that may develop at the Convention
15. oversee the design and production of "Official" Convention Badges for the Sergeant at Arms and Deputies
16. notify all State Legislatures of the decision the Convention made as to whether or not the SCHOOL VOUCHER AMENDMENT should be sent to Congress instructing Congress to send it to the States for ratification?

17. if the State Delegations voted to send the Amendment to the States for ratification, include the Convention's recommendation to the United States Congress as to whether it should be ratified by State Conventions or State Legislatures
18. declare the SCHOOL VOUCHER AMENDMENT Convention closed after the State Delegations have decided if the SCHOOL VOUCHER AMENDMENT should be sent to Congress instructing Congress to send it to the States for ratification?
19. arrange a Special News Conference to announce the decision by the SCHOOL VOUCHER AMENDMENT Convention
20. make available the proceedings of the Convention to the public 30 days after the Convention is closed

The first order of business for the "Convention Chairman" will be to open the Convention to nominations from State Delegations present for each of the following Convention Officials; one Assistant Convention Chairman, one Secretary, one Financial Officer, one Executive Administrator, one Sergeant at Arms and ten Deputies (the maximum number of nominees permitted for each Convention Official position is five. Only one nominee for each Convention Official position is permitted from any one State Delegation. The nominee with a plurality of votes from the State Delegations will be the winner). The "Convention Chairman" can call for nominations for more than 10 Deputies if and when circumstances warrant.

ASSISTANT CONVENTION CHAIRMAN
The "Assistant Convention Chairman" duties include:

1. be amenable to the "Convention Chairman"
2. provide assistance to the "Convention Chairman" in all matters pertaining to the business of the Convention
3. monitor activities at the Convention and report to the "Convention Chairman" violations or possible violations of the terms and/or conditions of this Legislative Call and Agreement
4. perform the duties of the "Convention Chairman" when called upon by the Chairman or when the Chairman is unable to perform the duties of his/her office
5. the "Assistant Convention Chairman" will take the following oath, administered by the Convention Chairman, while placing his/her right hand on the Bible

"I solemnly promise to officiate the office of Assistant Convention Chairman for the SCHOOL VOUCHER AMENDMENT Convention according to the terms and/or conditions set forth in the Legislative Calls from the Several States to the best of my ability, so help me God".

SECRETARY - The "Secretary's" duties include:

1. keep official minutes of all proceedings at the Convention
2. monitor activities at the Convention and report to the Convention Chairman violations or possible violations of Convention Rules and of the terms and/or conditions of this Legislative Call and Agreement
3. make available to the "Convention Chairman", upon request, the official minutes of the Convention
4. be amenable to the "Convention Chairman" and "Assistant Convention Chairman"
5. in the absence of the "Convention Chairman" and the "Assistant Convention Chairman" due to death or a disablement that prevents them from performing the duties of their offices at the Convention, the Secretary shall call the Convention to order for the purpose of nominating and electing a new "Convention Chairman" and "Assistant Convention Chairman". In this capacity the Secretary will assume the duties and authority of the "Convention Chairman". If the Secretary is unable to perform the duties described herein, then they will fall to the Financial Officer.
6. the "Secretary" will take the following oath while placing his/her right hand on the Bible

   "I solemnly promise to officiate the office of Secretary for the SCHOOL VOUCHER AMENDMENT Convention according to the terms and/or conditions set forth in the Legislative Calls from the Several States to the best of my ability, so help me God".

FINANCIAL OFFICER - The "Financial Officer's" duties include:

1. keep detailed accounting records of all financial matters at the Convention using generally accepted accounting principles
2. be amenable to the "Convention Chairman" and "Assistant Convention Chairman"
3. monitor activities at the Convention and report to the Convention Chairman violations or possible violations of the terms and/or conditions of this Legislative Call and Agreement
4. set up a checking account in the name of the SCHOOL VOUCHER AMENDMENT Convention requiring any two of the following three officers when signing a check or making withdrawals – Convention Chairman, Assistant Convention Chairman, Financial Officer
5. make available to the "Convention Chairman", upon request, all financial records at the Convention
6. provide to the Convention Chairman the financial needs of the Convention and the time lines as to when these monies are needed

7. in the absence of a "Convention Chairman", "Assistant Convention Chairman", and "Secretary" due to death or a disablement that prevents them from performing the duties of their offices at the Convention, the Financial Officer shall call the Convention to order for the purpose of nominating and electing a new "Convention Chairman", "Assistant Convention Chairman", and "Secretary". In this capacity the Financial Officer will assume the duties and authority of the "Convention Chairman"

8. the "Financial Officer" will take the following oath while placing his/her right hand on the Bible

"I solemnly promise to officiate the office of Financial Officer for the SCHOOL VOUCHER AMENDMENT Convention according to generally accepted accounting principles and according to the terms and/or conditions set forth in the Legislative Calls from the Several States to the best of my ability, so help me God".

EXECUTIVE ADMINISTRATOR - The "Executive Administrator's" duties include:

1. facilitate all Convention business as directed by the Convention Chairman
2. be amenable to the Convention Chairman and Assistant Convention Chairman
3. monitor activities at the Convention and report to the Convention Chairman violations or possible violations of the terms and/or conditions of this Legislative Call and Agreement
4. keep detailed reports of all administrative activities at the Convention
5. make available to the "Convention Chairman" upon request all administrative records and/or reports at the Convention
6. the "Executive Administrator" will take the following oath while placing his/her right hand on the Bible

"I solemnly promise to officiate the office of Executive Administrator for the SCHOOL VOUCHER AMENDMENT Convention according to the terms and/or conditions set forth in the Legislative Calls from the Several States to the best of my ability, so help me God".

SERGEANT AT ARMS – The "Sergeant at Arms'" duties include:

1. be amenable to the Convention Chairman and Assistant Convention Chairman
2. monitor all activities at the Convention and report to the Convention Chairman violations or possible violations of the terms and/or conditions of this Legislative Call and Agreement
3. maintain order at the Convention

4. enforce all remedies for violations of this Legislative Call and Agreement as directed by the Convention Chairman
5. organize and direct the activities of all Deputies at the Convention
6. oversee, train and manage all Deputies at the Convention
7. the "Sergeant at Arms" will take the following oath while placing his/her right hand on the Bible

"I solemnly promise to officiate the office of Sergeant at Arms for the SCHOOL VOUCHER AMENDMENT Convention according to the terms and/or conditions set forth in the Legislative Calls from the Several States to the best of my ability, so help me God".

DEPUTIES – The "Deputies'" duties include:

1. be amenable to the Convention Chairman, Assistant Convention Chairman and Sergeant at Arms
2. monitor all activities at the Convention and report to the Sergeant at Arms violations or possible violations of the terms and/or conditions of this Legislative Call and Agreement
3. maintain order at the Convention as directed by the Sergeant at Arms
4. enforce all remedies for violations of this Legislative Call and Agreement as directed by the Convention Chairman and/or the Sergeant at Arms
5. "Deputies" will take the following oath while placing his/her right hand on the Bible

"I solemnly promise to officiate the office of Deputy for the SCHOOL VOUCHER AMENDMENT Convention according to the terms and/or conditions set forth in the Legislative Calls from the Several States to the best of my ability, so help me God".

CHALLENGING THE QUALIFICATIONS OF CONVENTION OFFICIALS

A State Delegation can challenge the qualifications of any Convention Official at the SCHOOL VOUCHER AMENDMENT Convention by bringing its allegation(s), during a business session, to the Convention floor. The Convention Chairman will consider the allegation(s) and determine if it merits further investigation. If the Chairman decides that the allegation(s) merits further investigation, he/she will direct the Sergeant at Arms to conduct the necessary inquiry. He/she will then follow the instructions outlined in the section "Violating this Agreement" for proscribing a remedy or remedies.

The "Convention Chairman" can also reject a challenge to the qualifications of any Convention Official if he/she concludes that the Delegate making the allegation(s) is trying to disrupt and/or delay Convention business. If after following the instructions outlined in "Violating this Agreement" the Delegate is found to have made a false accusation against a Convention Official, the Delegate's State Delegation will be charged with a violation of the terms and/or conditions of this Call and Agreement.

PROHIBITIONS FOR STATE DELEGATES, STATE DELEGATIONS AND CONVENTION OFFICIALS AT THE CONVENTION

State Delegates, State Delegations and Convention Officials are prohibited from violating any of the following Convention prohibitions:

1. State Delegates, State Delegations and Convention Officials are prohibited, at the Convention, from introducing, discussing, voting on, or sending to the States for consideration and/or ratification any amendment to the United States Constitution other than the SCHOOL VOUCHER AMENDMENT, as herein written

2. State Delegates, State Delegations and Convention Officials are prohibited from altering or changing, in any way (which includes the wording, spelling, punctuation, or paragraph sections), the SCHOOL VOUCHER AMENDMENT from the written form shown in the section titled **"The full text of the SCHOOL VOUCHER AMENDMENT"**

3. State Delegates, State Delegations and Convention Officials are prohibited, at the Convention, from introducing, discussing, voting on, or sending to the States for consideration and/or ratification any alternate form of government for the United States of America

4. State Delegates, State Delegations and Convention Officials are prohibited, at the Convention, from introducing, discussing, voting on, or sending to the States for consideration and/or ratification any alternate constitution or governing document for the United States of America

5. State Delegates, State Delegations and Convention Officials are prohibited, at the Convention, from introducing, discussing, voting on, or sending to the States for consideration and/or ratification any changes, of any kind, to the existing Constitution of the United States of America other than the SCHOOL VOUCHER AMENDMENT

6. State Delegates, State Delegations and Convention Officials are prohibited, at the Convention, from introducing, discussing, voting on, or sending to the States for consideration any changes, of any kind, to this binding Agreement between the States Calling for the SCHOOL VOUCHER AMENDMENT Convention

7. State Delegates, State Delegations and Convention Officials are prohibited, at the Convention, from introducing, discussing, voting on, or sending to the States for consideration and/or ratification any subject matter, issue or topic (of any kind) other than the proposed SCHOOL

RECLAIMING AMERICA

VOUCHER AMENDMENT in its written form shown in the section titled "The full text of the SCHOOL VOUCHER AMENDMENT"

THE DATE, TIME, DURATION AND PLACE OF THE SCHOOL VOUCHER AMENDMENT CONVENTION.

The United States Congress will be responsible for determining and announcing to the Several States the date, time, and place that the SCHOOL VOUCHER AMENDMENT Convention is to convene immediately after two thirds of the States, under the authority given to the States in Article V of the United States Constitution, have completed their Calls on Congress to convene the SCHOOL VOUCHER AMENDMENT Convention. The Convention is expected to complete its business by the 180th day after convening. The Convention Chairman can extend the duration of the SCHOOL VOUCHER AMENDMENT Convention for one additional 180 day period. The maximum number of days the Convention is authorized to be in session are 360 days. If the Convention has not decided if the SCHOOL VOUCHER AMENDMENT should be sent to Congress with instructions to send the Amendment to the Several States for ratification by the end of 360 days, then the Call for the SCHOOL VOUCHER AMENDMENT Convention, which was approved by the Several States under the authority granted in Article V of the United States Constitution and this agreement, will be automatically withdrawn by the Calling States and the Convention will automatically terminate at 5:00 P.M. Eastern Standard Time on the 360th day after convening. Termination of the SCHOOL VOUCHER AMENDMENT Convention will automatically occur on the 360th day after convening the Convention, without requiring a formal notice by the States to the Convention, nor by the States to the United States Congress, nor by the Convention to the States, nor by the Convention to the United States Congress, although it is recommended that the Convention notify the United States Congress and the State Legislatures of its termination as a courtesy.

Under no circumstance(s) are the Delegates at the SCHOOL VOUCHER AMENDMENT Convention authorized to re-convene a new or different Convention, no matter what their purpose or intent. The official Legislative Call and authority granted by the Several States and the subsequent convening of the SCHOOL VOUCHER AMENDMENT Convention by Congress will be automatically invalidated and the Convention will be abolished at 5:00 P.M. Eastern Standard Time on the 360th day after the convening of the SCHOOL VOUCHER AMENDMENT Convention.

VIOLATING THIS AGREEMENT

The Convention Chairman (or in the absence of the Convention Chairman the Assistant Convention Chairman) will handle allegations of a violation(s) or actual violation(s) of the terms and/or conditions of this binding Agreement between the Several States, by any one or more Delegate(s) and/or Convention Official(s), as follows:

1. When an alleged violation has been presented to the Convention Chairman, and if the Chairman decides that the allegation(s) merits further investigation, he/she will instruct the Sergeant at Arms to conduct the necessary inquiry.

2. After the inquiry has been completed, and assuming the Convention Chairman concludes that the evidence does not substantiate further review by the Convention, the allegation(s) will be dismissed by the Chairman and the Convention will go forward with its business.

3. If however, after the inquiry has been completed, the Convention Chairman concludes that the evidence does substantiate further review by the Convention, the Chairman will present the allegation(s) and findings of the inquiry to the Convention for a discussion and vote. If a majority of the State Delegations (one vote per State Delegation) decide that no violation of the terms and/or conditions of this Legislative Call and Agreement has occurred, then the Chairman will declare that the alleged violation(s) of the terms and/or conditions of this Legislative Call and Agreement is/are dismissed. The Convention will then go forward with its business.

4. If however, after the inquiry has been completed, the Convention Chairman concludes that the evidence does substantiate further review by the Convention, the Chairman will present the allegation(s) and findings of the inquiry to the Convention for a discussion and vote. If a majority of the State Delegations (one vote per State Delegation) decide that one or more violation(s) of the terms and/or conditions of this Legislative Call and Agreement has/have occurred, then the Chairman will declare to the Convention that the Delegate(s) responsible for the violation(s), and their State Delegation(s), has/have been charged with "Violating this Agreement". The Convention will then go forward with its business.

5. If a State Delegation is charged with two violations of the terms and/or conditions of this Legislative Call and Agreement, the Convention Chairman will declare to the Convention that the State Delegation charged with violating this Agreement a second time has no further standing or authority at the Convention. The Chairman will notify the charged State Delegation that its entire delegation of Delegates must leave the Convention immediately and they will not be allowed back into the Convention. The Chairman will instruct the Sergeant at Arms that he should escort the charged State Delegation out of the Convention. The Convention Chairman will then notify the State

Legislature that sent the charged State Delegation of the actions that the Convention has taken and inform them that they can send a replacement State Delegation to the Convention as long as they do not disrupt the proceedings of the Convention. None of the original Delegates who were charged by the Convention will be allowed back into the Convention as part of a replacement delegation.

6. The Convention Chairman will not allow unreasonable delays in the proceedings of the Convention due to disruptive Delegates or State Delegations. He/she will move the business of the Convention forward expeditiously.

THE FULL TEXT OF THE SCHOOL VOUCHER AMENDMENT

The full text of the SCHOOL VOUCHER AMENDMENT to be submitted to the Several States by the United States Congress for ratification shall read as follows:

SCHOOL VOUCHER AMENDMENT
ARTICLE 28 (or alternate number to be assigned by Congress)

Section 1. It is the right of every citizen to train up their children according to their conscience, faith and capabilities without interference from the State. The rights of parents and legal guardians to choose how their children will be educated are foundational to a free people.

Section 2. School Vouchers consist of mandatory payments by the treasuries of Local, State and Federal authorities for student costs at private schools. Mandatory payments for student costs include tuition and related educational expenses.

Section 3. Private Schools can be pre-elementary, elementary, secondary, and higher education institutions.

Section 4. Private Schools that receive Local, State or Federal monies to pay for their students tuition and expenses are required to teach their students appropriate grade level academic subjects, good morals, good values, respect for the rights of others and respect for America's unique Christian heritage and Constitutional history. Private Schools are also required to teach their students civic responsibilities in Local, State and National communities, except at the pre-elementary level.

Section 5. Private Schools have the authority to discipline students which includes reasonable corporal punishment in elementary schools for the purpose of correcting wrong behavior.

Section 6. School Vouchers are initiated at the election of parents or legal guardians on behalf of their dependent children. For the purposes of this Article, dependent children are children up to the age of 21 and still dependent on their parents or legal guardians while

attending school. School Vouchers can be used to fund a student's private education at an elementary, secondary or higher education school when government funding is already authorized for the same or comparable education at a public or government school.

Section 7. School Vouchers must be paid to private schools in an amount equal to the sum of the amounts Local, State and/or Federal authorities are authorized to pay for the education of the same or similar student at a public or government school.

Section 8. Local, State and Federal authorities are prohibited from imposing on any private school certification requirements that exceed the academic requirements for public or government schools. Local, State and Federal authorities are prohibited from imposing laws, regulations or rules on private schools that are designed to inhibit the freedom of choice parents and legal guardians have when deciding to send their children to private schools. Local, State and Federal authorities are also prohibited from interfering in the academic instruction, moral and religious teaching, discipline and curriculum of private schools.

Section 9. This Article does not prevent Local, State and Federal authorities from enforcing reasonable laws that are for the protection and welfare of the American people.

Section 10. To secure the rights of parents, legal guardians and their dependent children, it is hereby prohibited to deny a student, who is a citizen of the United States the right to a private school education or deprive said student the appropriate funding for such education when the same or comparable funding is available at a public or government school. The provisions of this Article are enforceable within the United States which shall include the Several States, the District of Columbia, the Commonwealth of Puerto Rico, the Commonwealth of the Northern Mariana Islands and the territories and possessions of the United States.

Section 11. Congress shall have the power to enforce by appropriate legislation, the provisions of the Article.

_____

RECLAIMING AMERICA

RATIFICATION OF THE "SCHOOL VOUCHER AMENDMENT"

Under the requirements of Article V of the United States Constitution and also under Article IV, Section 4 which guarantees to every State a Republican form of Government, the SCHOOL VOUCHER AMENDMENT will become a ratified Amendment to the United States Constitution when three quarters of the Several States complete their ratifications of the Amendment.

"CONGRESSIONAL" OPTION

If the United States Congress voluntarily sends the SCHOOL VOUCHER AMENDMENT to the Several States for ratification without making any changes, of any kind (which includes the wording, spelling, punctuation and paragraph sections) in the proposed Amendment as herein written, and before two thirds of the States complete their Call for Congress to convene the SCHOOL VOUCHER AMENDMENT Convention, then the Legislature of the State of NORTH CAROLINA will withdraw its Call for the SCHOOL VOUCHER AMENDMENT Convention.

OFFICIAL AGREEMENT BY THE NORTH CAROLINA STATE LEGISLATURE BETWEEN ITSELF AND THE CALLING STATES

The Legislature of the State of NORTH CAROLINA enters into this binding Agreement with every other State Legislature that likewise agrees to the terms and/or conditions of this Legislative Call and Agreement as set forth herein. This is an irrevocable contract, during the term of this Agreement, between the State of NORTH CAROLINA and each and every State that signs this Agreement and completes its Call on the United States Congress directing Congress to convene a Federal Convention titled the SCHOOL VOUCHER AMENDMENT Convention. The Legislature of the State of NORTH CAROLINA agrees that it, and its delegates who are selected to attend the Convention, will abide by the purpose, terms, conditions, agenda, and "Convention Rules of Order" as explained in this Agreement.

The Legislature of the State of NORTH CAROLINA enters into this Agreement with every other State Legislature that likewise agrees to the terms and/or conditions of this Agreement and Legislative Call as set forth herein, understanding that the SCHOOL VOUCHER AMENDMENT Convention, by definition herein explained, is a "SINGLE ISSUE" Federal Convention and that the Convention will have no authority, under this Call and Agreement between the States, to review and/or consider any other subject matter, issue, or topic during its sessions other than business matters relating to the question, should the SCHOOL VOUCHER AMENDMENT, as herein written, be sent by the Convention to the United States Congress instructing Congress to send the Amendment to the Several States for ratification? The Legislature of the State of NORTH CAROLINA irrevocably declares by signing this Agreement that any subject matter, issue or topic (other than the SCHOOL VOUCHER AMENDMENT) that delegates might try to present to the Convention and subsequently to the States for review and/or ratification will be immediately, upon introduction at the Convention, unauthorized, invalid and automatically rejected by the Legislature of the State of NORTH CAROLINA, and the Legislature of the State of NORTH CAROLINA irrevocably declares that it will not review and/or consider for ratification any such subject matter, issue or topic, no matter how presented to it by the Convention. Only the SCHOOL VOUCHER AMENDMENT, as herein written, will be considered by the Legislature of the State of NORTH CAROLINA for ratification.

The Legislature of the State of NORTH CAROLINA also irrevocably declares that under no circumstance(s) will it consider for review and/or ratification any amendment to the United States Constitution, submitted to it by the SCHOOL VOUCHER AMENDMENT Convention other than the SCHOOL VOUCHER AMENDMENT as herein written.

The Legislature of the State of NORTH CAROLINA further irrevocably declares that under no circumstance(s) will it consider for review and/or ratification any modified form of the SCHOOL VOUCHER AMENDMENT submitted to it by the SCHOOL VOUCHER AMENDMENT Convention that would change, alter, or replace, in any way (which includes the wording, spelling, punctuation, or paragraph sections), the SCHOOL VOUCHER AMENDMENT from its written form herein.

The Legislature of the State of NORTH CAROLINA further irrevocably declares that under no circumstance(s) will it consider for review and/or ratification any proposal, of any kind, sent to it by the SCHOOL VOUCHER AMENDMENT Convention that would change, replace, or alter the United States Constitution other than the SCHOOL VOUCHER AMENDMENT as herein written.

The Legislature of the State of NORTH CAROLINA further irrevocably declares that under no circumstance(s) will it consider for review any proposal, of any kind, sent to it by the SCHOOL VOUCHER AMENDMENT Convention that would change, replace, or alter, in any way (which includes the wording, spelling, punctuation and section paragraphs), this Official Legislative Call for the SCHOOL VOUCHER AMENDMENT Convention and the terms and/or conditions of this Agreement between the States as herein written.

Under the authority reserved to the State of NORTH CAROLINA in Article V of the United States Constitution and also under Article IV, Section 4 which guarantees to every State a Republican form of Government, the Legislature of the State of NORTH CAROLINA hereby approves this Legislative Call on the United States Congress directing Congress to convene the SCHOOL

VOUCHER AMENDMENT Convention and binds itself with each and every State that likewise approves this identical Legislative Call according the terms and/or conditions set forth in this Agreement.

OFFICIAL CALL BY THE STATE OF NORTH CAROLINA ON THE UNITED STATES CONGRESS DIRECTING CONGRESS TO CONVENE THE SCHOOL VOUCHER AMENDMENT CONVENTION

The Legislature of the State of NORTH CAROLINA hereby Calls on the United States Congress directing Congress to convene a Federal Convention to be titled the SCHOOL VOUCHER AMENDMENT Convention. The Convention is to be convened immediately after two thirds of the Several States have completed their Calls for the SCHOOL VOUCHER AMENDMENT Convention.

The State of NORTH CAROLINA is authorized to make this Call for the SCHOOL VOUCHER AMENDMENT Convention under the authority reserved to the States in Article V of the United States Constitution and under Article IV, Section 4 which guarantees to every State a Republican form of Government. Both Articles give to each State an equal standing when calling for a Constitutional Convention. Article V and Article IV, Section 4 reserves to the Several States the right to Call for a Federal Convention for the purpose of amending the United States Constitution when Congress and/or the Courts refuse to address an egregious wrong suffered by the people.

Submitted to Both Houses of the United States Congress on this date _____, _____ by the Legislature of the State of NORTH CAROLINA.

State of NORTH CAROLINA Seal:

Authorized Signatures with titles:

_____Title_____

_____Title_____

_____Title_____

_____Title_____

CHAPTER 13

CONSTITUTIONAL HISTORY AMENDMENT

Text of proposed
CONSTITUTIONAL HISTORY AMENDMENT
ARTICLE 28 (or alternate number to be assigned by Congress)

Section 1. America's Constitutional history is unique among nations and sacred to the American people. It is the right of citizens to receive an accurate historical account of America's Constitutional history, which is foundational to a free people.

Section 2. To secure the rights of citizens it is hereby prohibited for any institution or individual to intentionally teach misleading, false or otherwise distorted accounts of America's Constitutional history. The provisions of this Article are enforceable within the United States which shall include the Several States, the District of Columbia, and the Commonwealth of Puerto Rico, the Commonwealth of the Northern Mariana Islands and the territories and possessions of the United States.

Section 3. Congress shall have the power to enforce by appropriate legislation, the provisions of the Article.

The American people have a Constitutional Right to learn about America's Constitutional History without intentional distortions, intentional falsehoods or intentionally misleading accounts of our Founders or Constitutional history. The Constitutional History Amendment will guard America's Constitutional History and leave for posterity accurate accounts of our past.

RECLAIMING AMERICA

AUTHORIZED CALL
BY THE TEXAS STATE LEGISLATURE
ON THE UNITED STATES CONGRESS INSTRUCTING
CONGRESS TO CONVENE A FEDERAL CONVENTION TO BE
TITLED THE CONSTITUTIONAL HISTORY AMENDMENT
CONVENTION

THIS AUTHORIZED CALL ALSO DEFINES THE AGREEMENT
THE TEXAS STATE LEGISLATURE IS ENTERING INTO
BETWEEN ITSELF AND OTHER CALLING STATES

To: **BOTH HOUSES OF UNITED STATES CONGRESS**

UNITED STATES SENATE:

President of the Senate, United States Vice President
Majority Leader Senator
Minority Leader Senator
President Pro Tempore Senator
Republican Whip Senator
Democratic Whip Senator

(Deliver this Official Call to every current leader and member of the United State Senate at Washington, DC)

HOUSE OF REPRESENTATIVE:

Speaker of the House Representative
House Majority Leader Representative
House Majority Whip Representative
House Minority Leader Representative
House Minority Whip Representative

(Deliver this Official Call to every current leader and member of the United State House of Representatives at Washington, DC)

From: **THE STATE LEGISLATURE OF THE STATE OF TEXAS**

The Legislature of the State of TEXAS hereby Calls on the United States Congress instructing Congress to convene a Federal Convention called the CONSTITUTIONAL HISTORY AMENDMENT Convention under the authority reserved to the States in Article V of the United States Constitution. Article IV, Section 4 guarantees to every State a Republican form of Government which gives each State equal standing when Calling for a Constitutional Convention. Article V reserves to the Several States the right to

Call for a Federal Constitutional Convention for the purpose of amending the United States Constitution when Congress and/or the Courts refuse to address an egregious wrong suffered by the people. The States *alone* have the authority to "limit" the agenda and authority of a Federal Convention. The States alone can Call for a "Single Issue" Convention by agreeing among themselves the purpose, terms, conditions, duration, and agenda for the Convention. Congress does not have the authority to define a "Single Issue" Convention. Congress' authority, under Article V of the United States Constitution, empowers it to convene a Convention as Called for and defined by the Several States. The Several States alone have the authority to enforce the terms and/or conditions set forth in this Agreement at the CONSTITUTIONAL HISTORY AMENDMENT Convention.

The CONSTITUTIONAL HISTORY AMENDMENT Convention will be a "Single Issue" Federal Convention as defined in this Legislative Call on the United States Congress and in this binding Agreement between the Several States. The delegates summoned to this Convention by Congress will have the authority to decide only one issue, should the CONSTITUTIONAL HISTORY AMENDMENT, as herein written, be sent to Congress with instructions to send the Amendment back to the Several States for ratification? The delegates at the CONSTITUTIONAL HISTORY AMENDMENT Convention will have no authority to change the wording of the proposed Amendment, neither are they authorized to deliberate on or discuss any other subject matter or issue at the Convention. The purpose, terms and/or conditions that will govern the agenda and affairs of the CONSTITUTIONAL HISTORY AMENDMENT Convention are as follows:

THE PURPOSE OF THE CONVENTION

The *only* purpose for convening the CONSTITUTIONAL HISTORY AMENDMENT Convention is for the State Delegations, representing the Several States, to decide if the CONSTITUTIONAL HISTORY AMENDMENT, as herein written, should be sent to the United States Congress with instructions for Congress to send the Amendment to the Several States for ratification? Absolutely no other business is authorized at this Convention.

CONVENTION RULES OF ORDER

The "Convention Rules of Order" that all Delegates and State Delegations are required to follow as a condition of participating at the CONSTITUTIONAL HISTORY AMENDMENT Convention are described in this Legislative Call on Congress. From time to time, in order to facilitate Convention business, the Convention Chairman may require the Convention to follow "Robert's Rules of Order" when a specific Rule of Order is not defined in this Legislative Call. The Delegates and State Delegations are required to honor the Convention

Chairman's instructions when applying Convention Rules of Order and/or Roberts Rules of Order.

CONSTITUTIONAL HISTORY AMENDMENT COMMITTEE

The CONSTITUTIONAL HISTORY AMENDMENT Committee is the citizens group that founded the CONSTITUTIONAL HISTORY AMENDMENT Initiative. This Committee will be responsible for pre-Convention planning and organization. The Chairman and Vice Chairman of the CONSTITUTIONAL HISTORY AMENDMENT Committee will be Ex-Officio (without voting rights) members of the Convention. They can be called upon by the Convention Chairman to clarify the CONSTITUTIONAL HISTORY AMENDMENT legislative strategy for the Delegates, provide progress reports in the States and also be available for questions and answers from Delegates at the Convention. They will be subject to the terms and/or conditions of this Legislative Call and Agreement between the States.

If they are also appointed as Delegates by their State Legislatures, then they will be entitled to voting privileges as Delegates at the Convention. The Chairman of the CONSTITUTIONAL HISTORY AMENDMENT Committee is R. C. "Kacprowicz" Casper.

If the Convention votes in favor of the Amendment, the CONSTITUTIONAL HISTORY AMENDMENT Committee will be responsible for post-convention planning and organization during the ratification process.

FUNDING THE CONVENTION AND STATE DELEGATIONS

The State Legislatures that send Delegates to the CONSTITUTIONAL HISTORY AMENDMENT Convention shall be responsible for providing monies necessary for their State Delegations to participate at the Convention. The amounts each State Delegation will require will be decided by each State Legislature. Other expenses or costs necessary to fund the Convention are to be shared by the Calling States equally. From time to time the Convention Chairman will notify the State Delegations what monies will be necessary to carry on the business of the Convention.

FUNDING FOR "PRE AND POST-CONVENTION PLANNING AND ORGANIZATION"

Each State Legislature making a Call on Congress to convene the CONSTITUTIONAL HISTORY AMENDMENT Convention will be asked to share expenses for "pre-Convention planning" and "pre-Convention organization". If the Convention votes to send the CONSTITUTIONAL HISTORY AMENDMENT to Congress to be ratified by the States, then the CONSTITUTIONAL HISTORY AMENDMENT Committee will ask the

Calling States to help fund post-convention planning and organization to cover expenses for the ratification process.

DELEGATES SUMMONED BY CONGRESS

Congress has the authority, under Article V, to summon Delegates from the Several States to the CONSTITUTIONAL HISTORY AMENDMENT Convention. Congress is hereby directed to summon to the Convention the appropriate number of Delegates that each State is entitled to immediately after two thirds of the States complete their Call directing Congress to convene the CONSTITUTIONAL HISTORY AMENDMENT Convention. The number of Delegates to be summoned to the Convention should be equal to the number of members each State has in the House of Representatives and in the Senate of the United States Congress.

DELEGATES AND STATE DELEGATIONS

Only State Delegates summoned by Congress to the CONSTITUTIONAL HISTORY AMENDMENT Convention and appointed by their State Legislatures to form State Delegations to represent their respective States are authorized to attend and speak at the CONSTITUTIONAL HISTORY AMENDMENT Convention. Each State Legislature has the responsibility to select, from within its State, individual Delegates who will represent its State at the Convention. The number of Delegates selected by a State Legislature can be no greater than the number of Delegates summoned by Congress from its State. Each State Delegation must select a Delegate from within its delegation to be its Spokesman at the Convention. Only a Delegation's Spokesman will be recognized by the Convention Chairman.

THE PRE-CONVENTION "ACTING CONVENTION CHAIRMAN" AND "ASSISTANT ACTING CONVENTION CHAIRMAN"

The Chairman and Vice Chairman of the CONSTITUTIONAL HISTORY AMENDMENT Committee will have exclusive authority to complete all pre-convention planning and organization for the CONSTITUTIONAL HISTORY AMENDMENT Convention. They will perform their duties under the titles "Acting Convention Chairman" and "Assistant Acting Convention Chairman" respectfully. They will also be available to State Legislatures to assist with their Legislative Calls and pre-Convention planning.

The Chairman and Vice Chairman of the CONSTITUTIONAL HISTORY AMENDMENT Committee will also be responsible for post-convention planning and organization if the Convention votes to send the CONSTITUTIONAL HISTORY AMENDMENT to Congress to be ratified by the States.

VOTING BY DELEGATES IN STATE DELEGATIONS

It is recommended that a simple majority of the Delegates within each State Delegation be required to decide a State Delegation's vote at the Convention. A quorum within each State Delegation will consist of one Delegate. The business of the Convention and voting will not be delayed if a State Delegation does not cast a vote during a roll call.

QUORUM REQUIRED FOR CONDUCTING BUSINESS AND VOTING AT THE CONVENTION

Each State Delegation will have one vote on all matters that are to be decided by the Convention. A simple majority vote by the State Delegations at the Convention is required to decide the outcome of all business brought before the Convention for a vote, including whether or not the CONSTITUTIONAL HISTORY AMENDMENT, as herein written, should be sent to the Several States, via Congress, for ratification. A quorum at the Convention for the purpose of conducting business and voting will consist of 17 State Delegations.

CLOSED DELIBERATIONS AT THE CONVENTION

The CONSTITUTIONAL HISTORY AMENDMENT Convention will be closed to all media and news groups. Only delegates appointed by their State Legislatures and the Chairman and Vice Chairman of the CONSTITUTIONAL HISTORY AMENDMENT Committee will be authorized to enter and speak at the Convention. No visitors, reporters, government officials, professionals or inquirers, of any kind, will be permitted to enter the Convention facilities. Unauthorized visitors will be escorted by the Sergeant of Arms out of the Convention. After the vote by the State Delegations is taken to determine if the CONSTITUTIONAL HISTORY AMENDMENT will be sent to the Several States, via Congress, for ratification, the Chairman of the Convention will call a special press conference to announce the Convention's decision. Within 30 days from the special press conference the Chairman will make available to the public the records kept by the Convention during its proceedings.

STATE LEGISLATURES NOT AUTHORIZING THIS CALL FOR THE CONSTITUTIONAL HISTORY AMENDMENT CONVENTION

State Legislatures that did not authorize this Call for the CONSTITUTIONAL HISTORY AMENDMENT Convention and yet agree to send delegates representing their State agree to follow the terms and/or conditions set forth in this Agreement and Legislative Call. They need to pay particular attention to the "Convention's Rules of Order" described in this Agreement and the prohibitions in the section titled "Prohibitions for Delegates, State Delegations and/or Convention Officials at the Convention". These non-calling States must notify the "Acting Convention Chairman" before the Convention convenes of

their intention to attend the Convention so accommodations can be completed for their Delegations. In order to receive Convention Passes, all Delegates attending the Convention, will be required to sign an agreement promising to abide by the terms and/or conditions in this Legislative Call and Agreement.

NO WEAPONS ALLOWED AT THE CONVENTION

Delegates and CONSTITUTIONAL HISTORY AMENDMENT Committee officials will not be allowed to bring into the CONSTITUTIONAL HISTORY AMENDMENT Convention any weapons or objects that can be construed as weapons.

PRESENTING ARGUMENTS AT THE CONVENTION BY STATE DELEGATIONS

Each State Delegation will be allotted a maximum of 60 minutes for presenting its argument(s) at the Convention for or against sending the CONSTITUTIONAL HISTORY AMENDMENT to the United States Congress with instruction for Congress to send the Amendment to the Several States for ratification. Only Delegates who have been officially selected by their State Legislatures and Ex-Officio members of the Convention are authorized to speak before the Convention. Each State Delegation can use one or more of its Delegates to present its position(s). However, the total time allotted for each State Delegation is 60 minutes, which includes any time that is necessary to replace one Delegate with another. The Chairman of the CONSTITUTIONAL HISTORY AMENDMENT Committee will also be limited to 60 minutes during his speaking segment. Speakers cannot reserve portions of their time to another time or day. Speakers must complete their arguments in the 60 minute segment assigned to them.

The order each State Delegation will follow when presenting their position(s) will be according to when each State completed its Legislative Call on Congress, or when it notified the "Acting Convention Chairman" that it intends to attend the Convention even though it may not complete a Legislative Call on Congress. The State Delegation presentations will be scheduled in the following manner: the first State making a Call on Congress will go first; the first State notifying the "Acting Convention Chairman" that it plans to attend will go second. The second State making a Call on Congress will go third; then the second State notifying the "Acting Convention Chairman" will go fourth, and so forth until all States wanting to present their positions have had an opportunity to do so. The Convention Chairman can rearrange the schedule if any conflicts arise at the Convention. The last speaker to be scheduled at the Convention for a 60 minute segment will be the Chairman of the CONSTITUTIONAL HISTORY AMENDMENT Committee.

DUTIES OF THE "ACTING CONVENTION CHAIRMAN"

The duties of the "Acting Convention Chairman include:

1. organize a pre-Convention support group for assisting Calling States with their Legislative Calls and non-calling States with their intentions to attend the Convention
2. set up an CONSTITUTIONAL HISTORY AMENDMENT Committee checking account
3. use generally accepted accounting principles when keeping records of all receipts and expenditures
4. provide financial reports and minutes of pre-convention activities as requested by States that are funding pre-convention operations
5. keep minutes of all business meetings of the CONSTITUTIONAL HISTORY AMENDMENT Committee
6. determine the budget that will be needed for pre-convention planning and organizing and notify each State Legislature of its share of the expenses
7. assist the Calling States and Attending States with their pre-convention planning
8. assist the Calling States with their Legislative Calls on Congress
9. after the CONSTITUTIONAL HISTORY AMENDMENT Convention has been convened call the Convention to order
10. invite nominations from the State Delegations present at the Convention to fill the "Convention Chairman's" position (the maximum number of nominees permitted is five and only one nominee from any one State Delegation is permitted)
11. take a roll call from the State Delegations for the nominee(s)
12. declare the winner based on the nominee who has received the most votes (a plurality of State Delegations). Each State Delegation will have one vote
13. officiate the installation of the "Convention Chairman" at the Convention by having the Chairman place his/her right hand on the Bible while repeating the following oath

    "I solemnly promise to officiate the office of Convention Chairman for the CONSTITUTIONAL HISTORY AMENDMENT Convention according to the terms and/or conditions set forth in the Legislative Calls from the Several States to the best of my ability, so help me God".

    In the event the "Acting Convention Chairman" is nominated and elected to the Convention Chairman position, the "Assistant Acting Convention Chairman" will conduct the installation ceremony for the Convention Chairman.

RECLAIMING AMERICA

ELECTION, AUTHORITY AND DUTIES OF CONVENTION OFFICIALS

CONVENTION CHAIRMAN: - The "Convention Chairman" is the senior official at the CONSTITUTIONAL HISTORY AMENDMENT Convention. He/she will have the requisite authority to oversee all activities at the Convention, including the nomination and election of all officials. The Convention Chairman's duties include:

1. organize and oversee all business and activities at the Convention
2. organize and officiate all nominations, elections and installations of officials at the Convention (this will be the Convention Chairman's first order of business)
3. organize and officiate all nominations, elections and installations of official positions that may become vacant at the Convention
4. oversee the enforcement of all Convention Rules
5. oversee the enforcement of the terms and/or conditions (herein described) of this Call and Agreement by the States
6. oversee the investigation of alleged and/or actual violations of this Agreement as defined in the section titled "Violating this Agreement"
7. bring before the Convention all matters that require a vote
8. bring before the Convention the financial needs of the Convention and time lines for when these monies are needed
9. cut off motions or discussions by State Delegations before the Convention if and when it seems appropriate
10. recognize the Spokesman within a State Delegation for the purpose of addressing a matter of importance to the Spokesman's Delegation (the Convention Chairman will have full authority to determine if a matter brought before the Convention by the Spokesman is appropriate for further discussion and/or if a decision by the Convention is necessary)
11. keep the business of the Convention moving forward expeditiously, cutting off all motions and discussions when it appears one or more Delegates are trying to hinder, delay or stop the work of the Convention
12. keep the business of the Convention focused on one objective which is, should the Convention send the CONSTITUTIONAL HISTORY AMENDMENT to Congress instructing Congress to send it to the Several States for ratification?
13. instruct Convention Officials (Assistant Convention Chairman, Secretary, Financial Officer, Executive Administrator, Sergeant at Arms, and Deputies) on their duties at the Convention
14. officiate and remedy any and all problems that may develop at the Convention
15. oversee the design and production of "Official" Convention Badges for the Sergeant at Arms and Deputies

16. notify all State Legislatures of the decision the Convention made as to whether or not the CONSTITUTIONAL HISTORY AMENDMENT should be sent to Congress instructing Congress to send it to the States for ratification?
17. if the State Delegations voted to send the Amendment to the States for ratification, include the Convention's recommendation to the United States Congress as to whether it should be ratified by State Conventions or State Legislatures
18. declare the CONSTITUTIONAL HISTORY AMENDMENT Convention closed after the State Delegations have decided if the CONSTITUTIONAL HISTORY AMENDMENT should be sent to Congress instructing Congress to send it to the States for ratification?
19. arrange a Special News Conference to announce the decision by the CONSTITUTIONAL HISTORY AMENDMENT Convention
20. make available the proceedings of the Convention to the public 30 days after the Convention is closed

The first order of business for the "Convention Chairman" will be to open the Convention to nominations from State Delegations present for each of the following Convention Officials; one Assistant Convention Chairman, one Secretary, one Financial Officer, one Executive Administrator, one Sergeant at Arms and ten Deputies (the maximum number of nominees permitted for each Convention Official position is five. Only one nominee for each Convention Official position is permitted from any one State Delegation. The nominee with a plurality of votes from the State Delegations will be the winner). The "Convention Chairman" can call for nominations for more than 10 Deputies if and when circumstances warrant.

ASSISTANT CONVENTION CHAIRMAN - The "Assistant Convention Chairman" duties include:

1. be amenable to the "Convention Chairman"
2. provide assistance to the "Convention Chairman" in all matters pertaining to the business of the Convention
3. monitor activities at the Convention and report to the "Convention Chairman" violations or possible violations of the terms and/or conditions of this Legislative Call and Agreement
4. perform the duties of the "Convention Chairman" when called upon by the Chairman or when the Chairman is unable to perform the duties of his/her office
5. the "Assistant Convention Chairman" will take the following oath, administered by the Convention Chairman, while placing his/her right hand on the Bible

"I solemnly promise to officiate the office of Assistant Convention Chairman for the CONSTITUTIONAL HISTORY AMENDMENT Convention according to the terms and/or conditions set forth in the Legislative Calls from the Several States to the best of my ability, so help me God".

SECRETARY - The "Secretary's" duties include:

1. keep official minutes of all proceedings at the Convention
2. monitor activities at the Convention and report to the Convention Chairman violations or possible violations of Convention Rules and of the terms and/or conditions of this Legislative Call and Agreement
3. make available to the "Convention Chairman", upon request, the official minutes of the Convention
4. be amenable to the "Convention Chairman" and "Assistant Convention Chairman"
5. in the absence of the "Convention Chairman" and the "Assistant Convention Chairman" due to death or a disablement that prevents them from performing the duties of their offices at the Convention, the Secretary shall call the Convention to order for the purpose of nominating and electing a new "Convention Chairman" and "Assistant Convention Chairman". In this capacity the Secretary will assume the duties and authority of the "Convention Chairman". If the Secretary is unable to perform the duties described herein, then they will fall to the Financial Officer.
6. the "Secretary" will take the following oath while placing his/her right hand on the Bible

   "I solemnly promise to officiate the office of Secretary for the CONSTITUTIONAL HISTORY AMENDMENT Convention according to the terms and/or conditions set forth in the Legislative Calls from the Several States to the best of my ability, so help me God".

FINANCIAL OFFICER - The "Financial Officer's" duties include:

1. keep detailed accounting records of all financial matters at the Convention using generally accepted accounting principles
2. be amenable to the "Convention Chairman" and "Assistant Convention Chairman"
3. monitor activities at the Convention and report to the Convention Chairman violations or possible violations of the terms and/or conditions of this Legislative Call and Agreement
4. set up a checking account in the name of the CONSTITUTIONAL HISTORY AMENDMENT Convention requiring any two of the

following three officers when signing a check or making withdrawals – Convention Chairman, Assistant Convention Chairman, Financial Officer

5. make available to the "Convention Chairman", upon request, all financial records at the Convention

6. provide to the Convention Chairman the financial needs of the Convention and the time lines as to when these monies are needed

7. in the absence of a "Convention Chairman", "Assistant Convention Chairman", and "Secretary" due to death or a disablement that prevents them from performing the duties of their offices at the Convention, the Financial Officer shall call the Convention to order for the purpose of nominating and electing a new "Convention Chairman", "Assistant Convention Chairman", and "Secretary". In this capacity the Financial Officer will assume the duties and authority of the "Convention Chairman"

8. the "Financial Officer" will take the following oath while placing his/her right hand on the Bible

"I solemnly promise to officiate the office of Financial Officer for the CONSTITUTIONAL HISTORY AMENDMENT Convention according to generally accepted accounting principles and according to the terms and/or conditions set forth in the Legislative Calls from the Several States to the best of my ability, so help me God".

EXECUTIVE ADMINISTRATOR - The "Executive Administrator's" duties include:

1. facilitate all Convention business as directed by the Convention Chairman

2. be amenable to the Convention Chairman and Assistant Convention Chairman

3. monitor activities at the Convention and report to the Convention Chairman violations or possible violations of the terms and/or conditions of this Legislative Call and Agreement

4. keep detailed reports of all administrative activities at the Convention

5. make available to the "Convention Chairman" upon request all administrative records and/or reports at the Convention

6. the "Executive Administrator" will take the following oath while placing his/her right hand on the Bible

"I solemnly promise to officiate the office of Executive Administrator for the CONSTITUTIONAL HISTORY AMENDMENT Convention according to the terms and/or conditions set forth in the Legislative Calls from the Several States to the best of my ability, so help me God".

SERGEANT AT ARMS – The "Sergeant at Arms'" duties include:

1. be amenable to the Convention Chairman and Assistant Convention Chairman
2. monitor all activities at the Convention and report to the Convention Chairman violations or possible violations of the terms and/or conditions of this Legislative Call and Agreement
3. maintain order at the Convention
4. enforce all remedies for violations of this Legislative Call and Agreement as directed by the Convention Chairman
5. organize and direct the activities of all Deputies at the Convention
6. oversee, train and manage all Deputies at the Convention
7. the "Sergeant at Arms" will take the following oath while placing his/her right hand on the Bible

"I solemnly promise to officiate the office of Sergeant at Arms for the CONSTITUTIONAL HISTORY AMENDMENT Convention according to the terms and/or conditions set forth in the Legislative Calls from the Several States to the best of my ability, so help me God".

DEPUTIES – The "Deputies'" duties include:

1. be amenable to the Convention Chairman, Assistant Convention Chairman and Sergeant at Arms
2. monitor all activities at the Convention and report to the Sergeant at Arms violations or possible violations of the terms and/or conditions of this Legislative Call and Agreement
3. maintain order at the Convention as directed by the Sergeant at Arms
4. enforce all remedies for violations of this Legislative Call and Agreement as directed by the Convention Chairman and/or the Sergeant at Arms
5. "Deputies" will take the following oath while placing his/her right hand on the Bible

"I solemnly promise to officiate the office of Deputy for the CONSTITUTIONAL HISTORY AMENDMENT Convention according to the terms and/or conditions set forth in the Legislative Calls from the Several States to the best of my ability, so help me God".

CHALLENGING THE QUALIFICATIONS OF CONVENTION OFFICIALS

A State Delegation can challenge the qualifications of any Convention Official at the CONSTITUTIONAL HISTORY AMENDMENT Convention by bringing its allegation(s), during a usiness session, to the Convention floor. The Convention Chairman will consider the allegation(s) and determine if it merits further investigation. If the Chairman decides that the allegation(s) merits further investigation, he/she will direct the Sergeant at Arms to conduct the necessary inquiry. He/she will then follow the instructions outlined in the section "Violating this Agreement" for proscribing a remedy or remedies.

The "Convention Chairman" can also reject a challenge to the qualifications of any Convention Official if he/she concludes that the Delegate making the allegation(s) is trying to disrupt and/or delay Convention business. If after following the instructions outlined in "Violating this Agreement" the Delegate is found to have made a false accusation against a Convention Official, the Delegate's State Delegation will be charged with a violation of the terms and/or conditions of this Call and Agreement.

PROHIBITIONS FOR STATE DELEGATES, STATE DELEGATIONS AND CONVENTION OFFICIALS AT THE CONVENTION

State Delegates, State Delegations and Convention Officials are prohibited from violating any of the following Convention prohibitions:

1. State Delegates, State Delegations and Convention Officials are prohibited, at the Convention, from introducing, discussing, voting on, or sending to the States for consideration and/or ratification any amendment to the United States Constitution other than the CONSTITUTIONAL HISTORY AMENDMENT, as herein written

2. State Delegates, State Delegations and Convention Officials are prohibited from altering or changing, in any way (which includes the wording, spelling, punctuation, or paragraph sections), the CONSTITUTIONAL HISTORY AMENDMENT from the written form shown in the section titled **"The full text of the CONSTITUTIONAL HISTORY AMENDMENT"**

3. State Delegates, State Delegations and Convention Officials are prohibited, at the Convention, from introducing, discussing, voting on, or sending to the States for consideration and/or ratification any alternate form of government for the United States of America

4. State Delegates, State Delegations and Convention Officials are prohibited, at the Convention, from introducing, discussing, voting on, or sending to the States for consideration and/or ratification any alternate constitution or governing document for the United States of America

5. State Delegates, State Delegations and Convention Officials are prohibited, at the Convention, from introducing, discussing, voting on, or sending to the States for consideration and/or ratification any changes, of any kind, to the existing Constitution of the United States

of America other than the CONSTITUTIONAL HISTORY AMENDMENT

6. State Delegates, State Delegations and Convention Officials are prohibited, at the Convention, from introducing, discussing, voting on, or sending to the States for consideration any changes, of any kind, to this binding Agreement between the States Calling for the CONSTITUTIONAL HISTORY AMENDMENT Convention

7. State Delegates, State Delegations and Convention Officials are prohibited, at the Convention, from introducing, discussing, voting on, or sending to the States for consideration and/or ratification any subject matter, issue or topic (of any kind) other than the proposed CONSTITUTIONAL HISTORY AMENDMENT in its written form shown in the section titled **"The full text of the CONSTITUTIONAL HISTORY AMENDMENT"**

THE DATE, TIME, DURATION AND PLACE OF THE CONSTITUTIONAL HISTORY AMENDMENT CONVENTION.

The United States Congress will be responsible for determining and announcing to the Several States the date, time, and place that the CONSTITUTIONAL HISTORY AMENDMENT Convention is to convene immediately after two thirds of the States, under the authority given to the States in Article V of the United States Constitution, have completed their Calls on Congress to convene the CONSTITUTIONAL HISTORY AMENDMENT Convention. The Convention is expected to complete its business by the 180th day after convening. The Convention Chairman can extend the duration of the CONSTITUTIONAL HISTORY AMENDMENT Convention for one additional 180 day period. The maximum number of days the Convention is authorized to be in session are 360 days. If the Convention has not decided if the CONSTITUTIONAL HISTORY AMENDMENT should be sent to Congress with instructions to send the Amendment to the Several States for ratification by the end of 360 days, then the Call for the CONSTITUTIONAL HISTORY AMENDMENT Convention, which was approved by the Several States under the authority granted in Article V of the United States Constitution and this agreement, will be automatically withdrawn by the Calling States and the Convention will automatically terminate at 5:00 P.M. Eastern Standard Time on the 360th day after convening. Termination of the CONSTITUTIONAL HISTORY AMENDMENT Convention will automatically occur on the 360th day after convening the Convention, without requiring a formal notice by the States to the Convention, nor by the States to the United States Congress, nor by the Convention to the States, nor by the Convention to the United States Congress, although it is recommended that the Convention notify the United States Congress and the State Legislatures of its termination as a courtesy.

Under no circumstance(s) are the Delegates at the CONSTITUTIONAL HISTORY AMENDMENT Convention authorized to re-convene a new or different Convention, no matter what their purpose or intent. The official Legislative Call and authority granted by the Several States and the subsequent convening of the CONSTITUTIONAL HISTORY AMENDMENT Convention by Congress will be automatically invalidated and the Convention will be abolished at 5:00 P.M. Eastern Standard Time on the 360th day after the convening of the CONSTITUTIONAL HISTORY AMENDMENT Convention.

VIOLATING THIS AGREEMENT

The Convention Chairman (or in the absence of the Convention Chairman the Assistant Convention Chairman) will handle allegations of a violation(s) or actual violation(s) of the terms and/or conditions of this binding Agreement between the Several States, by any one or more Delegate(s) and/or Convention Official(s), as follows:

1. When an alleged violation has been presented to the Convention Chairman, and if the Chairman decides that the allegation(s) merits further investigation, he/she will instruct the Sergeant at Arms to conduct the necessary inquiry.

2. After the inquiry has been completed, and assuming the Convention Chairman concludes that the evidence does not substantiate further review by the Convention, the allegation(s) will be dismissed by the Chairman and the Convention will go forward with its business.

3. If however, after the inquiry has been completed, the Convention Chairman concludes that the evidence does substantiate further review by the Convention, the Chairman will present the allegation(s) and findings of the inquiry to the Convention for a discussion and vote. If a majority of the State Delegations (one vote per State Delegation) decide that no violation of the terms and/or conditions of this Legislative Call and Agreement has occurred, then the Chairman will declare that the alleged violation(s) of the terms and/or conditions of this Legislative Call and Agreement is/are dismissed. The Convention will then go forward with its business.

4. If however, after the inquiry has been completed, the Convention Chairman concludes that the evidence does substantiate further review by the Convention, the Chairman will present the allegation(s) and findings of the inquiry to the Convention for a discussion and vote. If a majority of the State Delegations (one vote per State Delegation) decide that one or more violation(s) of the terms and/or conditions of this Legislative Call and Agreement has/have occurred, then the Chairman will declare to the Convention that the Delegate(s)

responsible for the violation(s), and their State Delegation(s), has/have been charged with "Violating this Agreement". The Convention will then go forward with its business.

5. If a State Delegation is charged with two violations of the terms and/or conditions of this Legislative Call and Agreement, the Convention Chairman will declare to the Convention that the State Delegation charged with violating this Agreement a second time has no further standing or authority at the Convention. The Chairman will notify the charged State Delegation that its entire delegation of Delegates must leave the Convention immediately and they will not be allowed back into the Convention. The Chairman will instruct the Sergeant at Arms that he should escort the charged State Delegation out of the Convention. The Convention Chairman will then notify the State Legislature that sent the charged State Delegation of the actions that the Convention has taken and inform them that they can send a replacement State Delegation to the Convention as long as they do not disrupt the proceedings of the Convention. None of the original Delegates who were charged by the Convention will be allowed back into the Convention as part of a replacement delegation.

6. The Convention Chairman will not allow unreasonable delays in the proceedings of the Convention due to disruptive Delegates or State Delegations. He/she will move the business of the Convention forward expeditiously.

THE FULL TEXT OF THE CONSTITUTIONAL HISTORY AMENDMENT

The full text of the CONSTITUTIONAL HISTORY AMENDMENT to be submitted to the Several States by the United States Congress for ratification shall read as follows:

CONSTITUTIONAL HISTORY AMENDMENT
ARTICLE 28 (or alternate number to be assigned by Congress)

Section 1. America's Constitutional history is unique among nations and sacred to the American people. It is the right of citizens to receive an accurate historical account of America's Constitutional history, which is foundational to a free people.

Section 2. To secure the rights of citizens it is hereby prohibited for any institution or individual to intentionally teach misleading, false or otherwise distorted accounts of America's Constitutional history. The provisions of this Article are enforceable within the United States which shall include the Several States, the District of Columbia, and the Commonwealth of Puerto Rico, the Commonwealth of the Northern Mariana Islands and the territories and possessions of the United States.

Section 3. Congress shall have the power to enforce by appropriate legislation, the provisions of the Article.

RATIFICATION OF THE "CONSTITUTIONAL HISTORY AMENDMENT"

Under the requirements of Article V of the United States Constitution and also under Article IV, Section 4 which guarantees to every State a Republican form of Government, the CONSTITUTIONAL HISTORY AMENDMENT will become a ratified Amendment to the United States Constitution when three quarters of the Several States complete their ratifications of the Amendment.

"CONGRESSIONAL" OPTION

If the United States Congress voluntarily sends the CONSTITUTIONAL HISTORY AMENDMENT to the Several States for ratification without making any changes, of any kind (which includes the wording, spelling, punctuation and paragraph sections) in the proposed Amendment as herein written, and before two thirds of the States complete their Call for Congress to convene the CONSTITUTIONAL HISTORY AMENDMENT Convention, then the Legislature of the State of TEXAS will withdraw its Call for the CONSTITUTIONAL HISTORY AMENDMENT Convention.

OFFICIAL AGREEMENT BY THE TEXAS STATE LEGISLATURE BETWEEN ITSELF AND THE CALLING STATES

The Legislature of the State of TEXAS enters into this binding Agreement with every other State Legislature that likewise agrees to the terms and/or conditions of this Legislative Call and Agreement as set forth herein. This is an irrevocable contract, during the term of this Agreement, between the State of TEXAS and each and every State that signs this Agreement and completes its Call on the United States Congress directing Congress to convene a Federal Convention titled the CONSTITUTIONAL HISTORY AMENDMENT Convention. The Legislature of the State of TEXAS agrees that it, and its delegates who are selected to attend the Convention, will abide by the purpose, terms, conditions, agenda, and "Convention Rules of Order" as explained in this Agreement.

The Legislature of the State of TEXAS enters into this Agreement with every other State Legislature that likewise agrees to the terms and/or conditions of this

Agreement and Legislative Call as set forth herein, understanding that the CONSTITUTIONAL HISTORY AMENDMENT Convention, by definition herein explained, is a "SINGLE ISSUE" Federal Convention and that the Convention will have no authority, under this Call and Agreement between the States, to review and/or consider any other subject matter, issue, or topic during its sessions other than business matters relating to the question, should the CONSTITUTIONAL HISTORY AMENDMENT, as herein written, be sent by the Convention to the United States Congress instructing Congress to send the Amendment to the Several States for ratification? The Legislature of the State of TEXAS irrevocably declares by signing this Agreement that any subject matter, issue or topic (other than the CONSTITUTIONAL HISTORY AMENDMENT) that delegates might try to present to the Convention and subsequently to the States for review and/or ratification will be immediately, upon introduction at the Convention, unauthorized, invalid and automatically rejected by the Legislature of the State of TEXAS, and the Legislature of the State of TEXAS irrevocably declares that it will not review and/or consider for ratification any such subject matter, issue or topic, no matter how presented to it by the Convention. Only the CONSTITUTIONAL HISTORY AMENDMENT, as herein written, will be considered by the Legislature of the State of TEXAS for ratification.

The Legislature of the State of TEXAS also irrevocably declares that under no circumstance(s) will it consider for review and/or ratification any amendment to the United States Constitution, submitted to it by the CONSTITUTIONAL HISTORY AMENDMENT Convention other than the CONSTITUTIONAL HISTORY AMENDMENT as herein written.

The Legislature of the State of TEXAS further irrevocably declares that under no circumstance(s) will it consider for review and/or ratification any modified form of the CONSTITUTIONAL HISTORY AMENDMENT submitted to it by the CONSTITUTIONAL HISTORY AMENDMENT Convention that would change, alter, or replace, in any way (which includes the wording, spelling, punctuation, or paragraph sections), the CONSTITUTIONAL HISTORY AMENDMENT from its written form herein.

The Legislature of the State of TEXAS further irrevocably declares that under no circumstance(s) will it consider for review and/or ratification any proposal, of any kind, sent to it by the CONSTITUTIONAL HISTORY AMENDMENT Convention that would change, replace, or alter the United States Constitution other than the CONSTITUTIONAL HISTORY AMENDMENT as herein written.

The Legislature of the State of TEXAS further irrevocably declares that under no circumstance(s) will it consider for review any proposal, of any kind, sent to it by the CONSTITUTIONAL HISTORY AMENDMENT Convention that would change, replace, or alter, in any way (which includes the wording, spelling, punctuation and section paragraphs), this Official Legislative Call for the CONSTITUTIONAL HISTORY AMENDMENT Convention and the terms and/or conditions of this Agreement between the States as herein written.

Under the authority reserved to the State of TEXAS in Article V of the United States Constitution and also under Article IV, Section 4 which guarantees to every State a Republican form of Government, the Legislature of the State of TEXAS hereby approves this Legislative Call on the United States Congress directing Congress to convene the CONSTITUTIONAL HISTORY AMENDMENT Convention and binds itself with each and every State that likewise approves this identical Legislative Call according the terms and/or conditions set forth in this Agreement.

OFFICIAL CALL BY THE STATE OF TEXAS ON THE UNITED STATES CONGRESS DIRECTING CONGRESS TO CONVENE THE CONSTITUTIONAL HISTORY AMENDMENT CONVENTION

The Legislature of the State of TEXAS hereby Calls on the United States Congress directing Congress to convene a Federal Convention to be titled the CONSTITUTIONAL HISTORY AMENDMENT Convention. The Convention is to be convened immediately after two thirds of the Several States have completed their Calls for the CONSTITUTIONAL HISTORY AMENDMENT Convention.

The State of TEXAS is authorized to make this Call for the CONSTITUTIONAL HISTORY AMENDMENT Convention under the authority reserved to the States in Article V of the United States Constitution and under Article IV, Section 4 which guarantees to every State a Republican form of Government. Both Articles give to each State an equal standing when calling for a Constitutional Convention. Article V and Article IV, Section 4 reserves to the Several States the right to Call for a Federal Convention for the purpose of amending the United States Constitution when Congress and/or the Courts refuse to address an egregious wrong suffered by the people.

Submitted to Both Houses of the United States Congress on this date _____, _____ by the Legislature of the State of TEXAS.

State of TEXAS Seal:

Authorized Signatures with titles:

RECLAIMING AMERICA

_____Title_____

_____Title_____

_____Title_____

_____Title_____

CHAPTER 14

UNBORN CHILD AMENDMENT

Text of proposed
UNBORN CHILD AMENDMENT
ARTICLE 28 (or alternate number to be assigned by Congress)

Section 1. The Unborn offspring of human beings are persons from the time of conception and continually thereafter throughout their subsequent development: No Unborn person shall be intentionally deprived of life or limb, or shall be subjected to intentionally inflicted harm.

Section 2. To secure the rights of Unborn persons, induced abortion is hereby prohibited within the United States which shall include the Several States, the District of Columbia, and the Commonwealth of Puerto Rico, the Commonwealth of the Northern Mariana Islands and the territories and possessions of the United States.

Section 3. Congress shall have the power to enforce by appropriate legislation, the provisions of the Article.

There can be no blacker blot on America's judicial history than Roe vs. Wade and subsequent rulings that extend the age of the Unborn Child beyond the first trimester during which the mother can abort. This incredibly evil ruling has effectively declared war on the Unborn Child, the father of the Unborn Child, the young mother (who in many cases understands little or nothing about the consequences of her choice) and the grandparents.

 It is impossible to calculate the human, social, and economic costs America has suffered because of Roe vs. Wade.. The carnage from the death of 48 million American babies has severely denigrated American life spiritually, morally, legally, politically, and intellectually. By legalizing abortion, we have discarded the first and most important principle that gives legitimacy to government – *HUMAN LIFE IS SACRED!*

RECLAIMING AMERICA

Government's first duty is to protect every human being. Sanctity of human life is the first principle upon which governments receive their legitimate mandate to govern. Abortion is an atrocity that carries incalculable costs for all of us. It must be stopped!

Pro Life Americans need to know that we can win a constitutional Amendment, protect the life of the Unborn Child, a father's and grandparent's right to a live heritage and restore to our young and vulnerable women a sane motherhood.

AUTHORIZED CALL
BY THE NORTH DAKOTA STATE LEGISLATURE
ON THE UNITED STATES CONGRESS INSTRUCTING CONGRESS
TO CONVENE A FEDERAL CONVENTION TO BE TITLED
THE UNBORN CHILD AMENDMENT CONVENTION

THIS AUTHORIZED CALL ALSO DEFINES THE AGREEMENT
THE NORTH DAKOTA STATE LEGISLATURE IS ENTERING INTO
BETWEEN ITSELF AND OTHER CALLING STATES

To: **BOTH HOUSES OF UNITED STATES CONGRESS**

UNITED STATES SENATE:

President of the Senate, United States Vice President
Majority Leader Senator
Minority Leader Senator
President Pro Tempore Senator
Republican Whip Senator
Democratic Whip Senator

(Deliver this Official Call to every current leader and member of the United State Senate at Washington, DC)

HOUSE OF REPRESENTATIVE:

Speaker of the House Representative
House Majority Leader Representative
House Majority Whip Representative
House Minority Leader Representative
House Minority Whip Representative

(Deliver this Official Call to every current leader and member of the United State House of Representatives at Washington, DC)

From: **THE STATE LEGISLATURE OF THE STATE OF NORTH DAKOTA**

The Legislature of the State of North Dakota hereby Calls on the United States Congress instructing Congress to convene a Federal Convention called the Unborn Child Amendment Convention under the authority reserved to the States in Article V of the United States Constitution. Article IV, Section 4 guarantees to every State a Republican form of Government which gives each State equal standing when Calling for a Constitutional Convention. Article V reserves to the Several States the right to Call for a

Federal Constitutional Convention for the purpose of amending the United States Constitution when Congress and/or the Courts refuse to address an egregious wrong suffered by the people. The States *alone* have the authority to "limit" the agenda and authority of a Federal Convention. The States alone can Call for a "Single Issue" Convention by agreeing among themselves the purpose, terms, conditions, duration, and agenda for the Convention. Congress does not have the authority to define a "Single Issue" Convention. Congress' authority, under Article V of the United States Constitution, empowers it to convene a Convention as Called for and defined by the Several States. The Several States alone have the authority to enforce the terms and/or conditions set forth in this Agreement at the Unborn Child Amendment Convention.

The Unborn Child Amendment Convention will be a "Single Issue" Federal Convention as defined in this Legislative Call on the United States Congress and in this binding Agreement between the Several States. The delegates summoned to this Convention by Congress will have the authority to decide only one issue, should the Unborn Child Amendment, as herein written, be sent to Congress with instructions to send the Amendment back to the Several States for ratification? The delegates at the Unborn Child Amendment Convention will have no authority to change the wording of the proposed Amendment, neither are they authorized to deliberate on or discuss any other subject matter or issue at the Convention. The purpose, terms and/or conditions that will govern the agenda and affairs of the Unborn Child Amendment Convention are as follows:

THE PURPOSE OF THE CONVENTION

The *only* purpose for convening the Unborn Child Amendment Convention is for the State Delegations, representing the Several States, to decide if the Unborn Child Amendment, as herein written, should be sent to the United States Congress with instructions for Congress to send the Amendment to the Several States for ratification? Absolutely no other business is authorized at this Convention.

CONVENTION RULES OF ORDER

The "Convention Rules of Order" that all Delegates and State Delegations are required to follow as a condition of participating at the Unborn Child Amendment Convention are described in this Legislative Call on Congress. From time to time, in order to facilitate Convention business, the Convention Chairman may require the Convention to follow "Robert's Rules of Order" when a specific Rule of Order is not defined in this Legislative Call. The Delegates and State Delegations are required to honor the Convention

Chairman's instructions when applying Convention Rules of Order and/or Roberts Rules of Order.

UNBORN CHILD AMENDMENT COMMITTEE

The Unborn Child Amendment Committee is the citizens group that founded the Unborn Child Amendment Initiative. This Committee will be responsible for pre-Convention planning and organization. The Chairman and Vice Chairman of the Unborn Child Amendment Committee will be Ex-Officio (without voting rights) members of the Convention. They can be called upon by the Convention Chairman to clarify the Unborn Child Amendment legislative strategy for the Delegates, provide progress reports in the States and also be available for questions and answers from Delegates at the Convention. They will be subject to the terms and/or conditions of this Legislative Call and Agreement between the States.

If they are also appointed as Delegates by their State Legislatures, then they will be entitled to voting privileges as Delegates at the Convention. The Chairman of the Unborn Child Amendment Committee is R.C. "Kacprowicz" Casper.

If the Convention votes in favor of the Amendment, the Unborn Child Amendment Committee will be responsible for post-convention planning and organization during the ratification process.

FUNDING THE CONVENTION AND STATE DELEGATIONS

The State Legislatures that send Delegates to the Unborn Child Amendment Convention shall be responsible for providing monies necessary for their State Delegations to participate at the Convention. The amounts each State Delegation will require will be decided by each State Legislature. Other expenses or costs necessary to fund the Convention are to be shared by the Calling States equally. From time to time the Convention Chairman will notify the State Delegations what monies will be necessary to carry on the business of the Convention.

FUNDING FOR "PRE AND POST-CONVENTION PLANNING AND ORGANIZATION"

Each State Legislature making a Call on Congress to convene the Unborn Child Amendment Convention will be asked to share expenses for "pre-Convention planning" and "pre-Convention organization". If the Convention votes to send the Unborn Child Amendment to Congress to be ratified by the States, then the Unborn Child Amendment Committee will ask the Calling States to help fund post-convention planning and organization to cover expenses for the ratification process.

DELEGATES SUMMONED BY CONGRESS

Congress has the authority, under Article V, to summon Delegates from the Several States to the Unborn Child Amendment Convention. Congress is hereby directed to summon to the Convention the appropriate number of Delegates that each State is entitled to immediately after two thirds of the States complete their Call directing Congress to convene the Unborn Child Amendment Convention. The number of Delegates to be summoned to the Convention should be equal to the number of members each State has in the House of Representatives and in the Senate of the United States Congress.

DELEGATES AND STATE DELEGATIONS

Only State Delegates summoned by Congress to the Unborn Child Amendment Convention and appointed by their State Legislatures to form State Delegations to represent their respective States are authorized to attend and speak at the Unborn Child Amendment Convention. Each State Legislature has the responsibility to select, from within its State, individual Delegates who will represent its State at the Convention. The number of Delegates selected by a State Legislature can be no greater than the number of Delegates summoned by Congress from its State. Each State Delegation must select a Delegate from within its delegation to be its Spokesman at the Convention. Only a Delegation's Spokesman will be recognized by the Convention Chairman.

THE PRE-CONVENTION "ACTING CONVENTION CHAIRMAN" AND "ASSISTANT ACTING CONVENTION CHAIRMAN"

The Chairman and Vice Chairman of the Unborn Child Amendment Committee will have exclusive authority to complete all pre-convention planning and organization for the Unborn Child Amendment Convention. They will perform their duties under the titles "Acting Convention Chairman" and "Assistant Acting Convention Chairman" respectfully. They will also be available to State Legislatures to assist with their Legislative Calls and pre-Convention planning.

The Chairman and Vice Chairman of the Unborn Child Amendment Committee will also be responsible for post-convention planning and organization if the Convention votes to send the Unborn Child Amendment to Congress to be ratified by the States.

VOTING BY DELEGATES IN STATE DELEGATIONS

It is recommended that a simple majority of the Delegates within each State Delegation be required to decide a State Delegation's vote at the Convention. A quorum within each State Delegation will consist of one Delegate. The business of the Convention and voting will not be delayed if a State Delegation does not cast a vote during a roll call.

QUORUM REQUIRED FOR CONDUCTING BUSINESS AND VOTING AT THE CONVENTION

Each State Delegation will have one vote on all matters that are to be decided by the Convention. A simple majority vote by the State Delegations at the Convention is required to decide the outcome of all business brought before the Convention for a vote, including whether or not the Unborn Child Amendment, as herein written, should be sent to the Several States, via Congress, for ratification. A quorum at the Convention for the purpose of conducting business and voting will consist of 17 State Delegations.

CLOSED DELIBERATIONS AT THE CONVENTION

The Unborn Child Amendment Convention will be closed to all media and news groups. Only delegates appointed by their State Legislatures and the Chairman and Vice Chairman of the Unborn Child Amendment Committee will be authorized to enter and speak at the Convention. No visitors, reporters, government officials, professionals or inquirers, of any kind, will be permitted to enter the Convention facilities. Unauthorized visitors will be escorted by the Sergeant of Arms out of the Convention. After the vote by the State Delegations is taken to determine if the Unborn Child Amendment will be sent to the Several States, via Congress, for ratification, the Chairman of the Convention will call a special press conference to announce the Convention's decision. Within 30 days from the special press conference the Chairman will make available to the public the records kept by the Convention during its proceedings.

STATE LEGISLATURES NOT AUTHORIZING THIS CALL FOR THE UNBORN CHILD AMENDMENT CONVENTION

State Legislatures that did not authorize this Call for the Unborn Child Amendment Convention and yet agree to send delegates representing their State agree to follow the terms and/or conditions set forth in this Agreement and Legislative Call. They need to pay particular attention to the "Convention's Rules of Order" described in this Agreement and the prohibitions in the section titled "Prohibitions for Delegates, State Delegations and/or Convention Officials at the Convention". These non-

calling States must notify the "Acting Convention Chairman" before the Convention convenes of their intention to attend the Convention so accommodations can be completed for their Delegations. In order to receive Convention Passes, all Delegates attending the Convention, will be required to sign an agreement promising to abide by the terms and/or conditions in this Legislative Call and Agreement.

NO WEAPONS ALLOWED AT THE CONVENTION

Delegates and Unborn Child Amendment Committee officials will not be allowed to bring into the Unborn Child Amendment Convention any weapons or objects that can be construed as weapons.

PRESENTING ARGUMENTS AT THE CONVENTION BY STATE DELEGATIONS

Each State Delegation will be allotted a maximum of 60 minutes for presenting its argument(s) at the Convention for or against sending the Unborn Child Amendment to the United States Congress with instruction for Congress to send the Amendment to the Several States for ratification. Only Delegates who have been officially selected by their State Legislatures and Ex-Officio members of the Convention are authorized to speak before the Convention. Each State Delegation can use one or more of its Delegates to present its position(s). However, the total time allotted for each State Delegation is 60 minutes, which includes any time that is necessary to replace one Delegate with another. The Chairman of the Unborn Child Amendment Committee will also be limited to 60 minutes during his speaking segment. Speakers cannot reserve portions of their time to another time or day. Speakers must complete their arguments in the 60 minute segment assigned to them.

The order each State Delegation will follow when presenting their position(s) will be according to when each State completed its Legislative Call on Congress, or when it notified the "Acting Convention Chairman" that it intends to attend the Convention even though it may not complete a Legislative Call on Congress. The State Delegation presentations will be scheduled in the following manner: the first State making a Call on Congress will go first; the first State notifying the "Acting Convention Chairman" that it plans to attend will go second. The second State making a Call on Congress will go third; then the second State notifying the "Acting Convention Chairman" will go fourth, and so forth until all States wanting to present their positions have had an opportunity to do so. The Convention Chairman can rearrange the schedule if any conflicts arise at the Convention. The last speaker to be scheduled at the Convention for a 60 minute segment will be the Chairman of the Unborn Child Amendment Committee.

DUTIES OF THE "ACTING CONVENTION CHAIRMAN"

The duties of the "Acting Convention Chairman include:

1. organize a pre-Convention support group for assisting Calling States with their Legislative Calls and non-calling States with their intentions to attend the Convention
2. set up an Unborn Child Amendment Committee checking account
3. use generally accepted accounting principles when keeping records of all receipts and expenditures
4. provide financial reports and minutes of pre-convention activities as requested by States that are funding pre-convention operations
5. keep minutes of all business meetings of the Unborn Child Amendment Committee
6. determine the budget that will be needed for pre-convention planning and organizing and notify each State Legislature of its share of the expenses
7. assist the Calling States and Attending States with their pre-convention planning
8. assist the Calling States with their Legislative Calls on Congress
9. after the Unborn Child Amendment Convention has been convened call the Convention to order
10. invite nominations from the State Delegations present at the Convention to fill the "Convention Chairman's" position (the maximum number of nominees permitted is five and only one nominee from any one State Delegation is permitted)
11. take a roll call from the State Delegations for the nominee(s)
12. declare the winner based on the nominee who has received the most votes (a plurality of State Delegations). Each State Delegation will have one vote
13. officiate the installation of the "Convention Chairman" at the Convention by having the Chairman place his/her right hand on the Bible while repeating the following oath

"I solemnly promise to officiate the office of Convention Chairman for the Unborn Child Amendment Convention according to the terms and/or conditions set forth in the Legislative Calls from the Several States to the best of my ability, so help me God".

In the event the "Acting Convention Chairman" is nominated and elected to the Convention Chairman position, the "Assistant Acting Convention Chairman" will conduct the installation ceremony for the Convention Chairman.

ELECTION, AUTHORITY AND DUTIES OF CONVENTION OFFICIALS

RECLAIMING AMERICA

CONVENTION CHAIRMAN: - The "Convention Chairman" is the senior official at the Unborn Child Amendment Convention. He/she will have the requisite authority to oversee all activities at the Convention, including the nomination and election of all officials. The Convention Chairman's duties include:

1. organize and oversee all business and activities at the Convention
2. organize and officiate all nominations, elections and installations of officials at the Convention (this will be the Convention Chairman's first order of business)
3. organize and officiate all nominations, elections and installations of official positions that may become vacant at the Convention
4. oversee the enforcement of all Convention Rules
5. oversee the enforcement of the terms and/or conditions (herein described) of this Call and Agreement by the States
6. oversee the investigation of alleged and/or actual violations of this Agreement as defined in the section titled "Violating this Agreement"
7. bring before the Convention all matters that require a vote
8. bring before the Convention the financial needs of the Convention and time lines for when these monies are needed
9. cut off motions or discussions by State Delegations before the Convention if and when it seems appropriate
10. recognize the Spokesman within a State Delegation for the purpose of addressing a matter of importance to the Spokesman's Delegation (the Convention Chairman will have full authority to determine if a matter brought before the Convention by the Spokesman is appropriate for further discussion and/or if a decision by the Convention is necessary)
11. keep the business of the Convention moving forward expeditiously, cutting off all motions and discussions when it appears one or more Delegates are trying to hinder, delay or stop the work of the Convention
12. keep the business of the Convention focused on one objective which is, should the Convention send the Unborn Child Amendment to Congress instructing Congress to send it to the Several States for ratification?
13. instruct Convention Officials (Assistant Convention Chairman, Secretary, Financial Officer, Executive Administrator, Sergeant at Arms, and Deputies) on their duties at the Convention
14. officiate and remedy any and all problems that may develop at the Convention
15. oversee the design and production of "Official" Convention Badges for the Sergeant at Arms and Deputies

16. notify all State Legislatures of the decision the Convention made as to whether or not the Unborn Child Amendment should be sent to Congress instructing Congress to send it to the States for ratification?
17. if the State Delegations voted to send the Amendment to the States for ratification, include the Convention's recommendation to the United States Congress as to whether it should be ratified by State Conventions or State Legislatures
18. declare the Unborn Child Amendment Convention closed after the State Delegations have decided if the Unborn Child Amendment should be sent to Congress instructing Congress to send it to the States for ratification?
19. arrange a Special News Conference to announce the decision by the Unborn Child Amendment Convention
20. make available the proceedings of the Convention to the public 30 days after the Convention is closed

> The first order of business for the "Convention Chairman" will be to open the Convention to nominations from State Delegations present for each of the following Convention Officials; one Assistant Convention Chairman, one Secretary, one Financial Officer, one Executive Administrator, one Sergeant at Arms and ten Deputies (the maximum number of nominees permitted for each Convention Official position is five. Only one nominee for each Convention Official position is permitted from any one State Delegation. The nominee with a plurality of votes from the State Delegations will be the winner). The "Convention Chairman" can call for nominations for more than 10 Deputies if and when circumstances warrant.

ASSISTANT CONVENTION CHAIRMAN

The "Assistant Convention Chairman" duties include:

1. be amenable to the "Convention Chairman"
2. provide assistance to the "Convention Chairman" in all matters pertaining to the business of the Convention
3. monitor activities at the Convention and report to the "Convention Chairman" violations or possible violations of the terms and/or conditions of this Legislative Call and Agreement
4. perform the duties of the "Convention Chairman" when called upon by the Chairman or when the Chairman is unable to perform the duties of his/her office the "Assistant Convention Chairman" will take the following oath, administered by the Convention Chairman, while placing his/her right hand on the Bible

"I solemnly promise to officiate the office of Assistant Convention Chairman for the Unborn Child Amendment Convention according to the terms and/or conditions set forth in the Legislative Calls from the Several States to the best of my ability, so help me God".

SECRETARY - The "Secretary's" duties include:

1. keep official minutes of all proceedings at the Convention
2. monitor activities at the Convention and report to the Convention Chairman violations or possible violations of Convention Rules and of the terms and/or conditions of this Legislative Call and Agreement
3. make available to the "Convention Chairman", upon request, the official minutes of the Convention
4. be amenable to the "Convention Chairman" and "Assistant Convention Chairman"
5. in the absence of the "Convention Chairman" and the "Assistant Convention Chairman" due to death or a disablement that prevents them from performing the duties of their offices at the Convention, the Secretary shall call the Convention to order for the purpose of nominating and electing a new "Convention Chairman" and "Assistant Convention Chairman". In this capacity the Secretary will assume the duties and authority of the "Convention Chairman". If the Secretary is unable to perform the duties described herein, then they will fall to the Financial Officer.
6. the "Secretary" will take the following oath while placing his/her right hand on the Bible

"I solemnly promise to officiate the office of Secretary for the Unborn Child Amendment Convention according to the terms and/or conditions set forth in the Legislative Calls from the Several States to the best of my ability, so help me God".

FINANCIAL OFFICER - The "Financial Officer's" duties include:
1. keep detailed accounting records of all financial matters at the Convention using generally accepted accounting principles
2. be amenable to the "Convention Chairman" and "Assistant Convention Chairman"
3. monitor activities at the Convention and report to the Convention Chairman violations or possible violations of the terms and/or conditions of this Legislative Call and Agreement
4. set up a checking account in the name of the Unborn Child Amendment Convention requiring any two of the following three officers when signing a check or making withdrawals –

Convention Chairman, Assistant Convention Chairman, Financial Officer

5. make available to the "Convention Chairman", upon request, all financial records at the Convention
6. provide to the Convention Chairman the financial needs of the Convention and the time lines as to when these monies are needed
7. in the absence of a "Convention Chairman", "Assistant Convention Chairman", and "Secretary" due to death or a disablement that prevents them from performing the duties of their offices at the Convention, the Financial Officer shall call the Convention to order for the purpose of nominating and electing a new "Convention Chairman", "Assistant Convention Chairman", and "Secretary". In this capacity the Financial Officer will assume the duties and authority of the "Convention Chairman"
8. the "Financial Officer" will take the following oath while placing his/her right hand on the Bible

"I solemnly promise to officiate the office of Financial Officer for the Unborn Child Amendment Convention according to generally accepted accounting principles and according to the terms and/or conditions set forth in the Legislative Calls from the Several States to the best of my ability, so help me God".

EXECUTIVE ADMINISTRATOR

The "Executive Administrator's" duties include:

1. facilitate all Convention business as directed by the Convention Chairman
2. be amenable to the Convention Chairman and Assistant Convention Chairman
3. monitor activities at the Convention and report to the Convention Chairman violations or possible violations of the terms and/or conditions of this Legislative Call and Agreement
4. keep detailed reports of all administrative activities at the Convention
5. make available to the "Convention Chairman" upon request all administrative records and/or reports at the Convention

6. the "Executive Administrator" will take the following oath while placing his/her right hand on the Bible

"I solemnly promise to officiate the office of Executive Administrator for the Unborn Child Amendment Convention according to the terms and/or conditions set forth in the Legislative Calls from the Several States to the best of my ability, so help me God".

SERGEANT AT ARMS

The "Sergeant at Arms'" duties include:

1. be amenable to the Convention Chairman and Assistant Convention Chairman
2. monitor all activities at the Convention and report to the Convention Chairman violations or possible violations of the terms and/or conditions of this Legislative Call and Agreement
3. maintain order at the Convention
4. enforce all remedies for violations of this Legislative Call and Agreement as directed by the Convention Chairman
5. organize and direct the activities of all Deputies at the Convention
6. oversee, train and manage all Deputies at the Convention
7. the "Sergeant at Arms" will take the following oath while placing his/her right hand on the Bible

   "I solemnly promise to officiate the office of Sergeant at Arms for the Unborn Child Amendment Convention according to the terms and/or conditions set forth in the Legislative Calls from the Several States to the best of my ability, so help me God".

DEPUTIES
The "Deputies'" duties include:

1. be amenable to the Convention Chairman, Assistant Convention Chairman and Sergeant at Arms
2. monitor all activities at the Convention and report to the Sergeant at Arms violations or possible violations of the terms and/or conditions of this Legislative Call and Agreement
3. maintain order at the Convention as directed by the Sergeant at Arms
4. enforce all remedies for violations of this Legislative Call and Agreement as directed by the Convention Chairman and/or the Sergeant at Arms
5. "Deputies" will take the following oath while placing his/her right hand on the Bible

"I solemnly promise to officiate the office of Deputy for the Unborn Child Amendment Convention according to the terms and/or conditions set forth in the Legislative Calls from the Several States to the best of my ability, so help me God".

CHALLENGING THE QUALIFICATIONS OF CONVENTION OFFICIALS

A State Delegation can challenge the qualifications of any Convention Official at the Unborn Child Amendment Convention by bringing its allegation(s), during a business session, to the Convention floor. The Convention Chairman will consider the allegation(s) and determine if it merits further investigation. If the Chairman decides that the allegation(s) merits further investigation, he/she will direct the Sergeant at Arms to conduct the necessary inquiry. He/she will then follow the instructions outlined in the section "Violating this Agreement" for proscribing a remedy or remedies.

The "Convention Chairman" can also reject a challenge to the qualifications of any Convention Official if he/she concludes that the Delegate making the allegation(s) is trying to disrupt and/or delay Convention business. If after following the instructions outlined in "Violating this Agreement" the Delegate is found to have made a false accusation against a Convention Official, the Delegate's State Delegation will be charged with a violation of the terms and/or conditions of this Call and Agreement.

PROHIBITIONS FOR STATE DELEGATES, STATE DELEGATIONS AND CONVENTION OFFICIALS AT THE CONVENTION

State Delegates, State Delegations and Convention Officials are prohibited from violating any of the following Convention prohibitions:

1. State Delegates, State Delegations and Convention Officials are prohibited, at the Convention, from introducing, discussing, voting on, or sending to the States for consideration and/or ratification any amendment to the United States Constitution other than the Unborn Child Amendment, as herein written
2. State Delegates, State Delegations and Convention Officials are prohibited from altering or changing, in any way (which includes the wording, spelling, punctuation, or paragraph sections), the Unborn Child Amendment from the written form shown in the section titled **"The full text of the Unborn Child Amendment"**
3. State Delegates, State Delegations and Convention Officials are prohibited, at the Convention, from introducing, discussing, voting on, or sending to the States for consideration and/or ratification any alternate form of government for the United States of America
4. State Delegates, State Delegations and Convention Officials are prohibited, at the Convention, from introducing, discussing, voting on, or sending to the States for consideration and/or ratification

any alternate constitution or governing document for the United States of America

5. State Delegates, State Delegations and Convention Officials are prohibited, at the Convention, from introducing, discussing, voting on, or sending to the States for consideration and/or ratification any changes, of any kind, to the existing Constitution of the United States of America other than the Unborn Child Amendment

6. State Delegates, State Delegations and Convention Officials are prohibited, at the Convention, from introducing, discussing, voting on, or sending to the States for consideration any changes, of any kind, to this binding Agreement between the States Calling for the Unborn Child Amendment Convention

7. State Delegates, State Delegations and Convention Officials are prohibited, at the Convention, from introducing, discussing, voting on, or sending to the States for consideration and/or ratification any subject matter, issue or topic (of any kind) other than the proposed Unborn Child Amendment in its written form shown in the section titled "The full text of the Unborn Child Amendment"

THE DATE, TIME, DURATION AND PLACE OF THE UNBORN CHILD AMENDMENT CONVENTION.

The United States Congress will be responsible for determining and announcing to the Several States the date, time, and place that the Unborn Child Amendment Convention is to convene immediately after two thirds of the States, under the authority given to the States in Article V of the United States Constitution, have completed their Calls on Congress to convene the Unborn Child Amendment Convention. The Convention is expected to complete its business by the 180th day after convening. The Convention Chairman can extend the duration of the Unborn Child Amendment Convention for one additional 180 day period. The maximum number of days the Convention is authorized to be in session are 360 days. If the Convention has not decided if the Unborn Child Amendment should be sent to Congress with instructions to send the Amendment to the Several States for ratification by the end of 360 days, then the Call for the Unborn Child Amendment Convention, which was approved by the Several States under the authority granted in Article V of the United States Constitution and this agreement, will be automatically withdrawn by the Calling States and the Convention will automatically terminate at 5:00 P.M. Eastern Standard Time on the 360th day after convening. Termination of the Unborn Child Amendment Convention will automatically occur on the 360th day after convening the Convention, without requiring a formal notice by the States to the Convention, nor by the States to the United States Congress, nor by the Convention to the States, nor by the Convention to the United States

Congress, although it is recommended that the Convention notify the United States Congress and the State Legislatures of its termination as a courtesy.

Under no circumstance(s) are the Delegates at the Unborn Child Amendment Convention authorized to re-convene a new or different Convention, no matter what their purpose or intent. The official Legislative Call and authority granted by the Several States and the subsequent convening of the Unborn Child Amendment Convention by Congress will be automatically invalidated and the Convention will be abolished at 5:00 P.M. Eastern Standard Time on the 360th day after the convening of the Unborn Child Amendment Convention.

VIOLATING THIS AGREEMENT

The Convention Chairman (or in the absence of the Convention Chairman the Assistant Convention Chairman) will handle allegations of a violation(s) or actual violation(s) of the terms and/or conditions of this binding Agreement between the Several States, by any one or more Delegate(s) and/or Convention Official(s), as follows:

1. When an alleged violation has been presented to the Convention Chairman, and if the Chairman decides that the allegation(s) merits further investigation, he/she will instruct the Sergeant at Arms to conduct the necessary inquiry.

2. After the inquiry has been completed, and assuming the Convention Chairman concludes that the evidence does not substantiate further review by the Convention, the allegation(s) will be dismissed by the Chairman and the Convention will go forward with its business.

3. If however, after the inquiry has been completed, the Convention Chairman concludes that the evidence does substantiate further review by the Convention, the Chairman will present the allegation(s) and findings of the inquiry to the Convention for a discussion and vote. If a majority of the State Delegations (one vote per State Delegation) decide that no violation of the terms and/or conditions of this Legislative Call and Agreement has occurred, then the Chairman will declare that the alleged violation(s) of the terms and/or conditions of this Legislative Call and Agreement is/are dismissed. The Convention will then go forward with its business.

4. If however, after the inquiry has been completed, the Convention Chairman concludes that the evidence does substantiate further review by the Convention, the Chairman will present the

allegation(s) and findings of the inquiry to the Convention for a discussion and vote. If a majority of the State Delegations (one vote per State Delegation) decide that one or more violation(s) of the terms and/or conditions of this Legislative Call and Agreement has/have occurred, then the Chairman will declare to the Convention that the Delegate(s) responsible for the violation(s), and their State Delegation(s), has/have been charged with "Violating this Agreement". The Convention will then go forward with its business.

5. If a State Delegation is charged with two violations of the terms and/or conditions of this Legislative Call and Agreement, the Convention Chairman will declare to the Convention that the State Delegation charged with violating this Agreement a second time has no further standing or authority at the Convention. The Chairman will notify the charged State Delegation that its entire delegation of Delegates must leave the Convention immediately and they will not be allowed back into the Convention. The Chairman will instruct the Sergeant at Arms that he should escort the charged State Delegation out of the Convention. The Convention Chairman will then notify the State Legislature that sent the charged State Delegation of the actions that the Convention has taken and inform them that they can send a replacement State Delegation to the Convention as long as they do not disrupt the proceedings of the Convention. None of the original Delegates who were charged by the Convention will be allowed back into the Convention as part of a replacement delegation.

6. The Convention Chairman will not allow unreasonable delays in the proceedings of the Convention due to disruptive Delegates or State Delegations. He/she will move the business of the Convention forward expeditiously.

THE FULL TEXT OF THE UNBORN CHILD AMENDMENT

The full text of the UNBORN CHILD AMENDMENT to be submitted to the Several States by the United States Congress for ratification shall read as follows:

UNBORN CHILD AMENDMENT
ARTICLE 28 (or alternate number to be assigned by Congress)

Section 1. The Unborn offspring of human beings are persons from the time of conception and continually thereafter throughout their subsequent development: No Unborn person shall be intentionally deprived of life or limb, or shall be subjected to intentionally inflicted harm.

Section 2. To secure the rights of Unborn persons, induced abortion is hereby prohibited within the United States which shall include the Several States, the District of Columbia, the Commonwealth of Puerto Rico, the Commonwealth of the Northern Mariana Islands and the territories and possessions of the United States.

Section 3. Congress shall have the power to enforce by appropriate legislation, the provisions of the Article.

RATIFICATION OF THE "UNBORN CHILD AMENDMENT"

Under the requirements of Article V of the United States Constitution and also under Article IV, Section 4 which guarantees to every State a Republican form of Government, the Unborn Child Amendment will become a ratified Amendment to the United States Constitution when three quarters of the Several States complete their ratifications of the Amendment.

"CONGRESSIONAL" OPTION

If the United States Congress voluntarily sends the Unborn Child Amendment to the Several States for ratification without making any

changes, of any kind (which includes the wording, spelling, punctuation and paragraph sections) in the proposed Amendment as herein written, and before two thirds of the States complete their Call for Congress to convene the Unborn Child Amendment Convention, then the Legislature of the State of North Dakota will withdraw its Call for the Unborn Child Amendment Convention.

OFFICIAL AGREEMENT BY THE NORTH DAKOTA STATE LEGISLATURE BETWEEN ITSELF AND THE CALLING STATES

The Legislature of the State of North Dakota enters into this binding Agreement with every other State Legislature that likewise agrees to the terms and/or conditions of this Legislative Call and Agreement as set forth herein. This is an irrevocable contract, during the term of this Agreement, between the State of North Dakota and each and every State that signs this Agreement and completes its Call on the United States Congress directing Congress to convene a Federal Convention titled the Unborn Child Amendment Convention. The Legislature of the State of North Dakota agrees that it, and its delegates who are selected to attend the Convention, will abide by the purpose, terms, conditions, agenda, and "Convention Rules of Order" as explained in this Agreement.

The Legislature of the State of North Dakota enters into this Agreement with every other State Legislature that likewise agrees to the terms and/or conditions of this Agreement and Legislative Call as set forth herein, understanding that the Unborn Child Amendment Convention, by definition herein explained, is a "SINGLE ISSUE" Federal Convention and that the Convention will have no authority, under this Call and Agreement between the States, to review and/or consider any other subject matter, issue, or topic during its sessions other than business matters relating to the question, should the Unborn Child Amendment, as herein written, be sent by the Convention to the United States Congress instructing Congress to send the Amendment to the Several States for ratification? The Legislature of the State of North Dakota irrevocably declares by signing this Agreement that any subject matter, issue or topic (other than the Unborn Child Amendment) that delegates might try to present to the Convention and subsequently to the States for review and/or ratification will be immediately, upon introduction at the Convention, unauthorized, invalid and automatically rejected by the Legislature of the State of North Dakota, and the Legislature of the State of North Dakota irrevocably declares that it will not review and/or consider for ratification any such subject matter, issue or topic, no matter how presented to it by the Convention. Only the Unborn Child Amendment, as herein written, will be considered by the Legislature of the State of North Dakota for ratification.

The Legislature of the State of North Dakota also irrevocably declares that under no circumstance(s) will it consider for review and/or ratification any amendment to the United States Constitution, submitted to it by the Unborn Child Amendment Convention other than the Unborn Child Amendment as herein written.

The Legislature of the State of North Dakota further irrevocably declares that under no circumstance(s) will it consider for review and/or ratification any modified form of the Unborn Child Amendment submitted to it by the Unborn Child Amendment Convention that would change, alter, or replace, in any way (which includes the wording, spelling, punctuation, or paragraph sections), the Unborn Child Amendment from its written form herein.

The Legislature of the State of North Dakota further irrevocably declares that under no circumstance(s) will it consider for review and/or ratification any proposal, of any kind, sent to it by the Unborn Child Amendment Convention that would change, replace, or alter the United States Constitution other than the Unborn Child Amendment as herein written.

The Legislature of the State of North Dakota further irrevocably declares that under no circumstance(s) will it consider for review any proposal, of any kind, sent to it by the Unborn Child Amendment Convention that would change, replace, or alter, in any way (which includes the wording, spelling, punctuation and section paragraphs), this Official Legislative Call for the Unborn Child Amendment Convention and the terms and/or conditions of this Agreement between the States as herein written.

Under the authority reserved to the State of North Dakota in Article V of the United States Constitution and also under Article IV, Section 4 which guarantees to every State a Republican form of Government, the Legislature of the State of North Dakota hereby approves this Legislative Call on the United States Congress directing Congress to convene the Unborn Child Amendment Convention and binds itself with each and every State that likewise approves this identical Legislative Call according the terms and/or conditions set forth in this Agreement.

OFFICIAL CALL BY THE STATE OF NORTH DAKOTA ON THE UNITED STATES CONGRESS DIRECTING CONGRESS TO CONVENE THE UNBORN CHILD AMENDMENT CONVENTION

The Legislature of the State of North Dakota hereby Calls on the United States Congress directing Congress to convene a Federal Convention to be titled the Unborn Child Amendment Convention. The Convention is to be

convened immediately after two thirds of the Several States have completed their Calls for the Unborn Child Amendment Convention.

The State of North Dakota is authorized to make this Call for the Unborn Child Amendment Convention under the authority reserved to the States in Article V of the United States Constitution and under Article IV, Section 4 which guarantees to every State a Republican form of Government. Both Articles give to each State an equal standing when calling for a Constitutional Convention. Article V and Article IV, Section 4 reserves to the Several States the right to Call for a Federal Convention for the purpose

of amending the United States Constitution when Congress and/or the Courts refuse to address an egregious wrong suffered by the people.

RECLAIMING AMERICA

Submitted to Both Houses of the United States Congress on this date
_____, _____ by the Legislature of the State of North
Dakota.

State of North Dakota Seal:

Authorized Signatures with titles:

_____Title_____

_____Title_____

_____Title_____

_____Title_____

_____Title_____

_____Title_____

CHAPTER 15

TRUTH IN EDUCATION AMENDMENT

Text of proposed
TRUTH IN EDUCATION AMENDMENT
ARTICLE 28 (or alternate number to be assigned by Congress)

Section 1. America's educational institutions have a unique importance to the American people. It is the right of American citizens to receive from their private and public educational institutions accurate accounts of America's history and academic subjects that is not intentionally false, or intentionally misleading, or deliberately distorted. This right is foundational to a free people.

Section 2. To secure the rights of citizens it is hereby prohibited for any educational institution, whether an individual or organization, whether private or public, to intentionally teach to students or to the American public false, misleading or distorted information on any and all subjects. The provisions of this Article are enforceable within the United States which shall include the Several States, the District of Columbia, and the Commonwealth of Puerto Rico, the Commonwealth of the Northern Mariana Islands and the territories and possessions of the United States.

Section 3. Congress shall have the power to enforce by appropriate legislation, the provisions of the Article.

Mao Tse Tung said that if he was able to control the education of China's children, he would rule the country. He successfully indoctrinated China's youth by forcing them to believe that the State, under Communist rule, was paramount. He was responsible for the death of nearly 60 million Chinese people. Communist China today continues to believe many of his intentional falsehoods. Stalin, Hitler, Pol Pot, and many others installed the same atheistic mandates on their people which led to unthinkable genocide and human suffering. The American people must be protected from intentional lies and distortions being taught by its educational institutions. The Truth in Education Amendment will require that

American educators to base their teachings on reliable and accurate facts and not intentional falsehoods or intentionally misleading instruction in the class room. This Amendment would not prevent personal opinion and personal theory from being taught and/or shared in the academic community.

AUTHORIZED CALL
BY THE MONTANA STATE LEGISLATURE
ON THE UNITED STATES CONGRESS INSTRUCTING CONGRESS
TO CONVENE A FEDERAL CONVENTION TO BE TITLED
THE TRUTH IN EDUCATION AMENDMENT CONVENTION

THIS AUTHORIZED CALL ALSO DEFINES THE AGREEMENT
THE MONTANA STATE LEGISLATURE IS ENTERING INTO
BETWEEN ITSELF AND OTHER CALLING STATES

To: **BOTH HOUSES OF UNITED STATES CONGRESS**

UNITED STATES SENATE:

President of the Senate, United States Vice President
Majority Leader Senator
Minority Leader Senator
President Pro Tempore Senator
Republican Whip Senator
Democratic Whip Senator

(Deliver this Official Call to every current leader and member of the United State Senate at Washington, DC)

HOUSE OF REPRESENTATIVE:

Speaker of the House Representative
House Majority Leader Representative
House Majority Whip Representative
House Minority Leader Representative
House Minority Whip Representative

(Deliver this Official Call to every current leader and member of the United State House of Representatives at Washington, DC)

From: **THE STATE LEGISLATURE OF THE STATE OF MONTANA**

The Legislature of the State of MONTANA hereby Calls on the United States Congress instructing Congress to convene a Federal Convention called the TRUTH IN EDUCATION AMENDMENT Convention under the authority reserved to the States in Article V of the United States Constitution. Article IV, Section 4 guarantees to every State a Republican form of Government which gives each State equal standing when Calling for a Constitutional

Convention. Article V reserves to the Several States the right to Call for a Federal Constitutional Convention for the purpose of amending the United States Constitution when Congress and/or the Courts refuse to address an egregious wrong suffered by the people. The States *alone* have the authority to "limit" the agenda and authority of a Federal Convention. The States alone can Call for a "Single Issue" Convention by agreeing among themselves the purpose, terms, conditions, duration, and agenda for the Convention. Congress does not have the authority to define a "Single Issue" Convention. Congress' authority, under Article V of the United States Constitution, empowers it to convene a Convention as Called for and defined by the Several States. The Several States alone have the authority to enforce the terms and/or conditions set forth in this Agreement at the TRUTH IN EDUCATION AMENDMENT Convention.

The TRUTH IN EDUCATION AMENDMENT Convention will be a "Single Issue" Federal Convention as defined in this Legislative Call on the United States Congress and in this binding Agreement between the Several States. The delegates summoned to this Convention by Congress will have the authority to decide only one issue, should the TRUTH IN EDUCATION AMENDMENT, as herein written, be sent to Congress with instructions to send the Amendment back to the Several States for ratification? The delegates at the TRUTH IN EDUCATION AMENDMENT Convention will have no authority to change the wording of the proposed Amendment, neither are they authorized to deliberate on or discuss any other subject matter or issue at the Convention. The purpose, terms and/or conditions that will govern the agenda and affairs of the TRUTH IN EDUCATION AMENDMENT Convention are as follows:

THE PURPOSE OF THE CONVENTION

The *only* purpose for convening the TRUTH IN EDUCATION AMENDMENT Convention is for the State Delegations, representing the Several States, to decide if the TRUTH IN EDUCATION AMENDMENT, as herein written, should be sent to the United States Congress with instructions for Congress to send the Amendment to the Several States for ratification? Absolutely no other business is authorized at this Convention.

CONVENTION RULES OF ORDER

The "Convention Rules of Order" that all Delegates and State Delegations are required to follow as a condition of participating at the TRUTH IN EDUCATION AMENDMENT Convention are described in this Legislative Call on Congress. From time to time, in order to facilitate Convention business, the Convention Chairman may require the Convention to follow "Robert's

Rules of Order" when a specific Rule of Order is not defined in this Legislative Call. The Delegates and State Delegations are required to honor the Convention Chairman's instructions when applying Convention Rules of Order and/or Roberts Rules of Order.

TRUTH IN EDUCATION AMENDMENT COMMITTEE

The TRUTH IN EDUCATION AMENDMENT Committee is the citizens group that founded the TRUTH IN EDUCATION AMENDMENT Initiative. This Committee will be responsible for pre-Convention planning and organization. The Chairman and Vice Chairman of the TRUTH IN EDUCATION AMENDMENT Committee will be Ex-Officio (without voting rights) members of the Convention. They can be called upon by the Convention Chairman to clarify the TRUTH IN EDUCATION AMENDMENT legislative strategy for the Delegates, provide progress reports in the States and also be available for questions and answers from Delegates at the Convention. They will be subject to the terms and/or conditions of this Legislative Call and Agreement between the States.

If they are also appointed as Delegates by their State Legislatures, then they will be entitled to voting privileges as Delegates at the Convention. The Chairman of the TRUTH IN EDUCATION AMENDMENT Committee is R. C. "Kacprowicz" Casper.

If the Convention votes in favor of the Amendment, the TRUTH IN EDUCATION AMENDMENT Committee will be responsible for post-convention planning and organization during the ratification process.

FUNDING THE CONVENTION AND STATE DELEGATIONS

The State Legislatures that send Delegates to the TRUTH IN EDUCATION AMENDMENT Convention shall be responsible for providing monies necessary for their State Delegations to participate at the Convention. The amounts each State Delegation will require will be decided by each State Legislature. Other expenses or costs necessary to fund the Convention are to be shared by the Calling States equally. From time to time the Convention Chairman will notify the State Delegations what monies will be necessary to carry on the business of the Convention.

FUNDING FOR "PRE AND POST-CONVENTION PLANNING AND ORGANIZATION"

Each State Legislature making a Call on Congress to convene the TRUTH IN EDUCATION AMENDMENT Convention will be asked to share expenses for "pre-Convention planning" and "pre-Convention organization". If the Convention votes to send the TRUTH IN EDUCATION AMENDMENT to

Congress to be ratified by the States, then the TRUTH IN EDUCATION AMENDMENT Committee will ask the Calling States to help fund post-convention planning and organization to cover expenses for the ratification process.

DELEGATES SUMMONED BY CONGRESS

Congress has the authority, under Article V, to summon Delegates from the Several States to the TRUTH IN EDUCATION AMENDMENT Convention. Congress is hereby directed to summon to the Convention the appropriate number of Delegates that each State is entitled to immediately after two thirds of the States complete their Call directing Congress to convene the TRUTH IN EDUCATION AMENDMENT Convention. The number of Delegates to be summoned to the Convention should be equal to the number of members each State has in the House of Representatives and in the Senate of the United States Congress.

DELEGATES AND STATE DELEGATIONS

Only State Delegates summoned by Congress to the TRUTH IN EDUCATION AMENDMENT Convention and appointed by their State Legislatures to form State Delegations to represent their respective States are authorized to attend and speak at the TRUTH IN EDUCATION AMENDMENT Convention. Each State Legislature has the responsibility to select, from within its State, individual Delegates who will represent its State at the Convention. The number of Delegates selected by a State Legislature can be no greater than the number of Delegates summoned by Congress from its State. Each State Delegation must select a Delegate from within its delegation to be its Spokesman at the Convention. Only a Delegation's Spokesman will be recognized by the Convention Chairman.

THE PRE-CONVENTION "ACTING CONVENTION CHAIRMAN" AND "ASSISTANT ACTING CONVENTION CHAIRMAN"

The Chairman and Vice Chairman of the TRUTH IN EDUCATION AMENDMENT Committee will have exclusive authority to complete all pre-convention planning and organization for the TRUTH IN EDUCATION AMENDMENT Convention. They will perform their duties under the titles "Acting Convention Chairman" and "Assistant Acting Convention Chairman" respectfully. They will also be available to State Legislatures to assist with their Legislative Calls and pre-Convention planning.

The Chairman and Vice Chairman of the TRUTH IN EDUCATION AMENDMENT Committee will also be responsible for post-convention planning and organization if the Convention votes to send the TRUTH IN EDUCATION AMENDMENT to Congress to be ratified by the States.

VOTING BY DELEGATES IN STATE DELEGATIONS

It is recommended that a simple majority of the Delegates within each State Delegation be required to decide a State Delegation's vote at the Convention. A quorum within each State Delegation will consist of one Delegate. The business of the Convention and voting will not be delayed if a State Delegation does not cast a vote during a roll call.

QUORUM REQUIRED FOR CONDUCTING BUSINESS AND VOTING AT THE CONVENTION

Each State Delegation will have one vote on all matters that are to be decided by the Convention. A simple majority vote by the State Delegations at the Convention is required to decide the outcome of all business brought before the Convention for a vote, including whether or not the TRUTH IN EDUCATION AMENDMENT, as herein written, should be sent to the Several States, via Congress, for ratification. A quorum at the Convention for the purpose of conducting business and voting will consist of 17 State Delegations.

CLOSED DELIBERATIONS AT THE CONVENTION

The TRUTH IN EDUCATION AMENDMENT Convention will be closed to all media and news groups. Only delegates appointed by their State Legislatures and the Chairman and Vice Chairman of the TRUTH IN EDUCATION AMENDMENT Committee will be authorized to enter and speak at the Convention. No visitors, reporters, government officials, professionals or inquirers, of any kind, will be permitted to enter the Convention facilities. Unauthorized visitors will be escorted by the Sergeant of Arms out of the Convention. After the vote by the State Delegations is taken to determine if the TRUTH IN EDUCATION AMENDMENT will be sent to the Several States, via Congress, for ratification, the Chairman of the Convention will call a special press conference to announce the Convention's decision. Within 30 days from the special press conference the Chairman will make available to the public the records kept by the Convention during its proceedings.

STATE LEGISLATURES NOT AUTHORIZING THIS CALL FOR THE TRUTH IN EDUCATION AMENDMENT CONVENTION

State Legislatures that did not authorize this Call for the TRUTH IN EDUCATION AMENDMENT Convention and yet agree to send delegates representing their State agree to follow the terms and/or conditions set forth in this Agreement and Legislative Call. They need to pay particular attention to the "Convention's Rules of Order" described in this Agreement and the prohibitions in the section titled "Prohibitions for Delegates, State Delegations and/or Convention Officials at the Convention". These non-calling States must notify the "Acting Convention Chairman" before the Convention convenes of their intention to attend the Convention so accommodations can be completed for their Delegations. In order to receive Convention Passes, all Delegates attending the Convention, will be required to sign an agreement promising to abide by the terms and/or conditions in this Legislative Call and Agreement.

NO WEAPONS ALLOWED AT THE CONVENTION

Delegates and TRUTH IN EDUCATION AMENDMENT Committee officials will not be allowed to bring into the TRUTH IN EDUCATION AMENDMENT Convention any weapons or objects that can be construed as weapons.

PRESENTING ARGUMENTS AT THE CONVENTION BY STATE DELEGATIONS

Each State Delegation will be allotted a maximum of 60 minutes for presenting its argument(s) at the Convention for or against sending the TRUTH IN EDUCATION AMENDMENT to the United States Congress with instruction for Congress to send the Amendment to the Several States for ratification. Only Delegates who have been officially selected by their State Legislatures and Ex-Officio members of the Convention are authorized to speak before the Convention. Each State Delegation can use one or more of its Delegates to present its position(s). However, the total time allotted for each State Delegation is 60 minutes, which includes any time that is necessary to replace one Delegate with another. The Chairman of the TRUTH IN EDUCATION AMENDMENT Committee will also be limited to 60 minutes during his speaking segment. Speakers cannot reserve portions of their time to another time or day. Speakers must complete their arguments in the 60 minute segment assigned to them.

The order each State Delegation will follow when presenting their position(s) will be according to when each State completed its Legislative Call on Congress, or when it notified the "Acting Convention Chairman" that it intends to attend the Convention even though it may not complete a Legislative Call on Congress. The State Delegation presentations will be scheduled in the following manner: the first State making a Call on Congress will go first; the first State notifying the "Acting Convention Chairman" that it plans to attend will go second. The second State making a Call on

Congress will go third; then the second State notifying the "Acting Convention Chairman" will go fourth, and so forth until all States wanting to present their positions have had an opportunity to do so. The Convention Chairman can rearrange the schedule if any conflicts arise at the Convention. The last speaker to be scheduled at the Convention for a 60 minute segment will be the Chairman of the TRUTH IN EDUCATION AMENDMENT Committee.

DUTIES OF THE "ACTING CONVENTION CHAIRMAN"

The duties of the "Acting Convention Chairman include:

1. organize a pre-Convention support group for assisting Calling States with their Legislative Calls and non-calling States with their intentions to attend the Convention
2. set up an TRUTH IN EDUCATION AMENDMENT Committee checking account
3. use generally accepted accounting principles when keeping records of all receipts and expenditures
4. provide financial reports and minutes of pre-convention activities as requested by States that are funding pre-convention operations
5. keep minutes of all business meetings of the TRUTH IN EDUCATION AMENDMENT Committee
6. determine the budget that will be needed for pre-convention planning and organizing and notify each State Legislature of its share of the expenses
7. assist the Calling States and Attending States with their pre-convention planning
8. assist the Calling States with their Legislative Calls on Congress
9. after the TRUTH IN EDUCATION AMENDMENT Convention has been convened call the Convention to order
10. invite nominations from the State Delegations present at the Convention to fill the "Convention Chairman's" position (the maximum number of nominees permitted is five and only one nominee from any one State Delegation is permitted)
11. take a roll call from the State Delegations for the nominee(s)
12. declare the winner based on the nominee who has received the most votes (a plurality of State Delegations). Each State Delegation will have one vote
13. officiate the installation of the "Convention Chairman" at the Convention by having the Chairman place his/her right hand on the Bible while repeating the following oath

"I solemnly promise to officiate the office of Convention Chairman for the TRUTH IN EDUCATION AMENDMENT Convention according to the terms and/or conditions set forth in the Legislative Calls from the Several States to the best of my ability, so help me God".

In the event the "Acting Convention Chairman" is nominated and elected to the Convention Chairman position, the "Assistant Acting Convention Chairman" will conduct the installation ceremony for the Convention Chairman.

ELECTION, AUTHORITY AND DUTIES OF CONVENTION OFFICIALS

CONVENTION CHAIRMAN: - The "Convention Chairman" is the senior official at the TRUTH IN EDUCATION AMENDMENT Convention. He/she will have the requisite authority to oversee all activities at the Convention, including the nomination and election of all officials. The Convention Chairman's duties include:

1. organize and oversee all business and activities at the Convention
2. organize and officiate all nominations, elections and installations of officials at the Convention (this will be the Convention Chairman's first order of business)
3. organize and officiate all nominations, elections and installations of official positions that may become vacant at the Convention
4. oversee the enforcement of all Convention Rules
5. oversee the enforcement of the terms and/or conditions (herein described) of this Call and Agreement by the States
6. oversee the investigation of alleged and/or actual violations of this Agreement as defined in the section titled "Violating this Agreement"
7. bring before the Convention all matters that require a vote
8. bring before the Convention the financial needs of the Convention and time lines for when these monies are needed
9. cut off motions or discussions by State Delegations before the Convention if and when it seems appropriate
10. recognize the Spokesman within a State Delegation for the purpose of addressing a matter of importance to the Spokesman's Delegation (the Convention Chairman will have full authority to determine if a matter brought before the Convention by the Spokesman is appropriate for further discussion and/or if a decision by the Convention is necessary)
11. keep the business of the Convention moving forward expeditiously, cutting off all motions and discussions when it appears one or more Delegates are trying to hinder, delay or stop the work of the Convention

12. keep the business of the Convention focused on one objective which is, should the Convention send the TRUTH IN EDUCATION AMENDMENT to Congress instructing Congress to send it to the Several States for ratification?
13. instruct Convention Officials (Assistant Convention Chairman, Secretary, Financial Officer, Executive Administrator, Sergeant at Arms, and Deputies) on their duties at the Convention
14. officiate and remedy any and all problems that may develop at the Convention
15. oversee the design and production of "Official" Convention Badges for the Sergeant at Arms and Deputies
16. notify all State Legislatures of the decision the Convention made as to whether or not the TRUTH IN EDUCATION AMENDMENT should be sent to Congress instructing Congress to send it to the States for ratification?
17. if the State Delegations voted to send the Amendment to the States for ratification, include the Convention's recommendation to the United States Congress as to whether it should be ratified by State Conventions or State Legislatures
18. declare the TRUTH IN EDUCATION AMENDMENT Convention closed after the State Delegations have decided if the TRUTH IN EDUCATION AMENDMENT should be sent to Congress instructing Congress to send it to the States for ratification?
19. arrange a Special News Conference to announce the decision by the TRUTH IN EDUCATION AMENDMENT Convention
20. make available the proceedings of the Convention to the public 30 days after the Convention is closed

The first order of business for the "Convention Chairman" will be to open the Convention to nominations from State Delegations present for each of the following Convention Officials; one Assistant Convention Chairman, one Secretary, one Financial Officer, one Executive Administrator, one Sergeant at Arms and ten Deputies (the maximum number of nominees permitted for each Convention Official position is five. Only one nominee for each Convention Official position is permitted from any one State Delegation. The nominee with a plurality of votes from the State Delegations will be the winner). The "Convention Chairman" can call for nominations for more than 10 Deputies if and when circumstances warrant.

ASSISTANT CONVENTION CHAIRMAN
The "Assistant Convention Chairman" duties include:

1. be amenable to the "Convention Chairman"

2. provide assistance to the "Convention Chairman" in all matters pertaining to the business of the Convention
3. monitor activities at the Convention and report to the "Convention Chairman" violations or possible violations of the terms and/or conditions of this Legislative Call and Agreement
4. perform the duties of the "Convention Chairman" when called upon by the Chairman or when the Chairman is unable to perform the duties of his/her office
5. the "Assistant Convention Chairman" will take the following oath, administered by the Convention Chairman, while placing his/her right hand on the Bible

"I solemnly promise to officiate the office of Assistant Convention Chairman for the TRUTH IN EDUCATION AMENDMENT Convention according to the terms and/or conditions set forth in the Legislative Calls from the Several States to the best of my ability, so help me God".

SECRETARY
The "Secretary's" duties include:

1. keep official minutes of all proceedings at the Convention
2. monitor activities at the Convention and report to the Convention Chairman violations or possible violations of Convention Rules and of the terms and/or conditions of this Legislative Call and Agreement
3. make available to the "Convention Chairman", upon request, the official minutes of the Convention
4. be amenable to the "Convention Chairman" and "Assistant Convention Chairman"
5. in the absence of the "Convention Chairman" and the "Assistant Convention Chairman" due to death or a disablement that prevents them from performing the duties of their offices at the Convention, the Secretary shall call the Convention to order for the purpose of nominating and electing a new "Convention Chairman" and "Assistant Convention Chairman". In this capacity the Secretary will assume the duties and authority of the "Convention Chairman".
6. If the Secretary is unable to perform the duties described herein, then they will fall to the Financial Officer.
7. the "Secretary" will take the following oath while placing his/her right hand on the Bible

"I solemnly promise to officiate the office of Secretary for the TRUTH IN EDUCATION AMENDMENT Convention according to the terms and/or conditions set forth in the Legislative Calls from the Several States to the best of my ability, so help me God".

FINANCIAL OFFICER
The "Financial Officer's" duties include:

1. keep detailed accounting records of all financial matters at the Convention using generally accepted accounting principles
2. be amenable to the "Convention Chairman" and "Assistant Convention Chairman"
3. monitor activities at the Convention and report to the Convention Chairman violations or possible violations of the terms and/or conditions of this Legislative Call and Agreement
4. set up a checking account in the name of the TRUTH IN EDUCATION AMENDMENT Convention requiring any two of the following three officers when signing a check or making withdrawals – Convention Chairman, Assistant Convention Chairman, Financial Officer
5. make available to the "Convention Chairman", upon request, all financial records at the Convention
6. provide to the Convention Chairman the financial needs of the Convention and the time lines as to when these monies are needed
7. in the absence of a "Convention Chairman", "Assistant Convention Chairman", and "Secretary" due to death or a disablement that prevents them from performing the duties of their offices at the Convention, the Financial Officer shall call the Convention to order for the purpose of nominating and electing a new "Convention Chairman", "Assistant Convention Chairman", and "Secretary". In this capacity the Financial Officer will assume the duties and authority of the "Convention Chairman" the "Financial Officer" will take the following oath while placing his/her right hand on the Bible

"I solemnly promise to officiate the office of Financial Officer for the TRUTH IN EDUCATION AMENDMENT Convention according to generally accepted accounting principles and according to the terms and/or conditions set forth in the Legislative Calls from the Several States to the best of my ability, so help me God".

EXECUTIVE ADMINISTRATOR
The "Executive Administrator's" duties include:

1. facilitate all Convention business as directed by the Convention Chairman
2. be amenable to the Convention Chairman and Assistant Convention Chairman

3. monitor activities at the Convention and report to the Convention Chairman violations or possible violations of the terms and/or conditions of this Legislative Call and Agreement keep detailed reports of all administrative activities at the Convention
4. make available to the "Convention Chairman" upon request all administrative records and/or reports at the Convention
5. the "Executive Administrator" will take the following oath while placing his/her right hand on the Bible

"I solemnly promise to officiate the office of Executive Administrator for the TRUTH IN EDUCATION AMENDMENT Convention according to the terms and/or conditions set forth in the Legislative Calls from the Several States to the best of my ability, so help me God".

SERGEANT AT ARMS
The "Sergeant at Arms'" duties include:

1. be amenable to the Convention Chairman and Assistant Convention Chairman
2. monitor all activities at the Convention and report to the Convention Chairman violations or possible violations of the terms and/or conditions of this Legislative Call and Agreement
3. maintain order at the Convention
4. enforce all remedies for violations of this Legislative Call and Agreement as directed by the Convention Chairman
5. organize and direct the activities of all Deputies at the Convention
6. oversee, train and manage all Deputies at the Convention
7. the "Sergeant at Arms" will take the following oath while placing his/her right hand on the Bible

"I solemnly promise to officiate the office of Sergeant at Arms for the TRUTH IN EDUCATION AMENDMENT Convention according to the terms and/or conditions set forth in the Legislative Calls from the Several States to the best of my ability, so help me God".

DEPUTIES
The "Deputies'" duties include:

1. be amenable to the Convention Chairman, Assistant Convention Chairman and Sergeant at Arms
2. monitor all activities at the Convention and report to the Sergeant at Arms violations or possible violations of the terms and/or conditions of this Legislative Call and Agreement

3. maintain order at the Convention as directed by the Sergeant at Arms
4. enforce all remedies for violations of this Legislative Call and Agreement as directed by the Convention Chairman and/or the Sergeant at Arms
5. "Deputies" will take the following oath while placing his/her right hand on the Bible

"I solemnly promise to officiate the office of Deputy for the TRUTH IN EDUCATION AMENDMENT Convention according to the terms and/or conditions set forth in the Legislative Calls from the Several States to the best of my ability, so help me God".

CHALLENGING THE QUALIFICATIONS OF CONVENTION OFFICIALS

A State Delegation can challenge the qualifications of any Convention Official at the TRUTH IN EDUCATION AMENDMENT Convention by bringing its allegation(s), during a business session, to the Convention floor. The Convention Chairman will consider the allegation(s) and determine if it merits further investigation. If the Chairman decides that the allegation(s) merits further investigation, he/she will direct the Sergeant at Arms to conduct the necessary inquiry. He/she will then follow the instructions outlined in the section "Violating this Agreement" for proscribing a remedy or remedies.

The "Convention Chairman" can also reject a challenge to the qualifications of any Convention Official if he/she concludes that the Delegate making the allegation(s) is trying to disrupt and/or delay Convention business. If after following the instructions outlined in "Violating this Agreement" the Delegate is found to have made a false accusation against a Convention Official, the Delegate's State Delegation will be charged with a violation of the terms and/or conditions of this Call and Agreement.

PROHIBITIONS FOR STATE DELEGATES, STATE DELEGATIONS AND CONVENTION OFFICIALS AT THE CONVENTION

State Delegates, State Delegations and Convention Officials are prohibited from violating any of the following Convention prohibitions:

1. State Delegates, State Delegations and Convention Officials are prohibited, at the Convention, from introducing, discussing, voting on, or sending to the States for consideration and/or ratification any amendment to the United States Constitution other than the TRUTH IN EDUCATION AMENDMENT, as herein written
2. State Delegates, State Delegations and Convention Officials are prohibited from altering or changing, in any way (which includes

- 233 -

the wording, spelling, punctuation, or paragraph sections), the TRUTH IN EDUCATION AMENDMENT from the written form shown in the section titled **"The full text of the TRUTH IN EDUCATION AMENDMENT"**

3. State Delegates, State Delegations and Convention Officials are prohibited, at the Convention, from introducing, discussing, voting on, or sending to the States for consideration and/or ratification any alternate form of government for the United States of America

4. State Delegates, State Delegations and Convention Officials are prohibited, at the Convention, from introducing, discussing, voting on, or sending to the States for consideration and/or ratification any alternate constitution or governing document for the United States of America

5. State Delegates, State Delegations and Convention Officials are prohibited, at the Convention, from introducing, discussing, voting on, or sending to the States for consideration and/or ratification any changes, of any kind, to the existing Constitution of the United States of America other than the TRUTH IN EDUCATION AMENDMENT

6. State Delegates, State Delegations and Convention Officials are prohibited, at the Convention, from introducing, discussing, voting on, or sending to the States for consideration any changes, of any kind, to this binding Agreement between the States Calling for the TRUTH IN EDUCATION AMENDMENT Convention

7. State Delegates, State Delegations and Convention Officials are prohibited, at the Convention, from introducing, discussing, voting on, or sending to the States for consideration and/or ratification any subject matter, issue or topic (of any kind) other than the proposed TRUTH IN EDUCATION AMENDMENT in its written form shown in the section titled "The full text of the TRUTH IN EDUCATION AMENDMENT"

THE DATE, TIME, DURATION AND PLACE OF THE TRUTH IN EDUCATION AMENDMENT CONVENTION.

The United States Congress will be responsible for determining and announcing to the Several States the date, time, and place that the TRUTH IN EDUCATION AMENDMENT Convention is to convene immediately after two thirds of the States, under the authority given to the States in Article V of the United States Constitution, have completed their Calls on Congress to convene the TRUTH IN EDUCATION AMENDMENT Convention. The Convention is expected to complete its business by the 180th day after convening. The Convention Chairman can extend the duration of the TRUTH IN EDUCATION AMENDMENT Convention for one additional 180 day period. The maximum number of days the Convention is authorized to be in session are 360 days. If the Convention has not decided if the TRUTH IN EDUCATION AMENDMENT should be sent to Congress with instructions to send the Amendment to the Several States for ratification by the end of 360 days, then the Call for the TRUTH IN EDUCATION AMENDMENT Convention, which was approved by the Several States under the authority granted in Article V of the United States Constitution and this agreement, will be automatically withdrawn by the Calling States and the Convention will automatically terminate at 5:00 P.M. Eastern Standard Time on the 360th day after convening. Termination of the TRUTH IN EDUCATION AMENDMENT Convention will automatically occur on the 360th day after convening the Convention, without requiring a formal notice by the States to the Convention, nor by the States to the United States Congress, nor by the Convention to the States, nor by the Convention to the United States Congress, although it is recommended that the Convention notify the United States Congress and the State Legislatures of its termination as a courtesy.

Under no circumstance(s) are the Delegates at the TRUTH IN EDUCATION AMENDMENT Convention authorized to re-convene a new or different Convention, no matter what their purpose or intent. The official Legislative Call and authority granted by the Several States and the subsequent convening of the TRUTH IN EDUCATION AMENDMENT Convention by Congress will be automatically invalidated and the Convention will be abolished at 5:00 P.M. Eastern Standard Time on the 360th day after the convening of the TRUTH IN EDUCATION AMENDMENT Convention.

VIOLATING THIS AGREEMENT

The Convention Chairman (or in the absence of the Convention Chairman the Assistant Convention Chairman) will handle allegations of a violation(s) or actual violation(s) of the terms and/or conditions of this binding Agreement between the Several States, by any one or more Delegate(s) and/or Convention Official(s), as follows:

1. When an alleged violation has been presented to the Convention Chairman, and if the Chairman decides that the allegation(s) merits further investigation, he/she will instruct the Sergeant at Arms to conduct the necessary inquiry.

2. After the inquiry has been completed, and assuming the Convention Chairman concludes that the evidence does not substantiate further review by the Convention, the allegation(s) will be dismissed by the Chairman and the Convention will go forward with its business.

3. If however, after the inquiry has been completed, the Convention Chairman concludes that the evidence does substantiate further review by the Convention, the Chairman will present the allegation(s) and findings of the inquiry to the Convention for a discussion and vote. If a majority of the State Delegations (one vote per State Delegation) decide that no violation of the terms and/or conditions of this Legislative Call and Agreement has occurred, then the Chairman will declare that the alleged violation(s) of the terms and/or conditions of this Legislative Call and Agreement is/are dismissed. The Convention will then go forward with its business.

4. If however, after the inquiry has been completed, the Convention Chairman concludes that the evidence does substantiate further review by the Convention, the Chairman will present the allegation(s) and findings of the inquiry to the Convention for a discussion and vote. If a majority of the State Delegations (one vote per State Delegation) decide that one or more violation(s) of the terms and/or conditions of this Legislative Call and Agreement has/have occurred, then the Chairman will declare to the Convention that the Delegate(s) responsible for the violation(s), and their State Delegation(s), has/have been charged with "Violating this Agreement". The Convention will then go forward with its business.

5. If a State Delegation is charged with two violations of the terms and/or conditions of this Legislative Call and Agreement, the Convention Chairman will declare to the Convention that the State Delegation charged with violating this Agreement a second time has no further standing or authority at the Convention. The Chairman will notify the charged State Delegation that its entire delegation of Delegates must leave the Convention immediately and they will not be allowed back into the Convention. The Chairman will instruct the Sergeant at Arms that he should escort the charged State Delegation out of the Convention. The Convention Chairman will then notify the State Legislature that sent the charged State Delegation of the actions that the Convention has taken and inform them that they can send a replacement State Delegation to the Convention as long as they do not disrupt the proceedings of the Convention. None of the original Delegates who were charged by the Convention will be allowed back into the Convention as part of a replacement delegation.

6. The Convention Chairman will not allow unreasonable delays in the proceedings of the Convention due to disruptive Delegates or State Delegations. He/she will move the business of the Convention forward expeditiously.

THE FULL TEXT OF THE TRUTH IN EDUCATION AMENDMENT

The full text of the TRUTH IN EDUCATION AMENDMENT to be submitted to the Several States by the United States Congress for ratification shall read as follows:

_____

TRUTH IN EDUCATION AMENDMENT
ARTICLE 28 (or alternate number to be assigned by Congress)

Section 1. America's educational institutions have a unique importance to the American people. It is the right of American citizens to receive from their private and public educational institutions accurate accounts of America's history and academic subjects that is not intentionally false, or intentionally misleading, or deliberately distorted. This right is foundational to a free people.

Section 2. To secure the rights of citizens it is hereby prohibited for any educational institution, whether an individual or organization, whether private or public, to intentionally teach to students or to the American public false, misleading or distorted information on any and all subjects. The provisions of this Article are enforceable within the United States which shall include the Several States, the District of Columbia, and the Commonwealth of Puerto Rico, the Commonwealth of the Northern Mariana Islands and the territories and possessions of the United States.

Section 3. Congress shall have the power to enforce by appropriate legislation, the provisions of the Article.

_____

RATIFICATION OF THE "TRUTH IN EDUCATION AMENDMENT"

Under the requirements of Article V of the United States Constitution and also under Article IV, Section 4 which guarantees to every State a Republican form of Government, the TRUTH IN EDUCATION AMENDMENT will become a ratified Amendment to the United States Constitution when three quarters of the Several States complete their ratifications of the Amendment.

"CONGRESSIONAL" OPTION

If the United States Congress voluntarily sends the TRUTH IN EDUCATION AMENDMENT to the Several States for ratification without making any changes, of any kind (which includes the wording, spelling, punctuation and paragraph sections) in the proposed Amendment as herein written, and before two thirds of the States complete their Call for Congress to convene the TRUTH IN EDUCATION AMENDMENT Convention, then the Legislature of the State of MONTANA will withdraw its Call for the TRUTH IN EDUCATION AMENDMENT Convention.

OFFICIAL AGREEMENT BY THE MONTANA STATE LEGISLATURE BETWEEN ITSELF AND THE CALLING STATES

The Legislature of the State of MONTANA enters into this binding Agreement with every other State Legislature that likewise agrees to the terms and/or conditions of this Legislative Call and Agreement as set forth herein. This is an irrevocable contract, during the term of this Agreement, between the State of MONTANA and each and every State that signs this Agreement and completes its Call on the United States Congress directing Congress to convene a Federal Convention titled the TRUTH IN EDUCATION AMENDMENT Convention. The Legislature of the State of MONTANA agrees that it, and its delegates who are selected to attend the Convention, will abide by the purpose, terms, conditions, agenda, and "Convention Rules of Order" as explained in this Agreement.

The Legislature of the State of MONTANA enters into this Agreement with every other State Legislature that likewise agrees to the terms and/or conditions of this Agreement and Legislative Call as set forth herein, understanding that the TRUTH IN EDUCATION AMENDMENT Convention, by definition herein explained, is a "SINGLE ISSUE" Federal Convention and that the Convention will have no authority, under this Call and Agreement between the States, to review and/or consider any other subject matter, issue, or topic during its sessions other than business matters relating to the question, should the TRUTH IN EDUCATION AMENDMENT, as herein written, be sent by the Convention to the United States Congress instructing Congress to send the Amendment to the Several States for ratification? The Legislature of the State of MONTANA irrevocably declares by signing this Agreement that any subject matter, issue or topic (other than the TRUTH IN EDUCATION AMENDMENT) that delegates might try to present to the Convention and subsequently to the States for review and/or ratification will be immediately, upon introduction at the Convention, unauthorized, invalid and automatically rejected by the Legislature of the State of MONTANA, and the Legislature of the State of MONTANA irrevocably declares that it will not review and/or consider for ratification any such subject matter, issue or topic, no matter how presented to it by the

Convention. Only the TRUTH IN EDUCATION AMENDMENT, as herein written, will be considered by the Legislature of the State of MONTANA for ratification.

The Legislature of the State of MONTANA also irrevocably declares that under no circumstance(s) will it consider for review and/or ratification any amendment to the United States Constitution, submitted to it by the TRUTH IN EDUCATION AMENDMENT Convention other than the TRUTH IN EDUCATION AMENDMENT as herein written.

The Legislature of the State of MONTANA further irrevocably declares that under no circumstance(s) will it consider for review and/or ratification any modified form of the TRUTH IN EDUCATION AMENDMENT submitted to it by the TRUTH IN EDUCATION AMENDMENT Convention that would change, alter, or replace, in any way (which includes the wording, spelling, punctuation, or paragraph sections), the TRUTH IN EDUCATION AMENDMENT from its written form herein.

The Legislature of the State of MONTANA further irrevocably declares that under no circumstance(s) will it consider for review and/or ratification any proposal, of any kind, sent to it by the TRUTH IN EDUCATION AMENDMENT Convention that would change, replace, or alter the United States Constitution other than the TRUTH IN EDUCATION AMENDMENT as herein written.

The Legislature of the State of MONTANA further irrevocably declares that under no circumstance(s) will it consider for review any proposal, of any kind, sent to it by the TRUTH IN EDUCATION AMENDMENT Convention that would change, replace, or alter, in any way (which includes the wording, spelling, punctuation and section paragraphs), this Official Legislative Call for the TRUTH IN EDUCATION AMENDMENT Convention and the terms and/or conditions of this Agreement between the States as herein written.

Under the authority reserved to the State of MONTANA in Article V of the United States Constitution and also under Article IV, Section 4 which guarantees to every State a Republican form of Government, the Legislature of the State of MONTANA hereby approves this Legislative Call on the United States Congress directing Congress to convene the TRUTH IN

EDUCATION AMENDMENT Convention and binds itself with each and every State that likewise approves this identical Legislative Call according the terms and/or conditions set forth in this Agreement.

OFFICIAL CALL BY THE STATE OF MONTANA ON THE UNITED STATES CONGRESS DIRECTING CONGRESS TO CONVENE THE TRUTH IN EDUCATION AMENDMENT CONVENTION

RECLAIMING AMERICA

The Legislature of the State of MONTANA hereby Calls on the United States Congress directing Congress to convene a Federal Convention to be titled the TRUTH IN EDUCATION AMENDMENT Convention. The Convention is to be convened immediately after two thirds of the Several States have completed their Calls for the TRUTH IN EDUCATION AMENDMENT Convention.

The State of MONTANA is authorized to make this Call for the TRUTH IN EDUCATION AMENDMENT Convention under the authority reserved to the States in Article V of the United States Constitution and under Article IV, Section 4 which guarantees to every State a Republican form of Government. Both Articles give to each State an equal standing when calling for a Constitutional Convention. Article V and Article IV, Section 4 reserves to the Several States the right to Call for a Federal Convention for the purpose of amending the United States Constitution when Congress and/or the Courts refuse to address an egregious wrong suffered by the people.

Submitted to Both Houses of the United States Congress on this date _____, _____ by the Legislature of the State of MONTANA.

State of MONTANA Seal:

Authorized Signatures with titles:

_____Title_____

_____Title_____

_____Title_____

_____Title_____

_____Title_____

CHAPTER 16

TRUTH IN MEDIA AMENDMENT

Text of proposed
TRUTH IN THE MEDIA AMENDMENT
ARTICLE 28 (or alternate number to be assigned by Congress)

Section 1. It is the right of every citizen to receive from any and all Media sources information that is not intentionally false or intentionally misleading which is foundational to a free people.

Section 2. The Media are all Broadcasters that disseminate information to and for consumption by the American public. The Media includes individuals, groups, corporations and any other type of institution or organization, whether domestic or foreign or whether located inside or outside the United States.

Section 3. Broadcast Formats used by the Media to disseminate information to the American public include news, entertainment, documentaries, editorials, opinion and any other Broadcast Format that is now being used or will be used in the future.

Section 4. Transmission Vehicles by which information is disseminated to the American public by the Media include cable, satellite, radio, television, airwaves, microwaves, telephone lines, print media, computers, computer disks, video tapes, travel disks and any other device or method that is now being used or in the future will be used to transmit information.

Section 5. To secure the rights of citizens the Media are hereby prohibited from intentionally disseminating false information and they are prohibited from intentionally disseminating misleading information to the American public through any Broadcast Format or through any Transmission Vehicle. The provisions of this Article are enforceable within the United States which shall include the Several States, the District of Columbia, and the Commonwealth of Puerto Rico, the Commonwealth of the Northern Mariana Islands and the territories and possessions of the United States.

Section 6.   Congress shall have the power to enforce by appropriate legislation, the provisions of the Article.

It is foundational to a free people that they receive from all media sources information that is not intentionally distorted, intentionally misleading or intentionally false. The 20th Century is replete with governments that intentionally propagandized their citizens with false, misleading and distorted information in order to gain and retain power. Governments have deliberately created national emergencies to drive its citizens to relinquish their God given natural rights. Nearly 200 million people were killed in the 20th Century through starvation, war, pestilences and mass genocide. The 20th Century is man's most evil experiment in human history. When you add 700 million plus Unborn Children who were aborted in the last 60 years, the horror count is nearly 1 billion human beings who lost their lives because governments deceived their citizens into believing untruths through the power of the media.

AUTHORIZED CALL
BY THE OKLAHOMA STATE LEGISLATURE
ON THE UNITED STATES CONGRESS INSTRUCTING CONGRESS
TO CONVENE A FEDERAL CONVENTION TO BE TITLED
THE TRUTH IN MEDIA AMENDMENT CONVENTION

THIS AUTHORIZED CALL ALSO DEFINES THE AGREEMENT
THE OKLAHOMA STATE LEGISLATURE IS ENTERING INTO
BETWEEN ITSELF AND OTHER CALLING STATES

To: **BOTH HOUSES OF UNITED STATES CONGRESS**

UNITED STATES SENATE:

President of the Senate, United States Vice President
Majority Leader Senator
Minority Leader Senator
President Pro Tempore Senator
Republican Whip Senator
Democratic Whip Senator

(Deliver this Official Call to every current leader and member of the United State Senate at Washington, DC)

HOUSE OF REPRESENTATIVE:

Speaker of the House Representative
House Majority Leader Representative
House Majority Whip Representative
House Minority Leader Representative
House Minority Whip Representative

(Deliver this Official Call to every current leader and member of the United State House of Representatives at Washington, DC)

From: **THE STATE LEGISLATURE OF THE STATE OF OKLAHOMA**

The Legislature of the State of OKLAHOMA hereby Calls on the United States Congress instructing Congress to convene a Federal Convention called the TRUTH IN MEDIA AMENDMENT Convention under the authority reserved to the States in Article V of the United States Constitution. Article IV, Section 4 guarantees to every State a Republican form of Government which gives each State equal standing when Calling for a Constitutional Convention. Article V reserves to the Several States the right to Call for a Federal Constitutional Convention for the purpose of amending the United

States Constitution when Congress and/or the Courts refuse to address an egregious wrong suffered by the people. The States *alone* have the authority to "limit" the agenda and authority of a Federal Convention. The States alone can Call for a "Single Issue" Convention by agreeing among themselves the purpose, terms, conditions, duration, and agenda for the Convention. Congress does not have the authority to define a "Single Issue" Convention. Congress' authority, under Article V of the United States Constitution, empowers it to convene a Convention as Called for and defined by the Several States. The Several States alone have the authority to enforce the terms and/or conditions set forth in this Agreement at the TRUTH IN MEDIA AMENDMENT Convention.

The TRUTH IN MEDIA AMENDMENT Convention will be a "Single Issue" Federal Convention as defined in this Legislative Call on the United States Congress and in this binding Agreement between the Several States. The delegates summoned to this Convention by Congress will have the authority to decide only one issue, should the TRUTH IN MEDIA AMENDMENT, as herein written, be sent to Congress with instructions to send the Amendment back to the Several States for ratification? The delegates at the TRUTH IN MEDIA AMENDMENT Convention will have no authority to change the wording of the proposed Amendment, neither are they authorized to deliberate on or discuss any other subject matter or issue at the Convention. The purpose, terms and/or conditions that will govern the agenda and affairs of the TRUTH IN MEDIA AMENDMENT Convention are as follows:

THE PURPOSE OF THE CONVENTION

The *only* purpose for convening the TRUTH IN MEDIA AMENDMENT Convention is for the State Delegations, representing the Several States, to decide if the TRUTH IN MEDIA AMENDMENT, as herein written, should be sent to the United States Congress with instructions for Congress to send the Amendment to the Several States for ratification? Absolutely no other business is authorized at this Convention.

CONVENTION RULES OF ORDER

The "Convention Rules of Order" that all Delegates and State Delegations are required to follow as a condition of participating at the TRUTH IN MEDIA AMENDMENT Convention are described in this Legislative Call on Congress. From time to time, in order to facilitate Convention business, the Convention Chairman may require the Convention to follow "Robert's Rules of Order" when a specific Rule of Order is not defined in this Legislative Call. The Delegates and State Delegations are required to honor the Convention

Chairman's instructions when applying Convention Rules of Order and/or Roberts Rules of Order.

TRUTH IN MEDIA AMENDMENT COMMITTEE

The TRUTH IN MEDIA AMENDMENT Committee is the citizens group that founded the TRUTH IN MEDIA AMENDMENT Initiative. This Committee will be responsible for pre-Convention planning and organization. The Chairman and Vice Chairman of the TRUTH IN MEDIA AMENDMENT Committee will be Ex-Officio (without voting rights) members of the Convention. They can be called upon by the Convention Chairman to clarify the TRUTH IN MEDIA AMENDMENT legislative strategy for the Delegates, provide progress reports in the States and also be available for questions and answers from Delegates at the Convention. They will be subject to the terms and/or conditions of this Legislative Call and Agreement between the States.

If they are also appointed as Delegates by their State Legislatures, then they will be entitled to voting privileges as Delegates at the Convention. The Chairman of the TRUTH IN MEDIA AMENDMENT Committee is R. C. "Kacprowicz" Casper.

If the Convention votes in favor of the Amendment, the TRUTH IN MEDIA AMENDMENT Committee will be responsible for post-convention planning and organization during the ratification process.

FUNDING THE CONVENTION AND STATE DELEGATIONS

The State Legislatures that send Delegates to the TRUTH IN MEDIA AMENDMENT Convention shall be responsible for providing monies necessary for their State Delegations to participate at the Convention. The amounts each State Delegation will require will be decided by each State Legislature. Other expenses or costs necessary to fund the Convention are to be shared by the Calling States equally. From time to time the Convention Chairman will notify the State Delegations what monies will be necessary to carry on the business of the Convention.

FUNDING FOR "PRE AND POST-CONVENTION PLANNING AND ORGANIZATION"

Each State Legislature making a Call on Congress to convene the TRUTH IN MEDIA AMENDMENT Convention will be asked to share expenses for "pre-Convention planning" and "pre-Convention organization". If the Convention votes to send the TRUTH IN MEDIA AMENDMENT to Congress to be ratified by the States, then the TRUTH IN MEDIA AMENDMENT Committee will ask the Calling States to help fund post-convention planning and organization to cover expenses for the ratification process.

DELEGATES SUMMONED BY CONGRESS

Congress has the authority, under Article V, to summon Delegates from the Several States to the TRUTH IN MEDIA AMENDMENT Convention. Congress is hereby directed to summon to the Convention the appropriate number of Delegates that each State is entitled to immediately after two thirds of the States complete their Call directing Congress to convene the TRUTH IN MEDIA AMENDMENT Convention. The number of Delegates to be summoned to the Convention should be equal to the number of members each State has in the House of Representatives and in the Senate of the United States Congress.

DELEGATES AND STATE DELEGATIONS

Only State Delegates summoned by Congress to the TRUTH IN MEDIA AMENDMENT Convention and appointed by their State Legislatures to form State Delegations to represent their respective States are authorized to attend and speak at the TRUTH IN MEDIA AMENDMENT Convention. Each State Legislature has the responsibility to
select, from within its State, individual Delegates who will represent its State at the Convention. The number of Delegates selected by a State Legislature can be no greater than the number of Delegates summoned by Congress from its State. Each State Delegation must select a Delegate from within its delegation to be its Spokesman at the Convention. Only a Delegation's Spokesman will be recognized by the Convention Chairman.

THE PRE-CONVENTION "ACTING CONVENTION CHAIRMAN" AND "ASSISTANT ACTING CONVENTION CHAIRMAN"

The Chairman and Vice Chairman of the TRUTH IN MEDIA AMENDMENT Committee will have exclusive authority to complete all pre-convention planning and organization for the TRUTH IN MEDIA AMENDMENT Convention. They will perform their duties under the titles "Acting Convention Chairman" and "Assistant Acting Convention Chairman" respectfully. They will also be available to State Legislatures to assist with their Legislative Calls and pre-Convention planning.

The Chairman and Vice Chairman of the TRUTH IN MEDIA AMENDMENT Committee will also be responsible for post-convention planning and organization if the Convention votes to send the TRUTH IN MEDIA AMENDMENT to Congress to be ratified by the States.

VOTING BY DELEGATES IN STATE DELEGATIONS

It is recommended that a simple majority of the Delegates within each State Delegation be required to decide a State Delegation's vote at the Convention. A quorum within each State Delegation will consist of one Delegate. The business of the Convention and voting will not be delayed if a State Delegation does not cast a vote during a roll call.

QUORUM REQUIRED FOR CONDUCTING BUSINESS AND VOTING AT THE CONVENTION

Each State Delegation will have one vote on all matters that are to be decided by the Convention. A simple majority vote by the State Delegations at the Convention is required to decide the outcome of all business brought before the Convention for a vote, including whether or not the TRUTH IN MEDIA AMENDMENT, as herein written, should be sent to the Several States, via Congress, for ratification. A quorum at the Convention for the purpose of conducting business and voting will consist of 17 State Delegations.

CLOSED DELIBERATIONS AT THE CONVENTION

The TRUTH IN MEDIA AMENDMENT Convention will be closed to all media and news groups. Only delegates appointed by their State Legislatures and the Chairman and Vice Chairman of the TRUTH IN MEDIA AMENDMENT Committee will be authorized to enter and speak at the Convention. No visitors, reporters, government officials, professionals or inquirers, of any kind, will be permitted to enter the Convention facilities. Unauthorized visitors will be escorted by the Sergeant of Arms out of the Convention. After the vote by the State Delegations is taken to determine if the TRUTH IN MEDIA AMENDMENT will be sent to the Several States, via Congress, for ratification, the Chairman of the Convention will call a special press conference to announce the Convention's decision. Within 30 days from the special press conference the Chairman will make available to the public the records kept by the Convention during its proceedings.

STATE LEGISLATURES NOT AUTHORIZING THIS CALL FOR THE TRUTH IN MEDIA AMENDMENT CONVENTION

State Legislatures that did not authorize this Call for the TRUTH IN MEDIA AMENDMENT Convention and yet agree to send delegates representing their State agree to follow the terms and/or conditions set forth in this Agreement and Legislative Call. They need to pay particular attention to the "Convention's Rules of Order" described in this Agreement and the prohibitions in the section titled "Prohibitions for Delegates, State Delegations and/or Convention Officials at the Convention". These non-calling States must notify the "Acting Convention Chairman" before the Convention convenes of their intention to attend the Convention so accommodations can be completed for their Delegations. In order to receive Convention Passes, all Delegates attending the Convention, will be required to sign an agreement promising to abide by the terms and/or conditions in this Legislative Call and Agreement.

NO WEAPONS ALLOWED AT THE CONVENTION

Delegates and TRUTH IN MEDIA AMENDMENT Committee officials will not be allowed to bring into the TRUTH IN MEDIA AMENDMENT Convention any weapons or objects that can be construed as weapons.

PRESENTING ARGUMENTS AT THE CONVENTION BY STATE DELEGATIONS

Each State Delegation will be allotted a maximum of 60 minutes for presenting its argument(s) at the Convention for or against sending the TRUTH IN MEDIA AMENDMENT to the United States Congress with instruction for Congress to send the Amendment to the Several States for ratification. Only Delegates who have been officially selected by their State Legislatures and Ex-Officio members of the Convention are authorized to speak before the Convention. Each State Delegation can use one or more of its Delegates to present its position(s). However, the total time allotted for each State Delegation is 60 minutes, which includes any time that is necessary to replace one Delegate with another. The Chairman of the TRUTH IN MEDIA AMENDMENT Committee will also be limited to 60 minutes during his speaking segment. Speakers cannot reserve portions of their time to another time or day. Speakers must complete their arguments in the 60 minute segment assigned to them.

The order each State Delegation will follow when presenting their position(s) will be according to when each State completed its Legislative Call on Congress, or when it notified the "Acting Convention Chairman" that it intends to attend the Convention even though it may not complete a Legislative Call on Congress. The State Delegation presentations will be scheduled in the following manner: the first State making a Call on Congress will go first; the first State notifying the "Acting Convention Chairman" that it plans to attend will go second. The second State making a Call on Congress will go third; then the second State notifying the "Acting Convention Chairman" will go fourth, and so forth until all States wanting to present their positions have had an opportunity to do so. The Convention

Chairman can rearrange the schedule if any conflicts arise at the Convention. The last speaker to be scheduled at the Convention for a 60 minute segment will be the Chairman of the TRUTH IN MEDIA AMENDMENT Committee.

DUTIES OF THE "ACTING CONVENTION CHAIRMAN"

The duties of the "Acting Convention Chairman include:

1. organize a pre-Convention support group for assisting Calling States with their Legislative Calls and non-calling States with their intentions to attend the Convention
2. set up an TRUTH IN MEDIA AMENDMENT Committee checking account
3. use generally accepted accounting principles when keeping records of all receipts and expenditures
4. provide financial reports and minutes of pre-convention activities as requested by States that are funding pre-convention operations
5. keep minutes of all business meetings of the TRUTH IN MEDIA AMENDMENT Committee
6. determine the budget that will be needed for pre-convention planning and organizing and notify each State Legislature of its share of the expenses
7. assist the Calling States and Attending States with their pre-convention planning
8. assist the Calling States with their Legislative Calls on Congress
9. after the TRUTH IN MEDIA AMENDMENT Convention has been convened call the Convention to order
10. invite nominations from the State Delegations present at the Convention to fill the "Convention Chairman's" position (the maximum number of nominees permitted is five and only one nominee from any one State Delegation is permitted)
11. take a roll call from the State Delegations for the nominee(s)
12. declare the winner based on the nominee who has received the most votes (a plurality of State Delegations). Each State Delegation will have one vote
13. officiate the installation of the "Convention Chairman" at the Convention by having the Chairman place his/her right hand on the Bible while repeating the following oath

    "I solemnly promise to officiate the office of Convention Chairman for the TRUTH IN MEDIA AMENDMENT Convention according to the terms and/or conditions set forth in the Legislative Calls from the Several States to the best of my ability, so help me God".

In the event the "Acting Convention Chairman" is nominated and elected to the Convention Chairman position, the "Assistant Acting Convention Chairman" will conduct the installation ceremony for the Convention Chairman.

ELECTION, AUTHORITY AND DUTIES OF CONVENTION OFFICIALS

CONVENTION CHAIRMAN: - The "Convention Chairman" is the senior official at the TRUTH IN MEDIA AMENDMENT Convention. He/she will have the requisite authority to oversee all activities at the Convention, including the nomination and election of all officials. The Convention Chairman's duties include:

1. organize and oversee all business and activities at the Convention
2. organize and officiate all nominations, elections and installations of officials at the Convention (this will be the Convention Chairman's first order of business)
3. organize and officiate all nominations, elections and installations of official positions that may become vacant at the Convention
4. oversee the enforcement of all Convention Rules
5. oversee the enforcement of the terms and/or conditions (herein described) of this Call and Agreement by the States
6. oversee the investigation of alleged and/or actual violations of this Agreement as defined in the section titled "Violating this Agreement"
7. bring before the Convention all matters that require a vote
8. bring before the Convention the financial needs of the Convention and time lines for when these monies are needed
9. cut off motions or discussions by State Delegations before the Convention if and when it seems appropriate
10. recognize the Spokesman within a State Delegation for the purpose of addressing a matter of importance to the Spokesman's Delegation (the Convention Chairman will have full authority to determine if a matter brought before the Convention by the Spokesman is appropriate for further discussion and/or if a decision by the Convention is necessary)
11. keep the business of the Convention moving forward expeditiously, cutting off all motions and discussions when it appears one or more Delegates are trying to hinder, delay or stop the work of the Convention
12. keep the business of the Convention focused on one objective which is, should the Convention send the TRUTH IN MEDIA AMENDMENT to Congress instructing Congress to send it to the Several States for ratification?

13. instruct Convention Officials (Assistant Convention Chairman, Secretary, Financial Officer, Executive Administrator, Sergeant at Arms, and Deputies) on their duties at the Convention
14. officiate and remedy any and all problems that may develop at the Convention
15. oversee the design and production of "Official" Convention Badges for the Sergeant at Arms and Deputies
16. notify all State Legislatures of the decision the Convention made as to whether or not the TRUTH IN MEDIA AMENDMENT should be sent to Congress instructing Congress to send it to the States for ratification?
17. if the State Delegations voted to send the Amendment to the States for ratification, include the Convention's recommendation to the United States
18. Congress as to whether it should be ratified by State Conventions or State Legislatures
19. declare the TRUTH IN MEDIA AMENDMENT Convention closed after the State Delegations have decided if the TRUTH IN MEDIA AMENDMENT should be sent to Congress instructing Congress to send it to the States for ratification?
20. arrange a Special News Conference to announce the decision by the TRUTH IN MEDIA AMENDMENT Convention
21. make available the proceedings of the Convention to the public 30 days after the Convention is closed

The first order of business for the "Convention Chairman" will be to open the Convention to nominations from State Delegations present for each of the following Convention Officials; one Assistant Convention Chairman, one Secretary, one Financial Officer, one Executive Administrator, one Sergeant at Arms and ten Deputies (the maximum number of nominees permitted for each Convention Official position is five. Only one nominee for each Convention Official position is permitted from any one State Delegation. The nominee with a plurality of votes from the State Delegations will be the winner). The "Convention Chairman" can call for nominations for more than 10 Deputies if and when circumstances warrant.

ASSISTANT CONVENTION CHAIRMAN
The "Assistant Convention Chairman" duties include:

1. be amenable to the "Convention Chairman"
2. provide assistance to the "Convention Chairman" in all matters pertaining to the business of the Convention

3. monitor activities at the Convention and report to the "Convention Chairman" violations or possible violations of the terms and/or conditions of this Legislative Call and Agreement
4. perform the duties of the "Convention Chairman" when called upon by the Chairman or when the Chairman is unable to perform the duties of his/her office
5. the "Assistant Convention Chairman" will take the following oath, administered by the Convention Chairman, while placing his/her right hand on the Bible

   "I solemnly promise to officiate the office of Assistant Convention Chairman for the TRUTH IN MEDIA AMENDMENT Convention according to the terms and/or conditions set forth in the Legislative Calls from the Several States to the best of my ability, so help me God".

SECRETARY
The "Secretary's" duties include:

1. keep official minutes of all proceedings at the Convention
2. monitor activities at the Convention and report to the Convention Chairman violations or possible violations of Convention Rules and of the terms and/or conditions of this Legislative Call and Agreement
3. make available to the "Convention Chairman", upon request, the official minutes of the Convention
4. be amenable to the "Convention Chairman" and "Assistant Convention Chairman"
5. in the absence of the "Convention Chairman" and the "Assistant Convention Chairman" due to death or a disablement that prevents them from performing the duties of their offices at the Convention, the Secretary shall call the Convention to order for the purpose of nominating and electing a new "Convention Chairman" and "Assistant Convention Chairman". In this capacity the Secretary will assume the duties and authority of the "Convention Chairman". If the Secretary is unable to perform the duties described herein, then they will fall to the Financial Officer.
6. the "Secretary" will take the following oath while placing his/her right hand on the Bible

   "I solemnly promise to officiate the office of Secretary for the TRUTH IN MEDIA AMENDMENT Convention according to the terms and/or conditions set forth in the Legislative Calls from the Several States to the best of my ability, so help me God".

FINANCIAL OFFICER
The "Financial Officer's" duties include:

1. keep detailed accounting records of all financial matters at the Convention using generally accepted accounting principles
2. be amenable to the "Convention Chairman" and "Assistant Convention Chairman"
3. monitor activities at the Convention and report to the Convention Chairman violations or possible violations of the terms and/or conditions of this Legislative Call and Agreement
4. set up a checking account in the name of the TRUTH IN MEDIA AMENDMENT Convention requiring any two of the following three officers when signing a check or making withdrawals – Convention Chairman, Assistant Convention Chairman, Financial Officer
5. make available to the "Convention Chairman", upon request, all financial records at the Convention
6. provide to the Convention Chairman the financial needs of the Convention and the time lines as to when these monies are needed
7. in the absence of a "Convention Chairman", "Assistant Convention Chairman", and "Secretary" due to death or a disablement that prevents them from performing the duties of their offices at the Convention, the Financial Officer shall call the Convention to order for the purpose of nominating and electing a new "Convention Chairman", "Assistant Convention Chairman", and "Secretary". In this capacity the Financial Officer will assume the duties and authority of the "Convention Chairman"
8. the "Financial Officer" will take the following oath while placing his/her right hand on the Bible

   "I solemnly promise to officiate the office of Financial Officer for the TRUTH IN MEDIA AMENDMENT Convention according to generally accepted accounting principles and according to the terms and/or conditions set forth in the Legislative Calls from the Several States to the best of my ability, so help me God".

EXECUTIVE ADMINISTRATOR
The "Executive Administrator's" duties include:

1. facilitate all Convention business as directed by the Convention Chairman
2. be amenable to the Convention Chairman and Assistant Convention Chairman
3. monitor activities at the Convention and report to the Convention Chairman violations or possible violations of the terms and/or conditions of this Legislative Call and Agreement

4. keep detailed reports of all administrative activities at the Convention
5. make available to the "Convention Chairman" upon request all administrative records and/or reports at the Convention
6. the "Executive Administrator" will take the following oath while placing his/her right hand on the Bible

"I solemnly promise to officiate the office of Executive Administrator for the TRUTH IN MEDIA AMENDMENT Convention according to the terms and/or conditions set forth in the Legislative Calls from the Several States to the best of my ability, so help me God".

SERGEANT AT ARMS
The "Sergeant at Arms'" duties include:

1. be amenable to the Convention Chairman and Assistant Convention Chairman
2. monitor all activities at the Convention and report to the Convention Chairman violations or possible violations of the terms and/or conditions of this Legislative Call and Agreement
3. maintain order at the Convention
4. enforce all remedies for violations of this Legislative Call and Agreement as directed by the Convention Chairman
5. organize and direct the activities of all Deputies at the Convention
6. oversee, train and manage all Deputies at the Convention
7. the "Sergeant at Arms" will take the following oath while placing his/her right hand on the Bible

"I solemnly promise to officiate the office of Sergeant at Arms for the TRUTH IN MEDIA AMENDMENT Convention according to the terms and/or conditions set forth in the Legislative Calls from the Several States to the best of my ability, so help me God".

DEPUTIES
The "Deputies'" duties include:

1. be amenable to the Convention Chairman, Assistant Convention Chairman and Sergeant at Arms
2. monitor all activities at the Convention and report to the Sergeant at Arms violations or possible violations of the terms and/or conditions of this Legislative Call and Agreement
3. maintain order at the Convention as directed by the Sergeant at Arms

4. enforce all remedies for violations of this Legislative Call and Agreement as directed by the Convention Chairman and/or the Sergeant at Arms
5. "Deputies" will take the following oath while placing his/her right hand on the Bible

"I solemnly promise to officiate the office of Deputy for the TRUTH IN MEDIA AMENDMENT Convention according to the terms and/or conditions set forth in the Legislative Calls from the Several States to the best of my ability, so help me God".

CHALLENGING THE QUALIFICATIONS OF CONVENTION OFFICIALS

A State Delegation can challenge the qualifications of any Convention Official at the TRUTH IN MEDIA AMENDMENT Convention by bringing its allegation(s), during a business session, to the Convention floor. The Convention Chairman will consider the allegation(s) and determine if it merits further investigation. If the Chairman decides that the allegation(s) merits further investigation, he/she will direct the Sergeant at Arms to conduct the necessary inquiry. He/she will then follow the instructions outlined in the section "Violating this Agreement" for proscribing a remedy or remedies.

The "Convention Chairman" can also reject a challenge to the qualifications of any Convention Official if he/she concludes that the Delegate making the allegation(s) is trying to disrupt and/or delay Convention business. If after following the instructions outlined in "Violating this Agreement" the Delegate is found to have made a false accusation against a Convention Official, the Delegate's State Delegation will be charged with a violation of the terms and/or conditions of this Call and Agreement.

PROHIBITIONS FOR STATE DELEGATES, STATE DELEGATIONS AND CONVENTION OFFICIALS AT THE CONVENTION

State Delegates, State Delegations and Convention Officials are prohibited from violating any of the following Convention prohibitions:

1. State Delegates, State Delegations and Convention Officials are prohibited, at the Convention, from introducing, discussing, voting on, or sending to the States for consideration and/or ratification any amendment to the United States Constitution other than the TRUTH IN MEDIA AMENDMENT, as herein written
2. State Delegates, State Delegations and Convention Officials are prohibited from altering or changing, in any way (which includes the wording, spelling, punctuation, or paragraph sections), the TRUTH IN MEDIA AMENDMENT from the written form shown in

the section titled "The full text of the TRUTH IN MEDIA AMENDMENT"

3. State Delegates, State Delegations and Convention Officials are prohibited, at the Convention, from introducing, discussing, voting on, or sending to the States for consideration and/or ratification any alternate form of government for the United States of America

4. State Delegates, State Delegations and Convention Officials are prohibited, at the Convention, from introducing, discussing, voting on, or sending to the States for consideration and/or ratification any alternate constitution or governing document for the United States of America

5. State Delegates, State Delegations and Convention Officials are prohibited, at the Convention, from introducing, discussing, voting on, or sending to the States for consideration and/or ratification any changes, of any kind, to the existing Constitution of the United States of America other than the TRUTH IN MEDIA AMENDMENT

6. State Delegates, State Delegations and Convention Officials are prohibited, at the Convention, from introducing, discussing, voting on, or sending to the States for consideration any changes, of any kind, to this binding Agreement between the States Calling for the TRUTH IN MEDIA AMENDMENT Convention

7. State Delegates, State Delegations and Convention Officials are prohibited, at the Convention, from introducing, discussing, voting on, or sending to the States for consideration and/or ratification any subject matter, issue or topic (of any kind) other than the proposed TRUTH IN MEDIA AMENDMENT in its

8. written form shown in the section titled "The full text of the TRUTH IN MEDIA AMENDMENT"

THE DATE, TIME, DURATION AND PLACE OF THE TRUTH IN MEDIA AMENDMENT CONVENTION.

The United States Congress will be responsible for determining and announcing to the Several States the date, time, and place that the TRUTH IN MEDIA AMENDMENT Convention is to convene immediately after two thirds of the States, under the authority given to the States in Article V of the United States Constitution, have completed their Calls on Congress to convene the TRUTH IN MEDIA AMENDMENT Convention. The Convention is expected to complete its business by the 180th day after convening. The Convention Chairman can extend the duration of the TRUTH IN MEDIA AMENDMENT Convention for one additional 180 day period. The maximum number of days the Convention is authorized to be in session are 360 days. If the Convention has not decided if the TRUTH IN MEDIA AMENDMENT should be sent to Congress with instructions to send the

Amendment to the Several States for ratification by the end of 360 days, then the Call for the TRUTH IN MEDIA AMENDMENT Convention, which was approved by the Several States under the authority granted in Article V of the United States Constitution and this agreement, will be automatically withdrawn by the Calling States and the Convention will automatically terminate at 5:00 P.M. Eastern Standard Time on the 360th day after convening. Termination of the TRUTH IN MEDIA AMENDMENT Convention will automatically occur on the 360th day after convening the Convention, without requiring a formal notice by the States to the Convention, nor by the States to the United States Congress, nor by the Convention to the States, nor by the Convention to the United States Congress, although it is recommended that the Convention notify the United States Congress and the State Legislatures of its termination as a courtesy.

Under no circumstance(s) are the Delegates at the TRUTH IN MEDIA AMENDMENT Convention authorized to re-convene a new or different Convention, no matter what their purpose or intent. The official Legislative Call and authority granted by the Several States and the subsequent convening of the TRUTH IN MEDIA AMENDMENT Convention by Congress will be automatically invalidated and the Convention will be abolished at 5:00 P.M. Eastern Standard Time on the 360th day after the convening of the TRUTH IN MEDIA AMENDMENT Convention.

VIOLATING THIS AGREEMENT

The Convention Chairman (or in the absence of the Convention Chairman the Assistant Convention Chairman) will handle allegations of a violation(s) or actual violation(s) of the terms and/or conditions of this binding Agreement between the Several States, by any one or more Delegate(s) and/or Convention Official(s), as follows:

1. When an alleged violation has been presented to the Convention Chairman, and if the Chairman decides that the allegation(s) merits further investigation, he/she will instruct the Sergeant at Arms to conduct the necessary inquiry.
2. After the inquiry has been completed, and assuming the Convention Chairman concludes that the evidence does not substantiate further review by the Convention, the allegation(s) will be dismissed by the Chairman and the Convention will go forward with its business.
3. If however, after the inquiry has been completed, the Convention Chairman concludes that the evidence does substantiate further review by the Convention, the Chairman will present the allegation(s) and findings of the inquiry to the Convention for a discussion and vote. If a majority of the State Delegations (one vote per State Delegation) decide that no violation of the terms and/or

conditions of this Legislative Call and Agreement has occurred, then the Chairman will declare that the alleged violation(s) of the terms and/or conditions of this Legislative Call and Agreement is/are dismissed. The Convention will then go forward with its business.

4. If however, after the inquiry has been completed, the Convention Chairman concludes that the evidence does substantiate further review by the Convention, the Chairman will present the allegation(s) and findings of the inquiry to the Convention for a discussion and vote. If a majority of the State Delegations (one vote per State Delegation) decide that one or more violation(s) of the terms and/or conditions of this Legislative Call and Agreement has/have occurred, then the Chairman will declare to the Convention that the Delegate(s) responsible for the violation(s), and their State Delegation(s), has/have been charged with "Violating this Agreement". The Convention will then go forward with its business.

5. If a State Delegation is charged with two violations of the terms and/or conditions of this Legislative Call and Agreement, the Convention Chairman will declare to the Convention that the State Delegation charged with violating this Agreement a second time has no further standing or authority at the Convention. The Chairman will notify the charged State Delegation that its entire delegation of Delegates must leave the Convention immediately and they will not be allowed back into the Convention. The Chairman will instruct the Sergeant at Arms that he should escort the charged State Delegation out of the Convention. The Convention Chairman will then notify the State Legislature that sent the charged State Delegation of the actions that the Convention has taken and inform them that they can send a replacement State Delegation to the Convention as long as they do not disrupt the proceedings of the Convention. None of the original Delegates who were charged by the Convention will be allowed back into the Convention as part of a replacement delegation.

6. The Convention Chairman will not allow unreasonable delays in the proceedings of the Convention due to disruptive Delegates or State Delegations. He/she will move the business of the Convention forward expeditiously.

THE FULL TEXT OF THE TRUTH IN MEDIA AMENDMENT

The full text of the TRUTH IN MEDIA AMENDMENT to be submitted to the Several States by the United States Congress for ratification shall read as follows:

TRUTH IN MEDIA AMENDMENT
ARTICLE 28 (or alternate number to be assigned by Congress)

Section 1. It is the right of every citizen to receive from any and all Media sources information that is not intentionally false or intentionally misleading which is foundational to a free people.

Section 2. The Media are all Broadcasters that disseminate information to and for consumption by the American public. The Media includes individuals, groups, corporations and any other type of institution or organization, whether domestic or foreign or whether located inside or outside the United States.

Section 3. Broadcast Formats used by the Media to disseminate information to the American public include news, entertainment, documentaries, editorials, opinion and any other Broadcast Format that is now being used or will be used in the future.

Section 4. Transmission Vehicles by which information is disseminated to the American public by the Media include cable, satellite, radio, television, airwaves, microwaves, telephone lines, print media, computers, computer disks, video tapes, travel disks and any other device or method that is now being used or in the future will be used to transmit information.

Section 5. To secure the rights of citizens the Media are hereby prohibited from intentionally disseminating false information and they are prohibited from intentionally disseminating misleading information to the American public through any Broadcast Format or through any Transmission Vehicle. The provisions of this Article are enforceable within the United States which shall include the Several States, the District of Columbia, and the Commonwealth of Puerto Rico, the Commonwealth of the Northern Mariana Islands and the territories and possessions of the United States.

Section 6. Congress shall have the power to enforce by appropriate legislation, the provisions of the Article.

RATIFICATION OF THE "TRUTH IN MEDIA AMENDMENT"

Under the requirements of Article V of the United States Constitution and also under Article IV, Section 4 which guarantees to every State a Republican form of Government, the TRUTH IN MEDIA AMENDMENT will become a ratified Amendment to the United States Constitution when three quarters of the Several States complete their ratifications of the Amendment.

"CONGRESSIONAL" OPTION

If the United States Congress voluntarily sends the TRUTH IN MEDIA AMENDMENT to the Several States for ratification without making any changes, of any kind (which includes the wording, spelling, punctuation and paragraph sections) in the proposed Amendment as herein written, and before two thirds of the States complete their Call for Congress to convene the TRUTH IN MEDIA AMENDMENT Convention, then the Legislature of the State of OKLAHOMA will withdraw its Call for the TRUTH IN MEDIA AMENDMENT Convention.

OFFICIAL AGREEMENT BY THE OKLAHOMA STATE LEGISLATURE BETWEEN ITSELF AND THE CALLING STATES

The Legislature of the State of OKLAHOMA enters into this binding Agreement with every other State Legislature that likewise agrees to the terms and/or conditions of this Legislative Call and Agreement as set forth herein. This is an irrevocable contract, during the term of this Agreement, between the State of OKLAHOMA and each and every State that signs this Agreement and completes its Call on the United States Congress directing Congress to convene a Federal Convention titled the TRUTH IN MEDIA AMENDMENT Convention. The Legislature of the State of OKLAHOMA agrees that it, and its delegates who are selected to attend the Convention, will abide by the purpose, terms, conditions, agenda, and "Convention Rules of Order" as explained in this Agreement.

The Legislature of the State of OKLAHOMA enters into this Agreement with every other State Legislature that likewise agrees to the terms and/or conditions of this Agreement and Legislative Call as set forth herein, understanding that the TRUTH IN MEDIA AMENDMENT Convention, by definition herein explained, is a "SINGLE ISSUE" Federal Convention and that the Convention will have no authority, under this Call and Agreement between the States, to review and/or consider any other subject matter, issue, or topic during its sessions other than business matters relating to the question, should the TRUTH IN MEDIA AMENDMENT, as herein written, be sent by the Convention to the United States Congress instructing Congress to send the Amendment to the Several States for ratification? The

Legislature of the State of OKLAHOMA irrevocably declares by signing this Agreement that any subject matter, issue or topic (other than the TRUTH IN MEDIA AMENDMENT) that delegates might try to present to the Convention and subsequently to the States for review and/or ratification will be immediately, upon introduction at the Convention, unauthorized, invalid and automatically rejected by the Legislature of the State of OKLAHOMA, and the Legislature of the State of OKLAHOMA irrevocably declares that it will not review and/or consider for ratification any such subject matter, issue or topic, no matter how presented to it by the Convention. Only the TRUTH IN MEDIA AMENDMENT, as herein written, will be considered by the Legislature of the State of OKLAHOMA for ratification.

The Legislature of the State of OKLAHOMA also irrevocably declares that under no circumstance(s) will it consider for review and/or ratification any amendment to the United States Constitution, submitted to it by the TRUTH IN MEDIA AMENDMENT Convention other than the TRUTH IN MEDIA AMENDMENT as herein written.

The Legislature of the State of OKLAHOMA further irrevocably declares that under no circumstance(s) will it consider for review and/or ratification any modified form of the TRUTH IN MEDIA AMENDMENT submitted to it by the TRUTH IN MEDIA AMENDMENT Convention that would change, alter, or replace, in any way (which includes the wording, spelling, punctuation, or paragraph sections), the TRUTH IN MEDIA AMENDMENT from its written form herein.

The Legislature of the State of OKLAHOMA further irrevocably declares that under no circumstance(s) will it consider for review and/or ratification any proposal, of any kind, sent to it by the TRUTH IN MEDIA AMENDMENT Convention that would change, replace, or alter the United States Constitution other than the TRUTH IN MEDIA AMENDMENT as herein written.

The Legislature of the State of OKLAHOMA further irrevocably declares that under no circumstance(s) will it consider for review any proposal, of any kind, sent to it by the TRUTH IN MEDIA AMENDMENT Convention that would change, replace, or alter, in any way (which includes the wording, spelling, punctuation and section paragraphs), this Official Legislative Call for the TRUTH IN MEDIA AMENDMENT Convention and the terms and/or conditions of this Agreement between the States as herein written.

Under the authority reserved to the State of OKLAHOMA in Article V of the United States Constitution and also under Article IV, Section 4 which guarantees to every State a Republican form of Government, the Legislature of the State of OKLAHOMA hereby approves this Legislative Call on the United States Congress directing Congress to convene the TRUTH IN MEDIA AMENDMENT Convention and binds itself with each and every State that likewise approves this identical Legislative Call according the terms and/or conditions set forth in this Agreement.

OFFICIAL CALL BY THE STATE OF OKLAHOMA ON THE UNITED STATES CONGRESS DIRECTING CONGRESS TO CONVENE THE TRUTH IN MEDIA AMENDMENT CONVENTION

The Legislature of the State of OKLAHOMA hereby Calls on the United States Congress directing Congress to convene a Federal Convention to be titled the TRUTH IN MEDIA AMENDMENT Convention. The Convention is to be convened immediately after two thirds of the Several States have completed their Calls for the TRUTH IN MEDIA AMENDMENT Convention.

The State of OKLAHOMA is authorized to make this Call for the TRUTH IN MEDIA AMENDMENT Convention under the authority reserved to the States in Article V of the United States Constitution and under Article IV, Section 4 which guarantees to every State a Republican form of Government. Both Articles give to each State an equal standing when calling for a Constitutional Convention. Article V and Article IV, Section 4 reserves to the Several States the right to Call for a Federal Convention for the purpose of amending the United States Constitution when Congress and/or the Courts refuse to address an egregious wrong suffered by the people.

Submitted to Both Houses of the United States Congress on this date _____, _____ by the Legislature of the State of OKLAHOMA.

State of OKLAHOMA Seal:

Authorized Signatures with titles:

_____Title_____

_____Title_____

_____Title_____

CHAPTER 17

PARENTAL RIGHTS AMENDMENT

Text of proposed
PARENTAL RIGHTS AMENDMENT
ARTICLE 28 (or alternate number to be assigned by Congress)

Section 1. It is the right of every citizen to train up their children according to their conscience, faith and capabilities without interference from the State. The rights of parents and legal guardians to choose how they will raise their children are foundational to a free people.

Section 2. Parental Rights consists of the responsible exercise of parental authority over their children for their children's instruction, welfare, discipline, education and training. Parental Rights also include the authority to discipline their children with reasonable corporal punishment for the purpose of correcting wrong behavior and to instill in their children good morals and good values that properly respect the rights of others and that foster respect for America's unique heritage and history.

Section 3. This Article does not prevent Local, State and Federal authorities from enforcing reasonable laws that are for the protection and welfare of the American people.

Section 4. To secure the rights of citizens, Parental Rights shall not be denied any parent or legal guardian within the United States which shall include the Several States, the District of Columbia, the Commonwealth of Puerto Rico, the Commonwealth of the Northern Mariana Islands and the territories and possessions of the United States.

Section 5. Congress shall have the power to enforce by appropriate legislation, the provisions of the Article.

American parents and legal guardians have a God given and Constitutional Right to train up their children in the way they should go without interference from the State that often disagrees with their values, faith and convictions. The Parental Rights Amendment will return to American parents and legal guardians the right to raise their children according to their consciences without unwarranted State interference.

AUTHORIZED CALL
BY THE FLORIDA STATE LEGISLATURE
ON THE UNITED STATES CONGRESS INSTRUCTING
CONGRESS TO CONVENE A FEDERAL CONVENTION TO BE
TITLED THE PARENTAL RIGHTS AMENDMENT
CONVENTION

THIS AUTHORIZED CALL ALSO DEFINES THE AGREEMENT
THE FLORIDA STATE LEGISLATURE IS ENTERING INTO
BETWEEN ITSELF AND OTHER CALLING STATES

To: **BOTH HOUSES OF UNITED STATES CONGRESS**

UNITED STATES SENATE:

President of the Senate, United States Vice President
Majority Leader Senator
Minority Leader Senator
President Pro Tempore Senator
Republican Whip Senator
Democratic Whip Senator

(Deliver this Official Call to every current leader and member of the United State Senate at Washington, DC)

HOUSE OF REPRESENTATIVE:

Speaker of the House Representative
House Majority Leader Representative
House Majority Whip Representative
House Minority Leader Representative
House Minority Whip Representative

(Deliver this Official Call to every current leader and member of the United State House of Representatives at Washington, DC)

From: **THE STATE LEGISLATURE OF THE STATE OF FLORIDA**

The Legislature of the State of FLORIDA hereby Calls on the United States Congress instructing Congress to convene a Federal Convention called the PARENTAL RIGHTS AMENDMENT Convention under the authority reserved to the States in Article V of the United States Constitution. Article IV, Section 4 guarantees to every State a Republican form of Government which gives each State equal standing when Calling for a Constitutional Convention. Article V reserves to the Several States the right to Call for a Federal Constitutional

Convention for the purpose of amending the United States Constitution when Congress and/or the Courts refuse to address an egregious wrong suffered by the people. The States *alone* have the authority to "limit" the agenda and authority of a Federal Convention. The States alone can Call for a "Single Issue" Convention by agreeing among themselves the purpose, terms, conditions, duration, and agenda for the Convention. Congress does not have the authority to define a "Single Issue" Convention. Congress' authority, under Article V of the United States Constitution, empowers it to convene a Convention as Called for and defined by the Several States. The Several States alone have the authority to enforce the terms and/or conditions set forth in this Agreement at the PARENTAL RIGHTS AMENDMENT Convention.

The PARENTAL RIGHTS AMENDMENT Convention will be a "Single Issue" Federal Convention as defined in this Legislative Call on the United States Congress and in this binding Agreement between the Several States. The delegates summoned to this Convention by Congress will have the authority to decide only one issue, should the PARENTAL RIGHTS AMENDMENT, as herein written, be sent to Congress with instructions to send the Amendment back to the Several States for ratification? The delegates at the PARENTAL RIGHTS AMENDMENT Convention will have no authority to change the wording of the proposed Amendment, neither are they authorized to deliberate on or discuss any other subject matter or issue at the Convention. The purpose, terms and/or conditions that will govern the agenda and affairs of the PARENTAL RIGHTS AMENDMENT Convention are as follows:

THE PURPOSE OF THE CONVENTION

The *only* purpose for convening the PARENTAL RIGHTS AMENDMENT Convention is for the State Delegations, representing the Several States, to decide if the PARENTAL RIGHTS AMENDMENT, as herein written, should be sent to the United States Congress with instructions for Congress to send the Amendment to the Several States for ratification? Absolutely no other business is authorized at this Convention.

CONVENTION RULES OF ORDER

The "Convention Rules of Order" that all Delegates and State Delegations are required to follow as a condition of participating at the PARENTAL RIGHTS AMENDMENT Convention are described in this Legislative Call on Congress. From time to time, in order to facilitate Convention business, the Convention Chairman may require the Convention to follow "Robert's Rules of Order" when a specific Rule of Order is not defined in this Legislative Call. The Delegates and State Delegations are required to honor the Convention Chairman's instructions when applying Convention Rules of Order and/or Roberts Rules of Order.

PARENTAL RIGHTS AMENDMENT COMMITTEE

The PARENTAL RIGHTS AMENDMENT Committee is the citizens group that founded the PARENTAL RIGHTS AMENDMENT Initiative. This Committee will be responsible for pre-Convention planning and organization. The Chairman and Vice Chairman of the PARENTAL RIGHTS AMENDMENT Committee will be Ex-Officio (without voting rights) members of the Convention. They can be called upon by the Convention Chairman to clarify the PARENTAL RIGHTS AMENDMENT legislative strategy for the Delegates, provide progress reports in the States and also be available for questions and answers from Delegates at the Convention. They will be subject to the terms and/or conditions of this Legislative Call and Agreement between the States.

If they are also appointed as Delegates by their State Legislatures, then they will be entitled to voting privileges as Delegates at the Convention. The Chairman of the PARENTAL RIGHTS AMENDMENT Committee is R. C. "Kacprowicz" Casper.

If the Convention votes in favor of the Amendment, the PARENTAL RIGHTS AMENDMENT Committee will be responsible for post-convention planning and organization during the ratification process.

FUNDING THE CONVENTION AND STATE DELEGATIONS

The State Legislatures that send Delegates to the PARENTAL RIGHTS AMENDMENT Convention shall be responsible for providing monies necessary for their State Delegations to participate at the Convention. The amounts each State Delegation will require will be decided by each State Legislature. Other expenses or costs necessary to fund the Convention are to be shared by the Calling States equally. From time to time the Convention Chairman will notify the State Delegations what monies will be necessary to carry on the business of the Convention.

FUNDING FOR "PRE AND POST-CONVENTION PLANNING AND ORGANIZATION"

Each State Legislature making a Call on Congress to convene the PARENTAL RIGHTS AMENDMENT Convention will be asked to share expenses for "pre-Convention planning" and "pre-Convention organization". If the Convention votes to send the PARENTAL RIGHTS AMENDMENT to Congress to be ratified by the States, then the PARENTAL RIGHTS AMENDMENT Committee will ask the Calling States to help fund post-convention planning and organization to cover expenses for the ratification process.

DELEGATES SUMMONED BY CONGRESS

Congress has the authority, under Article V, to summon Delegates from the Several States to the PARENTAL RIGHTS AMENDMENT Convention. Congress is hereby directed to summon to the Convention the appropriate number of Delegates that each State is entitled to immediately after two thirds of the States complete their Call directing Congress to convene the PARENTAL RIGHTS AMENDMENT Convention. The number of Delegates to be summoned to the Convention should be equal to the number of members each State has in the House of Representatives and in the Senate of the United States Congress.

DELEGATES AND STATE DELEGATIONS

Only State Delegates summoned by Congress to the PARENTAL RIGHTS AMENDMENT Convention and appointed by their State Legislatures to form State Delegations to represent their respective States are authorized to attend and speak at the PARENTAL RIGHTS AMENDMENT Convention. Each State Legislature has the responsibility to select, from within its State, individual Delegates who will represent its State at the Convention. The number of Delegates selected by a State Legislature can be no greater than the number of Delegates summoned by Congress from its State. Each State Delegation must select a Delegate from within its delegation to be its Spokesman at the Convention. Only a Delegation's Spokesman will be recognized by the Convention Chairman.

THE PRE-CONVENTION "ACTING CONVENTION CHAIRMAN" AND "ASSISTANT ACTING CONVENTION CHAIRMAN"

The Chairman and Vice Chairman of the PARENTAL RIGHTS AMENDMENT Committee will have exclusive authority to complete all pre-convention planning and organization for the PARENTAL RIGHTS AMENDMENT Convention. They will perform their duties under the titles "Acting Convention Chairman" and "Assistant Acting Convention Chairman" respectfully. They will also be available to State Legislatures to assist with their Legislative Calls and pre-Convention planning.

The Chairman and Vice Chairman of the PARENTAL RIGHTS AMENDMENT Committee will also be responsible for post-convention planning and organization if the Convention votes to send the PARENTAL RIGHTS AMENDMENT to Congress to be ratified by the States.

VOTING BY DELEGATES IN STATE DELEGATIONS

It is recommended that a simple majority of the Delegates within each State Delegation be required to decide a State Delegation's vote at the Convention. A quorum within each State Delegation will consist of one Delegate. The business of the Convention and voting will not be delayed if a State Delegation does not cast a vote during a roll call.

QUORUM REQUIRED FOR CONDUCTING BUSINESS AND VOTING AT THE CONVENTION

Each State Delegation will have one vote on all matters that are to be decided by the Convention. A simple majority vote by the State Delegations at the Convention is required to decide the outcome of all business brought before the Convention for a vote, including whether or not the PARENTAL RIGHTS AMENDMENT, as herein written, should be sent to the Several States, via Congress, for ratification. A quorum at the Convention for the purpose of conducting business and voting will consist of 17 State Delegations.

CLOSED DELIBERATIONS AT THE CONVENTION

The PARENTAL RIGHTS AMENDMENT Convention will be closed to all media and news groups. Only delegates appointed by their State Legislatures and the Chairman and Vice Chairman of the PARENTAL RIGHTS AMENDMENT Committee will be authorized to enter and speak at the Convention. No visitors, reporters, government officials, professionals or inquirers, of any kind, will be permitted to enter the Convention facilities. Unauthorized visitors will be escorted by the Sergeant of Arms out of the Convention. After the vote by the State Delegations is taken to determine if the PARENTAL RIGHTS AMENDMENT will be sent to the Several States, via Congress, for ratification, the Chairman of the Convention will call a special press conference to announce the Convention's decision. Within 30 days from the special press conference the Chairman will make available to the public the records kept by the Convention during its proceedings.

STATE LEGISLATURES NOT AUTHORIZING THIS CALL FOR THE PARENTAL RIGHTS AMENDMENT CONVENTION

State Legislatures that did not authorize this Call for the PARENTAL RIGHTS AMENDMENT Convention and yet agree to send delegates representing their State agree to follow the terms and/or conditions set forth in this Agreement and Legislative Call. They need to pay particular attention to the "Convention's Rules of Order" described in this Agreement and the prohibitions in the section titled "Prohibitions for Delegates, State Delegations and/or Convention Officials at the Convention". These non-calling States must notify the "Acting Convention Chairman" before the Convention convenes of their intention to attend the Convention so accommodations can be completed for their Delegations. In order to receive Convention Passes, all Delegates attending the Convention, will be required to sign an agreement promising to abide by the terms and/or conditions in this Legislative Call and Agreement.

NO WEAPONS ALLOWED AT THE CONVENTION

Delegates and PARENTAL RIGHTS AMENDMENT Committee officials will not be allowed to bring into the PARENTAL RIGHTS AMENDMENT Convention any weapons or objects that can be construed as weapons.

**PRESENTING ARGUMENTS AT THE CONVENTION
BY STATE DELEGATIONS**

Each State Delegation will be allotted a maximum of 60 minutes for presenting its argument(s) at the Convention for or against sending the PARENTAL RIGHTS AMENDMENT to the United States Congress with instruction for Congress to send the Amendment to the Several States for ratification. Only Delegates who have been officially selected by their State Legislatures and Ex-Officio members of the Convention are authorized to speak before the Convention. Each State Delegation can use one or more of its Delegates to present its position(s). However, the total time allotted for each State Delegation is 60 minutes, which includes any time that is necessary to replace one Delegate with another. The Chairman of the PARENTAL RIGHTS AMENDMENT Committee will also be limited to 60 minutes during his speaking segment. Speakers cannot reserve portions of their time to another time or day. Speakers must complete their arguments in the 60 minute segment assigned to them.

The order each State Delegation will follow when presenting their position(s) will be according to when each State completed its Legislative Call on Congress, or when it notified the "Acting Convention Chairman" that it intends to attend the Convention even though it may not complete a Legislative Call on Congress. The State Delegation presentations will be scheduled in the following manner: the first State making a Call on Congress will go first; the first State notifying the "Acting Convention Chairman" that it plans to attend will go second. The second State making a Call on Congress will go third; then the second State notifying the "Acting Convention Chairman" will go fourth, and so forth until all States wanting to present their positions have had an opportunity to do so. The Convention Chairman can rearrange the schedule if any conflicts arise at the Convention. The last speaker to be scheduled at the Convention for a 60 minute segment will be the Chairman of the PARENTAL RIGHTS AMENDMENT Committee.

DUTIES OF THE "ACTING CONVENTION CHAIRMAN"

The duties of the "Acting Convention Chairman include:

1. organize a pre-Convention support group for assisting Calling States with their Legislative Calls and non-calling States with their intentions to attend the Convention
2. set up an PARENTAL RIGHTS AMENDMENT Committee checking account
3. use generally accepted accounting principles when keeping records of all receipts and expenditures
4. provide financial reports and minutes of pre-convention activities as requested by States that are funding pre-convention operations
5. keep minutes of all business meetings of the PARENTAL RIGHTS AMENDMENT Committee
6. determine the budget that will be needed for pre-convention planning and organizing and notify each State Legislature of its share of the expenses
7. assist the Calling States and Attending States with their pre-convention planning
8. assist the Calling States with their Legislative Calls on Congress
9. after the PARENTAL RIGHTS AMENDMENT Convention has been convened call the Convention to order
10. invite nominations from the State Delegations present at the Convention to fill the "Convention Chairman's" position (the maximum number of nominees permitted is five and only one nominee from any one State Delegation is permitted)
11. take a roll call from the State Delegations for the nominee(s)
12. declare the winner based on the nominee who has received the most votes (a plurality of State Delegations). Each State Delegation will have one vote
13. officiate the installation of the "Convention Chairman" at the Convention by having the Chairman place his/her right hand on the Bible while repeating the following oath

"I solemnly promise to officiate the office of Convention Chairman for the PARENTAL RIGHTS AMENDMENT Convention according to the terms and/or conditions set forth in the Legislative Calls from the Several States to the best of my ability, so help me God".

In the event the "Acting Convention Chairman" is nominated and elected to the Convention Chairman position, the "Assistant Acting Convention Chairman" will conduct the installation ceremony for the Convention Chairman.

ELECTION, AUTHORITY AND DUTIES OF CONVENTION OFFICIALS

CONVENTION CHAIRMAN: - The "Convention Chairman" is the senior official at the PARENTAL RIGHTS AMENDMENT Convention. He/she will have the requisite authority to oversee all activities at the Convention, including the nomination and election of all officials. The Convention Chairman's duties include:

1. organize and oversee all business and activities at the Convention
2. organize and officiate all nominations, elections and installations of officials at the Convention (this will be the Convention Chairman's first order of business)
3. organize and officiate all nominations, elections and installations of official positions that may become vacant at the Convention
4. oversee the enforcement of all Convention Rules
5. oversee the enforcement of the terms and/or conditions (herein described) of this Call and Agreement by the States
6. oversee the investigation of alleged and/or actual violations of this Agreement as defined in the section titled "Violating this Agreement"
7. bring before the Convention all matters that require a vote
8. bring before the Convention the financial needs of the Convention and time lines for when these monies are needed
9. cut off motions or discussions by State Delegations before the Convention if and when it seems appropriate
10. recognize the Spokesman within a State Delegation for the purpose of addressing a matter of importance to the Spokesman's Delegation (the Convention Chairman will have full authority to determine if a matter brought before the Convention by the Spokesman is appropriate for further discussion and/or if a decision by the Convention is necessary)
11. keep the business of the Convention moving forward expeditiously, cutting off all motions and discussions when it appears one or more Delegates are trying to hinder, delay or stop the work of the Convention
12. keep the business of the Convention focused on one objective which is, should the Convention send the PARENTAL RIGHTS AMENDMENT to Congress instructing Congress to send it to the Several States for ratification?
13. instruct Convention Officials (Assistant Convention Chairman, Secretary, Financial Officer, Executive Administrator, Sergeant at Arms, and Deputies) on their duties at the Convention
14. officiate and remedy any and all problems that may develop at the Convention
15. oversee the design and production of "Official" Convention Badges for the Sergeant at Arms and Deputies
16. notify all State Legislatures of the decision the Convention made as to whether or not the PARENTAL RIGHTS AMENDMENT should be sent to Congress instructing Congress to send it to the States for ratification?
17. if the State Delegations voted to send the Amendment to the States for ratification, include the Convention's recommendation to the United

States Congress as to whether it should be ratified by State Conventions or State Legislatures

18. declare the PARENTAL RIGHTS AMENDMENT Convention closed after the State Delegations have decided if the PARENTAL RIGHTS AMENDMENT should be sent to Congress instructing Congress to send it to the States for ratification?

19. arrange a Special News Conference to announce the decision by the PARENTAL RIGHTS AMENDMENT Convention

20. make available the proceedings of the Convention to the public 30 days after the Convention is closed

The first order of business for the "Convention Chairman" will be to open the Convention to nominations from State Delegations present for each of the following Convention Officials; one Assistant Convention Chairman, one Secretary, one Financial Officer, one Executive Administrator, one Sergeant at Arms and ten Deputies (the maximum number of nominees permitted for each Convention Official position is five. Only one nominee for each Convention Official position is permitted from any one State Delegation. The nominee with a plurality of votes from the State Delegations will be the winner). The "Convention Chairman" can call for nominations for more than 10 Deputies if and when circumstances warrant.

ASSISTANT CONVENTION CHAIRMAN
The "Assistant Convention Chairman" duties include:

1. be amenable to the "Convention Chairman"
2. provide assistance to the "Convention Chairman" in all matters pertaining to the business of the Convention
3. monitor activities at the Convention and report to the "Convention Chairman" violations or possible violations of the terms and/or conditions of this Legislative Call and Agreement
4. perform the duties of the "Convention Chairman" when called upon by the Chairman or when the Chairman is unable to perform the duties of his/her office
5. the "Assistant Convention Chairman" will take the following oath, administered by the Convention Chairman, while placing his/her right hand on the Bible

"I solemnly promise to officiate the office of Assistant Convention Chairman for the PARENTAL RIGHTS AMENDMENT Convention according to the terms and/or conditions set forth in the Legislative Calls from the Several States to the best of my ability, so help me God".

SECRETARY

The "Secretary's" duties include:

1. keep official minutes of all proceedings at the Convention
2. monitor activities at the Convention and report to the Convention Chairman violations or possible violations of Convention Rules and of the terms and/or conditions of this Legislative Call and Agreement
3. make available to the "Convention Chairman", upon request, the official minutes of the Convention
4. be amenable to the "Convention Chairman" and "Assistant Convention Chairman"
5. in the absence of the "Convention Chairman" and the "Assistant Convention Chairman" due to death or a disablement that prevents them from performing the duties of their offices at the Convention, the Secretary shall call the Convention to order for the purpose of nominating and electing a new "Convention Chairman" and "Assistant Convention Chairman". In this capacity the Secretary will assume the duties and authority of the "Convention Chairman". If the Secretary is unable to perform the duties described herein, then they will fall to the Financial Officer.
6. the "Secretary" will take the following oath while placing his/her right hand on the Bible

    "I solemnly promise to officiate the office of Secretary for the PARENTAL RIGHTS AMENDMENT Convention according to the terms and/or conditions set forth in the Legislative Calls from the Several States to the best of my ability, so help me God".

FINANCIAL OFFICER - The "Financial Officer's" duties include:

1. keep detailed accounting records of all financial matters at the Convention using generally accepted accounting principles
2. be amenable to the "Convention Chairman" and "Assistant Convention Chairman"
3. monitor activities at the Convention and report to the Convention Chairman violations or possible violations of the terms and/or conditions of this Legislative Call and Agreement
4. set up a checking account in the name of the PARENTAL RIGHTS AMENDMENT Convention requiring any two of the following three officers when signing a check or making withdrawals – Convention Chairman, Assistant Convention Chairman, Financial Officer
5. make available to the "Convention Chairman", upon request, all financial records at the Convention
6. provide to the Convention Chairman the financial needs of the Convention and the time lines as to when these monies are needed

7. in the absence of a "Convention Chairman", "Assistant Convention Chairman", and "Secretary" due to death or a disablement that prevents them from performing the duties of their offices at the Convention, the Financial Officer shall call the Convention to order for the purpose of nominating and electing a new "Convention Chairman", "Assistant Convention Chairman", and "Secretary". In this capacity the Financial Officer will assume the duties and authority of the "Convention Chairman"

8. the "Financial Officer" will take the following oath while placing his/her right hand on the Bible

"I solemnly promise to officiate the office of Financial Officer for the PARENTAL RIGHTS AMENDMENT Convention according to generally accepted accounting principles and according to the terms and/or conditions set forth in the Legislative Calls from the Several States to the best of my ability, so help me God".

EXECUTIVE ADMINISTRATOR
The "Executive Administrator's" duties include:

1. facilitate all Convention business as directed by the Convention Chairman
2. be amenable to the Convention Chairman and Assistant Convention Chairman
3. monitor activities at the Convention and report to the Convention Chairman violations or possible violations of the terms and/or conditions of this Legislative Call and Agreement
4. keep detailed reports of all administrative activities at the Convention
5. make available to the "Convention Chairman" upon request all administrative records and/or reports at the Convention
6. the "Executive Administrator" will take the following oath while placing his/her right hand on the Bible

"I solemnly promise to officiate the office of Executive Administrator for the PARENTAL RIGHTS AMENDMENT Convention according to the terms and/or conditions set forth in the Legislative Calls from the Several States to the best of my ability, so help me God".

SERGEANT AT ARMS – The "Sergeant at Arms'" duties include:

1. be amenable to the Convention Chairman and Assistant Convention Chairman
2. monitor all activities at the Convention and report to the Convention Chairman violations or possible violations of the terms and/or conditions of this Legislative Call and Agreement
3. maintain order at the Convention

4. enforce all remedies for violations of this Legislative Call and Agreement as directed by the Convention Chairman
5. organize and direct the activities of all Deputies at the Convention
6. oversee, train and manage all Deputies at the Convention
7. the "Sergeant at Arms" will take the following oath while placing his/her right hand on the Bible

"I solemnly promise to officiate the office of Sergeant at Arms for the PARENTAL RIGHTS AMENDMENT Convention according to the terms and/or conditions set forth in the Legislative Calls from the Several States to the best of my ability, so help me God".

DEPUTIES – The "Deputies'" duties include:

1. be amenable to the Convention Chairman, Assistant Convention Chairman and Sergeant at Arms
2. monitor all activities at the Convention and report to the Sergeant at Arms violations or possible violations of the terms and/or conditions of this Legislative Call and Agreement
3. maintain order at the Convention as directed by the Sergeant at Arms
4. enforce all remedies for violations of this Legislative Call and Agreement as directed by the Convention Chairman and/or the Sergeant at Arms
5. "Deputies" will take the following oath while placing his/her right hand on the Bible

"I solemnly promise to officiate the office of Deputy for the PARENTAL RIGHTS AMENDMENT Convention according to the terms and/or conditions set forth in the Legislative Calls from the Several States to the best of my ability, so help me God".

CHALLENGING THE QUALIFICATIONS OF CONVENTION OFFICIALS

A State Delegation can challenge the qualifications of any Convention Official at the PARENTAL RIGHTS AMENDMENT Convention by bringing its allegation(s), during a business session, to the Convention floor. The Convention Chairman will consider the allegation(s) and determine if it merits further investigation. If the Chairman decides that the allegation(s) merits further investigation, he/she will direct the Sergeant at Arms to conduct the necessary inquiry. He/she will then follow the instructions outlined in the section "Violating this Agreement" for proscribing a remedy or remedies.

The "Convention Chairman" can also reject a challenge to the qualifications of any Convention Official if he/she concludes that the Delegate making the allegation(s) is trying to disrupt and/or delay Convention business. If after following the instructions outlined in "Violating this Agreement" the Delegate is found to have made a false accusation against a Convention Official, the Delegate's State Delegation will be charged with a violation of the terms and/or conditions of this Call and Agreement.

PROHIBITIONS FOR STATE DELEGATES, STATE DELEGATIONS AND CONVENTION OFFICIALS AT THE CONVENTION

State Delegates, State Delegations and Convention Officials are prohibited from violating any of the following Convention prohibitions:

1. State Delegates, State Delegations and Convention Officials are prohibited, at the Convention, from introducing, discussing, voting on, or sending to the States for consideration and/or ratification any amendment to the United States Constitution other than the PARENTAL RIGHTS AMENDMENT, as herein written
2. State Delegates, State Delegations and Convention Officials are prohibited from altering or changing, in any way (which includes the wording, spelling, punctuation, or paragraph sections), the PARENTAL RIGHTS AMENDMENT from the written form shown in the section titled **"The full text of the PARENTAL RIGHTS AMENDMENT"**
3. State Delegates, State Delegations and Convention Officials are prohibited, at the Convention, from introducing, discussing, voting on, or sending to the States for consideration and/or ratification any alternate form of government for the United States of America
4. State Delegates, State Delegations and Convention Officials are prohibited, at the Convention, from introducing, discussing, voting on, or sending to the States for consideration and/or ratification any alternate constitution or governing document for the United States of America
5. State Delegates, State Delegations and Convention Officials are prohibited, at the Convention, from introducing, discussing, voting on, or sending to the States for consideration and/or ratification any changes, of any kind, to the existing Constitution of the United States of America other than the PARENTAL RIGHTS AMENDMENT
6. State Delegates, State Delegations and Convention Officials are prohibited, at the Convention, from introducing, discussing, voting on, or sending to the States for consideration any changes, of any kind, to this binding Agreement between the States Calling for the PARENTAL RIGHTS AMENDMENT Convention State Delegates, State

   Delegations and Convention Officials are prohibited, at the Convention, from introducing, discussing, voting on, or sending to the States for consideration and/or ratification any subject matter, issue or topic (of any kind) other than the proposed PARENTAL RIGHTS

AMENDMENT in its written form shown in the section titled "The full text of the PARENTAL RIGHTS AMENDMENT"

THE DATE, TIME, DURATION AND PLACE OF THE PARENTAL RIGHTS AMENDMENT CONVENTION.

The United States Congress will be responsible for determining and announcing to the Several States the date, time, and place that the PARENTAL RIGHTS AMENDMENT Convention is to convene immediately after two thirds of the States, under the authority given to the States in Article V of the United States Constitution, have completed their Calls on Congress to convene the PARENTAL RIGHTS AMENDMENT Convention. The Convention is expected to complete its business by the 180th day after convening. The Convention Chairman can extend the duration of the PARENTAL RIGHTS AMENDMENT Convention for one additional 180 day period. The maximum number of days the Convention is authorized to be in session are 360 days. If the Convention has not decided if the PARENTAL RIGHTS AMENDMENT should be sent to Congress with instructions to send the Amendment to the Several States for ratification by the end of 360 days, then the Call for the PARENTAL RIGHTS AMENDMENT Convention, which was approved by the Several States under the authority granted in Article V of the United States Constitution and this agreement, will be automatically withdrawn by the Calling States and the Convention will automatically terminate at 5:00 P.M. Eastern Standard Time on the 360th day after convening. Termination of the PARENTAL RIGHTS AMENDMENT Convention will automatically occur on the 360th day after convening the Convention, without requiring a formal notice by the States to the Convention, nor by the States to the United States Congress, nor by the Convention to the States, nor by the Convention to the United States Congress, although it is recommended that the Convention notify the United States Congress and the State Legislatures of its termination as a courtesy.

Under no circumstance(s) are the Delegates at the PARENTAL RIGHTS AMENDMENT Convention authorized to re-convene a new or different Convention, no matter what their purpose or intent. The official Legislative Call and authority granted by the Several States and the subsequent convening of the PARENTAL RIGHTS AMENDMENT Convention by Congress will be automatically invalidated and the Convention will be abolished at 5:00 P.M. Eastern Standard Time on the 360th day after the convening of the PARENTAL RIGHTS AMENDMENT Convention.

VIOLATING THIS AGREEMENT
The Convention Chairman (or in the absence of the Convention Chairman the Assistant Convention Chairman) will handle allegations of a violation(s) or actual violation(s) of the terms and/or conditions of this binding Agreement

between the Several States, by any one or more Delegate(s) and/or Convention Official(s), as follows:

1. When an alleged violation has been presented to the Convention Chairman, and if the Chairman decides that the allegation(s) merits further investigation, he/she will instruct the Sergeant at Arms to conduct the necessary inquiry.

2. After the inquiry has been completed, and assuming the Convention Chairman concludes that the evidence does not substantiate further review by the Convention, the allegation(s) will be dismissed by the Chairman and the Convention will go forward with its business.

3. If however, after the inquiry has been completed, the Convention Chairman concludes that the evidence does substantiate further review by the Convention, the Chairman will present the allegation(s) and findings of the inquiry to the Convention for a discussion and vote. If a majority of the State Delegations (one vote per State Delegation) decide that no violation of the terms and/or conditions of this Legislative Call and Agreement has occurred, then the Chairman will declare that the alleged violation(s) of the terms and/or conditions of this Legislative Call and Agreement is/are dismissed. The Convention will then go forward with its business.

4. If however, after the inquiry has been completed, the Convention Chairman concludes that the evidence does substantiate further review by the Convention, the Chairman will present the allegation(s) and findings of the inquiry to the Convention for a discussion and vote. If a majority of the State Delegations (one vote per State Delegation) decide that one or more violation(s) of the terms and/or conditions of this Legislative Call and Agreement has/have occurred, then the Chairman will declare to the Convention that the Delegate(s) responsible for the violation(s), and their State Delegation(s), has/have been charged with "Violating this Agreement". The Convention will then go forward with its business.

5. If a State Delegation is charged with two violations of the terms and/or conditions of this Legislative Call and Agreement, the Convention Chairman will declare to the Convention that the State Delegation charged with violating this Agreement a second time has no further standing or authority at the Convention. The Chairman will notify the charged State Delegation that its entire delegation of Delegates must leave the Convention immediately and they will not be allowed back into the Convention. The Chairman will instruct the Sergeant at Arms that he should escort the charged State Delegation out of the Convention. The Convention Chairman will then notify the State

Legislature that sent the charged State Delegation of the actions that the Convention has taken and inform them that they can send a replacement State Delegation to the Convention as long as they do not disrupt the proceedings of the Convention. None of the original Delegates who were charged by the Convention will be allowed back into the Convention as part of a replacement delegation.

6. The Convention Chairman will not allow unreasonable delays in the proceedings of the Convention due to disruptive Delegates or State Delegations. He/she will move the business of the Convention forward expeditiously.

THE FULL TEXT OF THE PARENTAL RIGHTS AMENDMENT

The full text of the PARENTAL RIGHTS AMENDMENT to be submitted to the Several States by the United States Congress for ratification shall read as follows:

PARENTAL RIGHTS AMENDMENT
ARTICLE 28 (or alternate number to be assigned by Congress)

Section 1. It is the right of every citizen to train up their children according to their conscience, faith and capabilities without interference from the State. The rights of parents and legal guardians to choose how they will raise their children are foundational to a free people.

Section 2. Parental Rights consists of the responsible exercise of parental authority over their children for their children's instruction, welfare, discipline, education and training. Parental Rights also include the authority to discipline their children with reasonable corporal punishment for the purpose of correcting wrong behavior and to instill in their children good morals and good values that properly respect the rights of others and that foster respect for America's unique heritage and history.

Section 3. This Article does not prevent Local, State and Federal authorities from enforcing reasonable laws that are for the protection and welfare of the American people.

RATIFICATION OF THE "PARENTAL RIGHTS AMENDMENT"

Under the requirements of Article V of the United States Constitution and also under Article IV, Section 4 which guarantees to every State a Republican form of Government, the PARENTAL RIGHTS AMENDMENT will become a ratified Amendment to the United States Constitution when three quarters of the Several States complete their ratifications of the Amendment.

"CONGRESSIONAL" OPTION

If the United States Congress voluntarily sends the PARENTAL RIGHTS AMENDMENT to the Several States for ratification without making any changes, of any kind (which includes the wording, spelling, punctuation and paragraph sections) in the proposed Amendment as herein written, and before two thirds of the States complete their Call for Congress to convene the PARENTAL RIGHTS AMENDMENT Convention, then the Legislature of the State of FLORIDA will withdraw its Call for the PARENTAL RIGHTS AMENDMENT Convention.

OFFICIAL AGREEMENT BY THE FLORIDA STATE LEGISLATURE BETWEEN ITSELF AND THE CALLING STATES

The Legislature of the State of FLORIDA enters into this binding Agreement with every other State Legislature that likewise agrees to the terms and/or conditions of this Legislative Call and Agreement as set forth herein. This is an irrevocable contract, during the term of this Agreement, between the State of FLORIDA and each and every State that signs this Agreement and completes its Call on the United States Congress directing Congress to convene a Federal Convention titled the PARENTAL RIGHTS AMENDMENT Convention. The Legislature of the State of FLORIDA agrees that it, and its delegates who are selected to attend the Convention, will abide by the purpose, terms, conditions, agenda, and "Convention Rules of Order" as explained in this Agreement.

The Legislature of the State of FLORIDA enters into this Agreement with every other State Legislature that likewise agrees to the terms and/or conditions of this Agreement and Legislative Call as set forth herein, understanding that the PARENTAL RIGHTS AMENDMENT Convention, by definition herein explained, is a "SINGLE ISSUE" Federal Convention and that the Convention will have no authority, under this Call and Agreement between the States, to review and/or consider any other subject matter, issue, or topic during its sessions other than business matters relating to the question, should the PARENTAL RIGHTS AMENDMENT, as herein written, be sent by the Convention to the United States Congress instructing Congress to send the Amendment to the Several States for ratification? The Legislature of the State of FLORIDA

irrevocably declares by signing this Agreement that any subject matter, issue or topic (other than the PARENTAL RIGHTS AMENDMENT) that delegates might try to present to the Convention and subsequently to the States for review and/or ratification will be immediately, upon introduction at the Convention, unauthorized, invalid and automatically rejected by the Legislature of the State of FLORIDA, and the Legislature of the State of FLORIDA irrevocably declares that it will not review and/or consider for ratification any such subject matter, issue or topic, no matter how presented to it by the Convention. Only the PARENTAL RIGHTS AMENDMENT, as herein written, will be considered by the Legislature of the State of FLORIDA for ratification.

The Legislature of the State of FLORIDA also irrevocably declares that under no circumstance(s) will it consider for review and/or ratification any amendment to the United States Constitution, submitted to it by the PARENTAL RIGHTS AMENDMENT Convention other than the PARENTAL RIGHTS AMENDMENT as herein written.

The Legislature of the State of FLORIDA further irrevocably declares that under no circumstance(s) will it consider for review and/or ratification any modified form of the PARENTAL RIGHTS AMENDMENT submitted to it by the PARENTAL RIGHTS AMENDMENT Convention that would change, alter, or replace, in any way (which includes the wording, spelling, punctuation, or paragraph sections), the PARENTAL RIGHTS AMENDMENT from its written form herein.

The Legislature of the State of FLORIDA further irrevocably declares that under no circumstance(s) will it consider for review and/or ratification any proposal, of any kind, sent to it by the PARENTAL RIGHTS AMENDMENT Convention that would change, replace, or alter the United States Constitution other than the PARENTAL RIGHTS AMENDMENT as herein written.

The Legislature of the State of FLORIDA further irrevocably declares that under no circumstance(s) will it consider for review any proposal, of any kind, sent to it by the PARENTAL RIGHTS AMENDMENT Convention that would change, replace, or alter, in any way (which includes the wording, spelling, punctuation and section paragraphs), this Official Legislative Call for the PARENTAL RIGHTS AMENDMENT Convention and the terms and/or conditions of this Agreement between the States as herein written.

Under the authority reserved to the State of FLORIDA in Article V of the United States Constitution and also under Article IV, Section 4 which guarantees to every State a Republican form of Government, the Legislature of the State of FLORIDA hereby approves this Legislative Call on the United States Congress directing Congress to convene the PARENTAL RIGHTS AMENDMENT Convention and binds itself with each and every State that likewise approves this identical Legislative Call according the terms and/or conditions set forth in this Agreement.

OFFICIAL CALL BY THE STATE OF FLORIDA ON THE UNITED STATES CONGRESS DIRECTING CONGRESS TO CONVENE THE PARENTAL RIGHTS AMENDMENT CONVENTION

The Legislature of the State of FLORIDA hereby Calls on the United States Congress directing Congress to convene a Federal Convention to be titled the PARENTAL RIGHTS AMENDMENT Convention. The Convention is to be convened immediately after two thirds of the Several States have completed their Calls for the PARENTAL RIGHTS AMENDMENT Convention.

The State of FLORIDA is authorized to make this Call for the PARENTAL RIGHTS AMENDMENT Convention under the authority reserved to the States in Article V of the United States Constitution and under Article IV, Section 4 which guarantees to every State a Republican form of Government. Both Articles give to each State an equal standing when calling for a Constitutional Convention. Article V and Article IV, Section 4 reserves to the Several States the right to Call for a Federal Convention for the purpose of amending the United States Constitution when Congress and/or the Courts refuse to address an egregious wrong suffered by the people.

Submitted to Both Houses of the United States Congress on this date _____, _____ by the Legislature of the State of FLORIDA.

State of FLORIDA Seal:

Authorized Signatures with titles:

_____Title_____

_____Title_____

_____Title_____

_____Title_____

_____Title_____

RECLAIMING AMERICA

CHAPTER 18

FREE MARKETS AMENDMENT

Text of proposed
FREE MARKETS AMENDMENT
ARTICLE 28 (or alternate number to be assigned by Congress)

Section 1. It is the right of citizens to enjoy the pursuit of happiness in an economy that is governed by free market principles. This is foundational to a free people and must not be violated by the State.

Section 2. To secure the rights of citizens it is prohibited for any branch or agency of government, to prevent the free exercise of free market principles in the nation's economy. It is further prohibited for the government to impose on individuals or companies unreasonable regulations that prohibit the free exercise of an open market economy. These prohibitions do not prevent the government from restricting, regulating or stopping unfair trade practices of foreign governments, foreign companies or foreign individuals. The government can also restrict or prevent ownership in American companies or American assets by foreign governments, foreign companies or foreign individuals. The provisions of this Article are enforceable within the United States which shall include the Several States, the District of Columbia, and the Commonwealth of Puerto Rico, the Commonwealth of the Northern Mariana Islands and the territories and possessions of the United States.

Section 3. Congress shall have the power to enforce by appropriate legislation, the provisions of the Article.

Wealth building is essential for a Free Market Economy to prosper. As the value of American industries increase, so does America's tax revenue. For an example of how wealth building works, assume that a small retail company does $10,000,000 in annual sales and has received a grant of $100,000 to grow its business. The $100,000 could actually come from many sources including stock holders. Every business must turn its inventory or saleable services over periodically. Most retail business try to turn their inventories over every 90 days. If a retailer invests its $100,000 on January 1st, at the end of 90 days the retailer would have its $100,000 back with an additional amount coming from planned growth. We will assume for this analysis that at the end of 90 days the retailer has $200,000 from sales and services. This same retailer will take the $200,000 and repeat the business cycle so that in 180 days it has $400,000. By the end of the year, the $100,000 has grown into $1,600,000 which represents an annual growth of 13.7% of the company's annual sales.   Throughout the year this retailer will hire new people who pay their own taxes. It will also pay taxes on the $1,600,000 it has generated.   This is a win win scenario for the government, employees and the retailer. Only Free Markets allow businesses to grow based on potential market conditions. You cannot borrow and spend your way into prosperity.

There is a separate benefit that can come from the above scenario. As the company grows it generates excitement in the economy, which transfers to consumers and in turn consumer confidence increases.   Consumers in turn are encouraged to buy more of the retailer's products and services.

Free Market Economies create healthy government treasuries which in turn reduce State and Federal debt.

America has historically been a Free Market Economy and the envy of the world.   For many decades, however, we have allowed socialists, liberals, environmentalists, progressives, communists, etc. to undermine our most important Capitalist principle – multipli-cation by division (this is also God's first principle in nature and economies – "...be fruitful and multiply...").   Wealth building is not an evil strategy and the environment does not have to be sacrificed when practicing it.   It is not an either/or alternative. We can once again have a robust, wealth building economy while protecting wildlife and the environment at the same time.   The Free Markets Amendment will restore America's free markets and growth in the economy.   America can once again be the economic engine of the world.

CHAPTER 19

ENERGY AMENDMENT

Text of proposed
ENERGY AMENDMENT
ARTICLE 28 (or alternate number to be assigned by Congress)

Section 1. It is the right of citizens to enjoy the full use of America's natural resources for the betterment of their society and personal pursuits. This right is foundational to a free people and must not be violated by the State.

Section 2. To secure the rights of citizens to fully enjoy America's natural resources, it is hereby prohibited for any individual, group, organization or government to restrict or interfere with the exploration, development or full utilization of America's natural resources which include, but are not limited to, crude oil, natural gas, coal, nuclear, solar, wind, water and any other natural resource that can be utilized or in the future will be utilized to meet America's energy needs. It is further prohibited for the government to impose on individuals or companies unreasonable regulations that prohibit the free development of natural energy resources. The provisions of this Article are enforceable within the United States which shall include the Several States, the District of Columbia, and the Commonwealth of Puerto Rico, the Commonwealth of the Northern Mariana Islands and the territories and possessions of the United States.

Section 3. Congress shall have the power to enforce by appropriate legislation, the provisions of the Article.

America's economy has been crippled over the last 40 years by environmentalist who have through advocacy organizations installed State and Congressional legislation that has foolishly prevented the development of America's natural energy resources. For over 30 years energy and power companies have been prevented from building nuclear facilities, utilize one of America's most abundant resources coal, explore, extract and refine crude oil and natural gas, etc. This ill conceived regulatory environment has crippled our national economy and forced us to buy, at inflated prices, energy resources from other countries.

There is a proper balance that can protect our environment and wildlife while producing essential energy to energize America's industries.

The Energy Amendment will allow American companies to supply American industry economical energy that will cause the national economy to soar.

CHAPTER 20

AMERICAN SOVEREIGNTY AMENDMENT

Text of proposed
AMERICAN SOVEREIGNTY AMENDMENT
ARTICLE 28 (or alternate number to be assigned by Congress)

Section 1. America's constitutional history and historical experience is unique among nations and revered by the American people. It is the right of citizens to require their government to retain its sovereignty among nations.

Section 2. To secure the rights of citizens it is prohibited to pass any law, enact any regulation or adjudicate any matter that would diminish, in any way, the authority the United States has to govern itself as an independent and sovereign nation. The provisions of this Article are enforceable within the United States which shall include the Several States, the District of Columbia, and the Commonwealth of Puerto Rico, the Commonwealth of the Northern Mariana Islands and the territories and possessions of the United States.

Section 3. Congress shall have the power to enforce by appropriate legislation, the provisions of the Article.

There are many backdoor ways to abdicate American sovereignty. United States sovereignty can be abdicated through United Nations agreements, NATO agreements, flawed immigration policies, international agreements between nations, Federal judicial decisions, Congressional legislation, etc. It is imperative that the United States Constitution remain the final authority for American government. It must never to compromised to foreign governments, international courts, United Nations, NATO, agreements between nations, international commerce agreements, etc. The American Sovereignty Amendment will safeguard our nations sovereignty by assuring that our Constitution is always the foundation of government's authority.

RECLAIMING AMERICA

CHAPTER 21

AMENDMENTS BEING CONSIDERED

- **RESTORING THE 2ND AMENDMENT**
- **HEALTH CARE CHOICE AMENDMENT**
- **STATES RIGHTS AMENDMENT**
- **PRAYER IN AMERICA AMENDMENT**
- **TERM LIMITS AMENDMENT**
- **POL.ITICAL CORRECTNESS AMENDMENT**

The reader can keep abreast of developments by going to http://CitizenInitiatives.org. CITIZEN INITIATIVES welcomes ideas and comments from its readers.

RECLAIMING AMERICA

CHAPTER 22

UNITED STATES CONSTITUTION

We the People of the United States, in Order to form a more perfect Union, establish Justice, insure domestic Tranquility, provide for the common defence, promote the general Welfare, and secure the Blessings of Liberty to ourselves and our Posterity, do ordain and establish this Constitution for the United States of America.

Article. I.

Section. 1. All legislative Powers herein granted shall be vested in a Congress of the United States, which shall consist of a Senate and House of Representatives.

Section. 2. The House of Representatives shall be composed of Members chosen every second Year by the People of the several States, and the Electors in each State shall have the Qualifications requisite for Electors of the most numerous Branch of the State Legislature.

No Person shall be a Representative who shall not have attained to the Age of twenty five Years, and been seven Years a Citizen of the United States, and who shall not, when elected, be an Inhabitant of that State in which he shall be chosen.

Representatives and direct Taxes shall be apportioned among the several States which may be included within this Union, according to their respective Numbers, which shall be determined by adding to the whole Number of free Persons, including those bound to Service for a Term of Years, and excluding Indians not taxed, three fifths of all other Persons [Modified by Amendment XIV]. The actual Enumeration shall be made within three Years after the first Meeting of the Congress of the United States, and within every subsequent Term of ten Years, in such Manner as they shall by Law direct. The Number of Representatives shall not exceed one for every thirty Thousand, but each State shall have at Least one Representative; and until such enumeration shall be made, the State of New Hampshire shall be entitled to chuse three, Massachusetts eight, Rhode-Island and Providence Plantations one, Connecticut five, New-York six, New Jersey four, Pennsylvania eight, Delaware one, Maryland six, Virginia ten, North Carolina five, South Carolina five, and Georgia three.

When vacancies happen in the Representation from any State, the Executive Authority thereof shall issue Writs of Election to fill such Vacancies.

The House of Representatives shall chuse their Speaker and other Officers; and shall have the sole Power of Impeachment.

Section. 3. The Senate of the United States shall be composed of two Senators from each State, chosen by the Legislature thereof [Modified by Amendment XVII], for six Years; and each Senator shall have one Vote.

Immediately after they shall be assembled in Consequence of the first Election, they shall be divided as equally as may be into three Classes. The Seats of the Senators of the first Class shall be vacated at the Expiration of the second Year, of the second Class at the Expiration of the fourth Year, and of the third Class at the Expiration of the sixth Year, so that one third may be chosen every second Year; and if Vacancies happen by Resignation, or otherwise, during the Recess of the Legislature of any State, the Executive thereof may make temporary Appointments until the next Meeting of the Legislature, which shall then fill such Vacancies [Modified by Amendment XVII].

No Person shall be a Senator who shall not have attained to the Age of thirty Years, and been nine Years a Citizen of the United States, and who shall not, when elected, be an Inhabitant of that State for which he shall be chosen.

The Vice President of the United States shall be President of the Senate, but shall have no Vote, unless they be equally divided.

The Senate shall chuse their other Officers, and also a President pro tempore, in the Absence of the Vice President, or when he shall exercise the Office of President of the United States.

The Senate shall have the sole Power to try all Impeachments. When sitting for that Purpose, they shall be on Oath or Affirmation. When the President of the United States is tried, the Chief Justice shall preside: And no Person shall be convicted without the Concurrence of two thirds of the Members present.

Judgment in Cases of Impeachment shall not extend further than to removal from Office, and disqualification to hold and enjoy any Office of honor, Trust or Profit under the United States: but the Party convicted shall nevertheless be liable and subject to Indictment, Trial, Judgment and Punishment, according to Law.

Section. 4. The Times, Places and Manner of holding Elections for Senators and Representatives, shall be prescribed in each State by the Legislature thereof; but the Congress may at any time by Law make or alter such Regulations, except as to the Places of chusing Senators.

The Congress shall assemble at least once in every Year, and such Meeting shall be on the first Monday in December [Modified by Amendment XX], unless they shall by Law appoint a different Day.

Section. 5. Each House shall be the Judge of the Elections, Returns and Qualifications of its own Members, and a Majority of each shall constitute a Quorum to do

Business; but a smaller Number may adjourn from day to day, and may be authorized to compel the Attendance of absent Members, in such Manner, and under such Penalties as each House may provide.

Each House may determine the Rules of its Proceedings, punish its Members for disorderly Behaviour, and, with the Concurrence of two thirds, expel a Member.

Each House shall keep a Journal of its Proceedings, and from time to time publish the same, excepting such Parts as may in their Judgment require Secrecy; and the Yeas and Nays of the Members of either House on any question shall, at the Desire of one fifth of those Present, be entered on the Journal.

Neither House, during the Session of Congress, shall, without the Consent of the other, adjourn for more than three days, nor to any other Place than that in which the two Houses shall be sitting.

Section. 6. The Senators and Representatives shall receive a Compensation for their Services, to be ascertained by Law, and paid out of the Treasury of the United States. They shall in all Cases, except Treason, Felony and Breach of the Peace, be privileged from Arrest during their Attendance at the Session of their respective Houses, and in going to and returning from the same; and for any Speech or Debate in either House, they shall not be questioned in any other Place.

No Senator or Representative shall, during the Time for which he was elected, be appointed to any civil Office under the Authority of the United States, which shall have been created, or the Emoluments whereof shall have been encreased during such time; and no Person holding any Office under the United States, shall be a Member of either House during his Continuance in Office.

Section. 7. All Bills for raising Revenue shall originate in the House of Representatives; but the Senate may propose or concur with Amendments as on other Bills.

Every Bill which shall have passed the House of Representatives and the Senate, shall, before it become a Law, be presented to the President of the United States: If he approve he shall sign it, but if not he shall return it, with his Objections to that House in which it shall have originated, who shall enter the Objections at large on their Journal, and proceed to reconsider it. If after such Reconsideration two thirds of that House shall agree to pass the Bill, it shall be sent, together with the Objections, to the other House, by which it shall likewise be reconsidered, and if approved by two thirds of that House, it shall become a Law. But in all such Cases the Votes of both Houses shall be determined by yeas and Nays, and the Names of the Persons voting for and against the Bill shall be entered on the Journal of each House respectively. If any Bill shall not be returned by the President within ten Days (Sundays excepted) after it shall have been presented to him, the Same shall be a Law, in like Manner as if he had signed it, unless the Congress by their Adjournment prevent its Return, in which Case it shall not be a Law.

Every Order, Resolution, or Vote to which the Concurrence of the Senate and House of Representatives may be necessary (except on a question of Adjournment) shall be presented to the President of the United States; and before the Same shall take

Effect, shall be approved by him, or being disapproved by him, shall be repassed by two thirds of the Senate and House of Representatives, according to the Rules and Limitations prescribed in the Case of a Bill.

Section. 8. The Congress shall have Power To lay and collect Taxes, Duties, Imposts and Excises, to pay the Debts and provide for the common Defence and general Welfare of the United States; but all Duties, Imposts and Excises shall be uniform throughout the United States;

To borrow Money on the credit of the United States;

To regulate Commerce with foreign Nations, and among the several States, and with the Indian Tribes;

To establish an uniform Rule of Naturalization, and uniform Laws on the subject of Bankruptcies throughout the United States;

To coin Money, regulate the Value thereof, and of foreign Coin, and fix the Standard of Weights and Measures;

To provide for the Punishment of counterfeiting the Securities and current Coin of the United States;

To establish Post Offices and post Roads;

To promote the Progress of Science and useful Arts, by securing for limited Times to Authors and Inventors the exclusive Right to their respective Writings and Discoveries;

To constitute Tribunals inferior to the Supreme Court;

To define and punish Piracies and Felonies committed on the high Seas, and Offences against the Law of Nations;

To declare War, grant Letters of Marque and Reprisal, and make Rules concerning Captures on Land and Water;

To raise and support Armies, but no Appropriation of Money to that Use shall be for a longer Term than two Years;

To provide and maintain a Navy;

To make Rules for the Government and Regulation of the land and naval Forces;

To provide for calling forth the Militia to execute the Laws of the Union, suppress Insurrections and repel Invasions;

To provide for organizing, arming, and disciplining, the Militia, and for governing such Part of them as may be employed in the Service of the United States, reserving to the States respectively, the Appointment of the Officers, and the Authority of training the Militia according to the discipline prescribed by Congress;

To exercise exclusive Legislation in all Cases whatsoever, over such District (not exceeding ten Miles square) as may, by Cession of particular States, and the Acceptance of Congress, become the Seat of the Government of the United States, and to exercise like Authority over all Places purchased by the Consent of the Legislature of the State in which the Same shall be, for the Erection of Forts, Magazines, Arsenals, dock-Yards, and other needful Buildings;--And

To make all Laws which shall be necessary and proper for carrying into Execution the foregoing Powers, and all other Powers vested by this Constitution in the Government of the United States, or in any Department or Officer thereof.

Section. 9. The Migration or Importation of such Persons as any of the States now existing shall think proper to admit, shall not be prohibited by the Congress prior to the Year one thousand eight hundred and eight, but a Tax or duty may be imposed on such Importation, not exceeding ten dollars for each Person.

The Privilege of the Writ of Habeas Corpus shall not be suspended, unless when in Cases of Rebellion or Invasion the public Safety may require it.

No Bill of Attainder or ex post facto Law shall be passed.

No Capitation, or other direct, Tax shall be laid, unless in Proportion to the Census or Enumeration herein before directed to be taken.

No Tax or Duty shall be laid on Articles exported from any State.
No Preference shall be given by any Regulation of Commerce or Revenue to the Ports of one State over those of another; nor shall Vessels bound to, or from, one State, be obliged to enter, clear, or pay Duties in another.

No Money shall be drawn from the Treasury, but in Consequence of Appropriations made by Law; and a regular Statement and Account of the Receipts and Expenditures of all public Money shall be published from time to time.

No Title of Nobility shall be granted by the United States: And no Person holding any Office of Profit or Trust under them, shall, without the Consent of the Congress, accept of any present, Emolument, Office, or Title, of any kind whatever, from any King, Prince, or foreign State.

Section. 10. No State shall enter into any Treaty, Alliance, or Confederation; grant Letters of Marque and Reprisal; coin Money; emit Bills of Credit; make any Thing but gold and silver Coin a Tender in Payment of Debts; pass any Bill of Attainder, ex post facto Law, or Law impairing the Obligation of Contracts, or grant any Title of Nobility.

No State shall, without the Consent of the Congress, lay any Imposts or Duties on Imports or Exports, except what may be absolutely necessary for executing it's inspection Laws; and the net Produce of all Duties and Imposts, laid by any State on

Imports or Exports, shall be for the Use of the Treasury of the United States; and all such Laws shall be subject to the Revision and Controul of the Congress.

No State shall, without the Consent of Congress, lay any Duty of Tonnage, keep Troops, or Ships of War in time of Peace, enter into any Agreement or Compact with another State, or with a foreign Power, or engage in War, unless actually invaded, or in such imminent Danger as will not admit of delay.

Article. II.

Section. 1. The executive Power shall be vested in a President of the United States of America. He shall hold his Office during the Term of four Years, and, together with the Vice President, chosen for the same Term, be elected, as follows:

Each State shall appoint, in such Manner as the Legislature thereof may direct, a Number of Electors, equal to the whole Number of Senators and Representatives to which the State may be entitled in the Congress: but no Senator or Representative, or Person holding an Office of Trust or Profit under the United States, shall be appointed an Elector.

The Electors shall meet in their respective States, and vote by Ballot for two Persons, of whom one at least shall not be an Inhabitant of the same State with themselves. And they shall make a List of all the Persons voted for, and of the Number of Votes for each; which List they shall sign and certify, and transmit sealed to the Seat of the Government of the United States, directed to the President of the Senate. The President of the Senate shall, in the Presence of the Senate and House of Representatives, open all the Certificates, and the Votes shall then be counted. The Person having the greatest Number of Votes shall be the President, if such Number be a Majority of the whole Number of Electors appointed; and if there be more than one who have such Majority, and have an equal Number of Votes, then the House of Representatives shall immediately chuse by Ballot one of them for President; and if no Person have a Majority, then from the five highest on the List the said House shall in like Manner chuse the President. But in chusing the President, the Votes shall be taken by States, the Representation from each State having one Vote; a quorum for this Purpose shall consist of a Member or Members from two thirds of the States, and a Majority of all the States shall be necessary to a Choice. In every Case, after the Choice of the President, the Person having the greatest Number of Votes of the Electors shall be the Vice President. But if there should remain two or more who have equal Votes, the Senate shall chuse from them by Ballot the Vice President [Modified by Amendment XII].

The Congress may determine the Time of chusing the Electors, and the Day on which they shall give their Votes; which Day shall be the same throughout the United States.

No Person except a natural born Citizen, or a Citizen of the United States, at the time of the Adoption of this Constitution, shall be eligible to the Office of President; neither shall any Person be eligible to that Office who shall not have attained to the Age of thirty five Years, and been fourteen Years a Resident within the United States.

In Case of the Removal of the President from Office, or of his Death, Resignation, or Inability to discharge the Powers and Duties of the said Office, the Same shall devolve on the Vice President, and the Congress may by Law provide for the Case of Removal, Death, Resignation or Inability, both of the President and Vice President, declaring what Officer shall then act as President, and such Officer shall act accordingly, until the Disability be removed, or a President shall be elected [Modified by Amendment XXV].

The President shall, at stated Times, receive for his Services, a Compensation, which shall neither be increased nor diminished during the Period for which he shall have been elected, and he shall not receive within that Period any other Emolument from the United States, or any of them.

Before he enter on the Execution of his Office, he shall take the following Oath or Affirmation:--"I do solemnly swear (or affirm) that I will faithfully execute the Office of President of the United States, and will to the best of my Ability, preserve, protect and defend the Constitution of the United States."

Section. 2. The President shall be Commander in Chief of the Army and Navy of the United States, and of the Militia of the several States, when called into the actual Service of the United States; he may require the Opinion, in writing, of the principal Officer in each of the executive Departments, upon any Subject relating to the Duties of their respective Offices, and he shall have Power to grant Reprieves and Pardons for Offences against the United States, except in Cases of Impeachment.

He shall have Power, by and with the Advice and Consent of the Senate, to make Treaties, provided two thirds of the Senators present concur; and he shall nominate, and by and with the Advice and Consent of the Senate, shall appoint Ambassadors, other public Ministers and Consuls, Judges of the supreme Court, and all other Officers of the United States, whose Appointments are not herein otherwise provided for, and which shall be established by Law: but the Congress may by Law vest the Appointment of such inferior Officers, as they think proper, in the President alone, in the Courts of Law, or in the Heads of Departments.

The President shall have Power to fill up all Vacancies that may happen during the Recess of the Senate, by granting Commissions which shall expire at the End of their next Session.

Section. 3. He shall from time to time give to the Congress Information of the State of the Union, and recommend to their Consideration such Measures as he shall judge necessary and expedient; he may, on extraordinary Occasions, convene both Houses, or either of them, and in Case of Disagreement between them, with Respect to the Time of Adjournment, he may adjourn them to such Time as he shall think proper; he shall receive Ambassadors and other public Ministers; he shall take Care that the Laws be faithfully executed, and shall Commission all the Officers of the United States.

Section. 4. The President, Vice President and all civil Officers of the United States, shall be removed from Office on Impeachment for, and Conviction of, Treason, Bribery, or other high Crimes and Misdemeanors.

Article. III.

Section. 1. The judicial Power of the United States shall be vested in one supreme Court, and in such inferior Courts as the Congress may from time to time ordain and establish. The Judges, both of the supreme and inferior Courts, shall hold their Offices during good Behaviour, and shall, at stated Times, receive for their Services a Compensation, which shall not be diminished during their Continuance in Office.

Section. 2. The judicial Power shall extend to all Cases, in Law and Equity, arising under this Constitution, the Laws of the United States, and Treaties made, or which shall be made, under their Authority;--to all Cases affecting Ambassadors, other public Ministers and Consuls;--to all Cases of admiralty and maritime Jurisdiction;-- to Controversies to which the United States shall be a Party;--to Controversies between two or more States;--between a State and Citizens of another State [Modified by Amendment XI];--between Citizens of different States;--between Citizens of the same State claiming Lands under Grants of different States, and between a State, or the Citizens thereof, and foreign States, Citizens or Subjects.

In all Cases affecting Ambassadors, other public Ministers and Consuls, and those in which a State shall be Party, the supreme Court shall have original Jurisdiction. In all the other Cases before mentioned, the supreme Court shall have appellate Jurisdiction, both as to Law and Fact, with such Exceptions, and under such Regulations as the Congress shall make.

The Trial of all Crimes, except in Cases of Impeachment, shall be by Jury; and such Trial shall be held in the State where the said Crimes shall have been committed; but when not committed within any State, the Trial shall be at such Place or Places as the Congress may by Law have directed.

Section. 3. Treason against the United States shall consist only in levying War against them, or in adhering to their Enemies, giving them Aid and Comfort. No Person shall be convicted of Treason unless on the Testimony of two Witnesses to the same overt Act, or on Confession in open Court.

The Congress shall have Power to declare the Punishment of Treason, but no Attainder of Treason shall work Corruption of Blood, or Forfeiture except during the Life of the Person attainted.

Article. IV.

Section. 1. Full Faith and Credit shall be given in each State to the public Acts, Records, and judicial Proceedings of every other State. And the Congress may by general Laws prescribe the Manner in which such Acts, Records and Proceedings shall be proved, and the Effect thereof.

Section. 2. The Citizens of each State shall be entitled to all Privileges and Immunities of Citizens in the several States.

A Person charged in any State with Treason, Felony, or other Crime, who shall flee from Justice, and be found in another State, shall on Demand of the executive

Authority of the State from which he fled, be delivered up, to be removed to the State having Jurisdiction of the Crime.

No Person held to Service or Labour in one State, under the Laws thereof, escaping into another, shall, in Consequence of any Law or Regulation therein, be discharged from such Service or Labour, but shall be delivered up on Claim of the Party to whom such Service or Labour may be due [Modified by Amendment XIII].

Section. 3. New States may be admitted by the Congress into this Union; but no new State shall be formed or erected within the Jurisdiction of any other State; nor any State be formed by the Junction of two or more States, or Parts of States, without the Consent of the Legislatures of the States concerned as well as of the Congress.

The Congress shall have Power to dispose of and make all needful Rules and Regulations respecting the Territory or other Property belonging to the United States; and nothing in this Constitution shall be so construed as to Prejudice any Claims of the United States, or of any particular State.

Section. 4. The United States shall guarantee to every State in this Union a Republican Form of Government, and shall protect each of them against Invasion; and on Application of the Legislature, or of the Executive (when the Legislature cannot be convened), against domestic Violence.

Article. V.
The Congress, whenever two thirds of both Houses shall deem it necessary, shall propose Amendments to this Constitution, or, on the Application of the Legislatures of two thirds of the several States, shall call a Convention for proposing Amendments, which, in either Case, shall be valid to all Intents and Purposes, as Part of this Constitution, when ratified by the Legislatures of three fourths of the several States, or by Conventions in three fourths thereof, as the one or the other Mode of Ratification may be proposed by the Congress; Provided that no Amendment which may be made prior to the Year One thousand eight hundred and eight shall in any Manner affect the first and fourth Clauses in the Ninth Section of the first Article; and that no State, without its Consent, shall be deprived of its equal Suffrage in the Senate [Possibly abrogated by Amendment XVII].

Article. VI.
All Debts contracted and Engagements entered into, before the Adoption of this Constitution, shall be as valid against the United States under this Constitution, as under the Confederation.

This Constitution, and the Laws of the United States which shall be made in Pursuance thereof; and all Treaties made, or which shall be made, under the Authority of the United States, shall be the supreme Law of the Land; and the Judges in every State shall be bound thereby, any Thing in the Constitution or Laws of any State to the Contrary notwithstanding.

The Senators and Representatives before mentioned, and the Members of the several State Legislatures, and all executive and judicial Officers, both of the United States and of the several States, shall be bound by Oath or Affirmation, to support this Constitution; but no religious Test shall ever be required as a Qualification to any Office or public Trust under the United States.

Article. VII.

The Ratification of the Conventions of nine States, shall be sufficient for the Establishment of this Constitution between the States so ratifying the Same.

The Word, "the," being interlined between the seventh and eighth Lines of the first Page, The Word "Thirty" being partly written on an Erazure in the fifteenth Line of the first Page, The Words "is tried" being interlined between the thirty second and thirty third Lines of the first Page and the Word "the" being interlined between the forty third and forty fourth Lines of the second Page.

Attest William Jackson
Secretary

done in Convention by the Unanimous Consent of the States present the Seventeenth Day of September in the Year of our Lord one thousand seven hundred and Eighty seven and of the Independence of the United States of America the Twelfth In witness whereof We have hereunto subscribed our Names,

Go. WASHINGTON—
    Presidt. And deputy from Virginia

New Hampshire {
    JOHN LANGDON
    NICHOLAS GILMAN

Massachusetts {
    NATHANIEL GORHAM
    RUFUS KING

Connecticut {
    WM. SAML. JOHNSON
    ROGER SHERMAN

New York . . . .
    ALEXANDER HAMILTON

New Jersey {
    WIL: LIVINGSTON
    DAVID BREARLEY
    WM. PATERSON
    JONA: DAYTON

Pennsylvania {
    B FRANKLIN
    THOMAS MIFFLIN

ROBT MORRIS
GEO. CLYMER
THOS. FITZSIMONS
JARED INGERSOLL
JAMES WILSON
GOUV MORRIS

Delaware {
GEO: READ
GUNNING BEDFORD jun
JOHN DICKINSON
RICHARD BASSETT
JACO: BROOM

Maryland {
JAMES MCHENRY
DAN OF ST THOS. JENIFER
DANL CARROLL

Virginia {
JOHN BLAIR—
JAMES MADISON Jr.

North Carolina {
WM. BLOUNT
RICHD. DOBBS SPAIGHT
HU WILLIAMSON
J. RUTLEDGE

South Carolina {
CHARLES COTESWORTH PINCKNEY
CHARLES PINCKNEY
PIERCE BUTLER

Georgia {
WILLIAM FEW
ABR BALDWIN

In Convention Monday, September 17th, 1787.

Present
The States of

New Hampshire, Massachusetts, Connecticut, MR. Hamilton from New York, New Jersey, Pennsylvania, Delaware, Maryland, Virginia, North Carolina, South Carolina and Georgia.

Resolved,

That the preceeding Constitution be laid before the United States in Congress assembled, and that it is the Opinion of this Convention, that it should afterwards be submitted to a Convention of Delegates, chosen in each State by the People thereof, under the Recommendation of its Legislature, for their Assent and Ratification; and that each Convention assenting to, and ratifying the Same, should give Notice thereof to the United States in Congress assembled. Resolved, That it is the Opinion of this Convention, that as soon as the Conventions of nine States shall have ratified this Constitution, the United States in Congress assembled should fix a Day on which Electors should be appointed by the States which have ratified the same, and a Day on which the Electors should assemble to vote for the President, and the Time and Place for commencing Proceedings under this Constitution. That after such Publication the Electors should be appointed, and the Senators and Representatives elected: That the Electors should meet on the Day fixed for the Election of the President, and should transmit their Votes certified, signed, sealed and directed, as the Constitution requires, to the Secretary of the United States in Congress assembled, that the Senators and Representatives should convene at the Time and Place assigned; that the Senators should appoint a President of the Senate, for the sole purpose of receiving, opening and counting the Votes for President; and, that after he shall be chosen, the Congress, together with the President, should, without Delay, proceed to execute this Constitution.

By the Unanimous Order of the Convention
Go. WASHINGTON—Presidt.
W. JACKSON Secretary.

CHAPTER 23

UNITED STATES BILL OF RIGHTS

Congress OF THE United States begun and held at the City of New-York, on Wednesday the Fourth of March, one thousand seven hundred and eighty nine.

THE Conventions of a number of the States having at the time of their adopting the Constitution, expressed a desire, in order to prevent misconstruction or abuse of its powers, that further declaratory and restrictive clauses should be added: And as extending the ground of public confidence in the Government, will best insure the beneficent ends of its institution.

RESOLVED by the Senate and House of Representatives of the United States of America, in Congress assembled, two thirds of both Houses concurring, that the following Articles be proposed to the Legislatures of the several States, as Amendments to the Constitution of the United States, all or any of which Articles, when ratified by three fourths of the said Legislatures, to be valid to all intents and purposes, as part of the said Constitution; viz.:

ARTICLES in addition to, and Amendment of the Constitution of the United States of America, proposed by Congress, and ratified by the Legislatures of the several States, pursuant to the fifth Article of the original Constitution.

Article the first
[Not Ratified]
After the first enumeration required by the first Article of the Constitution, there shall be one Representative for every thirty thousand, until the number shall amount to one hundred, after which the proportion shall be so regulated by Congress, that there shall be not less than one hundred Representatives, nor less than one Representative for every forty thousand persons, until the number of Representatives shall amount to two hundred; after which the proportion shall be so regulated by Congress, that there shall not be less than two hundred

Representatives, nor more than one Representative for every fifty thousand persons.

Article the second
[Amendment XXVII – Ratified 1992]
No law, varying the compensation for the services of the Senators and Representatives, shall take effect, until an election of Representatives shall have intervened.

Article the third
[Amendment I]
Congress shall make no law respecting an establishment of religion, or prohibiting the free exercise thereof; or abridging the freedom of speech, or of the press; or the right of the people peaceably to assemble, and to petition the Government for a redress of grievances.

Article the fourth
[Amendment II]
A well regulated Militia, being necessary to the security of a free State, the right of the people to keep and bear Arms, shall not be infringed.

Article the fifth
[Amendment III]
No Soldier shall, in time of peace be quartered in any house, without the consent of the Owner, nor in time of war, but in a manner to be prescribed by law.

Article the sixth
[Amendment IV]
The right of the people to be secure in their persons, houses, papers, and effects, against unreasonable searches and seizures, shall not be violated, and no Warrants shall issue, but upon probable cause, supported by Oath or affirmation, and particularly describing the place to be searched, and the persons or things to be seized.

Article the seventh
[Amendment V]
No person shall be held to answer for a capital, or otherwise infamous crime, unless on a presentment or indictment of a Grand Jury, except in cases arising in the land or naval forces, or in the Militia, when in actual service in time of War or public danger; nor shall any person be subject for the same offence to be twice put in jeopardy of life or limb; nor shall be compelled in any criminal case to be a witness against himself, nor be deprived of life, liberty, or property, without due process of law; nor shall private property be taken for public use, without just compensation.

Article the eighth
[Amendment VI]
In all criminal prosecutions, the accused shall enjoy the right to a speedy and public trial, by an impartial jury of the State and district wherein the crime shall have been committed, which district shall have been previously ascertained by law, and to be

informed of the nature and cause of the accusation; to be confronted with the witnesses against him; to have compulsory process for obtaining witnesses in his favor, and to have the Assistance of Counsel for his defence.

Article the ninth
[Amendment VII]
In Suits at common law, where the value in controversy shall exceed twenty dollars, the right of trial by jury shall be preserved, and no fact tried by a jury, shall be otherwise re-examined in any Court of the United States, than according to the rules of the common law.

Article the tenth
[Amendment VIII]
Excessive bail shall not be required, nor excessive fines imposed, nor cruel and unusual punishments inflicted.

Article the eleventh
[Amendment IX]
The enumeration in the Constitution, of certain rights, shall not be construed to deny or disparage others retained by the people.

Article the twelfth
[Amendment X]
The powers not delegated to the United States by the Constitution, nor prohibited by it to the States, are reserved to the States respectively, or to the people.

ATTEST: Frederick Augustus Muhlenberg, Speaker of the House of Representatives

ARTICLES in addition to, and Amendment of, the Constitution of the United States of America, proposed by Congress, and ratified by the Legislatures of the several States, pursuant to the fifth Article of the original Constitution

AMENDMENTS
[Article. XI.]
[Proposed 1794; Ratified 1798]
The Judicial power of the United States shall not be construed to extend to any suit in law or equity, commenced or prosecuted against one of the United States by Citizens of another State, or by Citizens or Subjects of any Foreign State.

[Article. XII.]
[Proposed 1803; Ratified 1804]
The Electors shall meet in their respective states, and vote by ballot for President and Vice-President, one of whom, at least, shall not be an inhabitant of the same state with themselves; they shall name in their ballots the person voted for as President, and in distinct ballots the person voted for as Vice-President, and they shall make distinct lists of all persons voted for as President, and of all persons voted for as Vice-President, and of the number of votes for each, which lists they shall sign and certify, and transmit sealed to the seat of the government of the United States, directed to the President of the Senate;—The President of the Senate shall, in the presence of the Senate and House of Representatives, open all the

certificates and the votes shall then be counted;—The person having the greatest number of votes for President, shall be the President, if such number be a majority of the whole number of Electors appointed; and if no person have such majority, then from the persons having the highest numbers not exceeding three on the list of those voted for as President, the House of Representatives shall choose immediately, by ballot, the President. But in choosing the President, the votes shall be taken by states, the representation from each state having one vote; a quorum for this purpose shall consist of a member or members from two-thirds of the states, and a majority of all the states shall be necessary to a choice. And if the House of Representatives shall not choose a President whenever the right of choice shall devolve upon them, before the fourth day of March next following, then the Vice-President shall act as President, as in the case of the death or other constitutional disability of the President.—The person having the greatest number of votes as Vice-President, shall be the Vice-President, if such number be a majority of the whole number of Electors appointed, and if no person have a majority, then from the two highest numbers on the list, the Senate shall choose the Vice-President; a quorum for the purpose shall consist of two-thirds of the whole number of Senators, and a majority of the whole number shall be necessary to a choice. But no person constitutionally ineligible to the office of President shall be eligible to that of Vice-President of the United States.

[Contested Article.]
[Proposed 1810; Probably Ratified 1819]
If any Citizen of the United States shall accept, claim, receive or retain any Title of Nobility or Honour, or shall, without the Consent of Congress, accept and retain any present, Pension, Office or Emolument of any kind whatever, from any Emperor, King, Prince or foreign Power, such Person shall cease to be a Citizen of the United States, and shall be incapable of holding any Office of Trust or Profit under them, or either of them.

[Unratified Article.]
[Proposed 1861; Signed by President Lincoln; Unratified]
Article Thirteen. No amendment shall be made to the Constitution which will authorize or give to Congress the power to abolish or interfere, within any State, with the domestic institutions thereof, including that of persons held to labor or service by the laws of said State.

Article. XIII.
[Proposed 1865; Ratified 1865]
Section. 1. Neither slavery nor involuntary servitude, except as a punishment for crime whereof the party shall have been duly convicted, shall exist within the United States, or any place subject to their jurisdiction.

Section. 2. Congress shall have power to enforce this article by appropriate legislation.

Article. XIV.
[Proposed 1866; Ratified Under Duress 1868]

Section. 1. All persons born or naturalized in the United States, and subject to the jurisdiction thereof, are citizens of the United States and of the State wherein they reside. No State shall make or enforce any law which shall abridge the privileges or immunities of citizens of the United States; nor shall any State deprive any person of life, liberty, or property, without due process of law; nor deny to any person within its jurisdiction the equal protection of the laws.

Section. 2. Representatives shall be apportioned among the several States according to their respective numbers, counting the whole number of persons in each State, excluding Indians not taxed. But when the right to vote at any election for the choice of electors for President and Vice President of the United States, Representatives in Congress, the Executive and Judicial officers of a State, or the members of the Legislature thereof, is denied to any of the male inhabitants of such State, being twenty-one years of age, and citizens of the United States, or in any way abridged, except for participation in rebellion, or other crime, the basis of representation therein shall be reduced in the proportion which the number of such male citizens shall bear to the whole number of male citizens twenty-one years of age in such State.

Section. 3. No person shall be a Senator or Representative in Congress, or elector of President and Vice President, or hold any office, civil or military, under the United States, or under any State, who, having previously taken an oath, as a member of Congress, or as an officer of the United States, or as a member of any State legislature, or as an executive or judicial officer of any State, to support the Constitution of the United States, shall have engaged in insurrection or rebellion against the same, or given aid or comfort to the enemies thereof. But Congress may by a vote of two-thirds of each House, remove such disability.

Section. 4. The validity of the public debt of the United States, authorized by law, including debts incurred for payment of pensions and bounties for services in suppressing insurrection or rebellion, shall not be questioned. But neither the United States nor any State shall assume or pay any debt or obligation incurred in aid of insurrection or rebellion against the United States, or any claim for the loss or emancipation of any slave; but all such debts, obligations and claims shall be held illegal and void.

Section. 5. The Congress shall have power to enforce, by appropriate legislation, the provisions of this article.

Article. XV.
[Proposed 1869; Ratified 1870]

Section. 1. The right of citizens of the United States to vote shall not be denied or abridged by the United States or by any State on account of race, color, or previous condition of servitude.

Section. 2. The Congress shall have power to enforce this article by appropriate legislation.

Article. XVI.
[Proposed 1909; Questionably Ratified 1913]

The Congress shall have power to lay and collect taxes on incomes, from whatever source derived, without apportionment among the several States, and without regard to any census or enumeration.

[Article. XVII.]
[Proposed 1912; Ratified 1913;
Possibly Unconstitutional
(See Article V, Clause 3 of the Constitution)]

The Senate of the United States shall be composed of two Senators from each State, elected by the people thereof, for six years; and each Senator shall have one vote. The electors in each State shall have the qualifications requisite for electors of the most numerous branch of the State legislatures.

When vacancies happen in the representation of any State in the Senate, the executive authority of such State shall issue writs of election to fill such vacancies: Provided, That the legislature of any State may empower the executive thereof to make temporary appointments until the people fill the vacancies by election as the legislature may direct.

This amendment shall not be so construed as to affect the election or term of any Senator chosen before it becomes valid as part of the Constitution.

Article. [XVIII.]
[Proposed 1917; Ratified 1919;
Repealed 1933 (See Amendment XXI, Section 1)]

Section. 1. After one year from the ratification of this article the manufacture, sale, or transportation of intoxicating liquors within, the importation thereof into, or the exportation thereof from the United States and all territory subject to the jurisdiction thereof for beverage purposes is hereby prohibited.

Section. 2. The Congress and the several States shall have concurrent power to enforce this article by appropriate legislation.

Section. 3. This article shall be inoperative unless it shall have been ratified as an amendment to the Constitution by the legislatures of the several States, as provided in the Constitution, within seven years from the date of the submission hereof to the States by the Congress.

Article. [XIX.]
[Proposed 1919; Ratified 1920]

The right of citizens of the United States to vote shall not be denied or abridged by the United States or by any State on account of sex.

Congress shall have power to enforce this article by appropriate legislation.

[Unratified Article.]
[Proposed 1926; Unratified]
Article—

Section. 1. The Congress shall have power to limit, regulate, and prohibit the labor of persons under eighteen years of age.

Section. 2. The power of the several States is unimpaired by this article except that the operation of State laws shall be suspended to the extent necessary to give effect to legislation enacted by the Congress.

Article. [XX.]
[Proposed 1932; Ratified 1933]

Section. 1. The terms of the President and Vice President shall end at noon on the 20th day of January, and the terms of Senators and Representatives at noon on the 3d day of January, of the years in which such terms would have ended if this article had not been ratified; and the terms of their successors shall then begin.

Section. 2. The Congress shall assemble at least once in every year, and such meeting shall begin at noon on the 3d day of January, unless they shall by law appoint a different day.

Section. 3. If, at the time fixed for the beginning of the term of the President, the President elect shall have died, the Vice President elect shall become President. If a President shall not have been chosen before the time fixed for the beginning of his term, or if the President elect shall have failed to qualify, then the Vice President elect shall act as President until a President shall have qualified; and the Congress may by law provide for the case wherein neither a President elect nor a Vice President elect shall have qualified, declaring who shall then act as President, or the manner in which one who is to act shall be selected, and such person shall act accordingly until a President or Vice President shall have qualified.

Section. 4. The Congress may by law provide for the case of the death of any of the persons from whom the House of Representatives may choose a President whenever the right of choice shall have devolved upon them, and for the case of the death of any of the persons from whom the Senate may choose a Vice President whenever the right of choice shall have devolved upon them.

Section. 5. Sections 1 and 2 shall take effect on the 15th day of October following the ratification of this article.

Section. 6. This article shall be inoperative unless it shall have been ratified as an amendment to the Constitution by the legislatures of three-fourths of the several States within seven years from the date of its submission.

Article. [XXI.]
[Proposed 1933; Ratified 1933]

Section. 1. The eighteenth article of amendment to the Constitution of the United States is hereby repealed.

Section. 2. The transportation or importation into any State, Territory, or possession of the United States for delivery or use therein of intoxicating liquors, in violation of the laws thereof, is hereby prohibited.

Section. 3. This article shall be inoperative unless it shall have been ratified as an amendment to the Constitution by conventions in the several States, as provided in the Constitution, within seven years from the date of the submission hereof to the States by the Congress.

Article. [XXII.]
[Proposed 1947; Ratified 1951]

Section. 1. No person shall be elected to the office of the President more than twice, and no person who has held the office of President, or acted as President, for more than two years of a term to which some other person was elected President shall be elected to the office of the President more than once. But this Article shall not apply to any person holding the office of President when this Article was proposed by the Congress, and shall not prevent any person who may be holding the office of President, or acting as President, during the term within which this Article becomes operative from holding the office of President or acting as President during the remainder of such term.

Section. 2. This article shall be inoperative unless it shall have been ratified as an amendment to the Constitution by the legislatures of three-fourths of the several States within seven years from the date of its submission to the States by the Congress.

Article. [XXIII.]
[Proposed 1960; Ratified 1961]

Section. 1. The District constituting the seat of Government of the United States shall appoint in such manner as the Congress may direct:

A number of electors of President and Vice President equal to the whole number of Senators and Representatives in Congress to which the District would be entitled if it were a State, but in no event more than the least populous State; they shall be in addition to those appointed by the States, but they shall be considered, for the purposes of the election of President and Vice President, to be electors appointed by a State; and they shall meet in the District and perform such duties as provided by the twelfth article of amendment.

Section. 2. The Congress shall have power to enforce this article by appropriate legislation.

Article. [XXIV.]
[Proposed 1962; Ratified 1964]

Section. 1. The right of citizens of the United States to vote in any primary or other election for President or Vice President, for electors for President or Vice President, or for Senator or Representative in Congress, shall not be denied or abridged by the United States or any State by reason of failure to pay any poll tax or other tax.

Section. 2. The Congress shall have power to enforce this article by appropriate legislation.

Article. [XXV.]

[Proposed 1965; Ratified 1967]
Section. 1. In case of the removal of the President from office or of his death or resignation, the Vice President shall become President.

Section. 2. Whenever there is a vacancy in the office of the Vice President, the President shall nominate a Vice President who shall take office upon confirmation by a majority vote of both Houses of Congress.

Section. 3. Whenever the President transmits to the President pro tempore of the Senate and the Speaker of the House of Representatives his written declaration that he is unable to discharge the powers and duties of his office, and until he transmits to them a written declaration to the contrary, such powers and duties shall be discharged by the Vice President as Acting President.

Section. 4. Whenever the Vice President and a majority of either the principal officers of the executive departments or of such other body as Congress may by law provide, transmit to the President pro tempore of the Senate and the Speaker of the House of Representatives their written declaration that the President is unable to discharge the powers and duties of his office, the Vice President shall immediately assume the powers and duties of the office as Acting President.

Thereafter, when the President transmits to the President pro tempore of the Senate and the Speaker of the House of Representatives his written declaration that no inability exists, he shall resume the powers and duties of his office unless the Vice President and a majority of either the principal officers of the executive department or of such other body as Congress may by law provide, transmit within four days to the President pro tempore of the Senate and the Speaker of the House of Representatives their written declaration that the President is unable to discharge the powers and duties of his office. Thereupon Congress shall decide the issue, assembling within forty-eight hours for that purpose if not in session. If the Congress, within twenty-one days after receipt of the latter written declaration, or, if Congress is not in session, within twenty-one days after Congress is required to assemble, determines by two-thirds vote of both Houses that the President is unable to discharge the powers and duties of his office, the Vice President shall continue to discharge the same as Acting President; otherwise, the President shall resume the powers and duties of his office.

Article. [XXVI.]
[Proposed 1971; Ratified 1971]
Section. 1. The right of citizens of the United States, who are eighteen years of age or older, to vote shall not be denied or abridged by the United States or by any State on account of age.

Section. 2. The Congress shall have power to enforce this article by appropriate legislation.

[Inoperative Article.]
[Proposed 1972; Expired Unratified 1982]
Article—

Section. 1. Equality of rights under the law shall not be denied or abridged by the United States or by any State on account of sex.

Section. 2. The Congress shall have the power to enforce, by appropriate legislation, the provisions of this article.

Section. 3. This amendment shall take effect two years after the date of ratification.

[Inoperative Article.]
[Proposed 1978; Expired Unratified 1985]
Article—
Section. 1. For purposes of representation in the Congress, election of the President and Vice President, and article V of this Constitution, the District constituting the seat of government of the United States shall be treated as though it were a State.

Section. 2. The exercise of the rights and powers conferred under this article shall be by the people of the District constituting the seat of government, and as shall be provided by the Congress.

Section. 3. The twenty-third article of amendment to the Constitution of the United States is hereby repealed.

Section. 4. This article shall be inoperative, unless it shall have been ratified as an amendment to the Constitution by the legislatures of three-fourths of the several States within seven years from the date of its submission.

Article. [XXVII].
[Proposed 1789; Ratified 1992; Second of twelve Articles comprising the Bill of Rights]
No law, varying the compensation for the services of the Senators and Representatives, shall take effect, until an election of Representatives shall have intervened.

Bibliography

Barnhouse, Donald Grey. *THE INVISIBLE WAR.* Zondervan Publishing House, 1965.

[4]Black, Henry Campbell, M.A. *Black's Law Dictionary.* West Publishing Company, 1968, 4th Ed.

Blankenhorn, David. *FATHERLESS AMERICA.* Basic Books, 1995.

Blumenfeld, Samuel L. *NEA - TROJAN HORSE IN AMERICAN EDUCATION.* Paradigm Company, 1984.

Brown, Judie. *It Is I Who Have Chosen You.* American Life League, Inc., 1992.

Legrand, Jacques. *Chronicle of the 20th Century.* Chronicle Publications, 1986

Colson, Charles. *Kingdoms in Conflict,* Zondervan Publishing. 1988

[3]Foundation, The Arthur S. DeMoss. *THE REBIRTH OF AMERICA.* The Arthur S. DeMoss Foundation, 1986.

Gills, James P. *DARWINISM Under the Microscope.* Charisma House. 2002

Goff, Kenneth. *BRAIN WASHING A Synthesis of the Russian Textbook on Psychopolitics.*

Grant, George. *GRAND ILLUSIONS The Legacy of Planned Parenthood.* Adroit Press, 1992

Hall, Verna M. *Christian History of the Constitution.* Foundation for American Christian Education, 1960

Johnson, Derric. *What Price Freedom.* Zondervan Publishers, 1973

[1]Kacprowicz, Charles. *The UNBORN CHILD AMENDMENT- a National Strategy to Amend the U.S. Constitution through State Legislatures.* Markets Global Publishing, 2003

Litzenberger, T. Wilson. *Startling Trends in Our Generation.* Gibbs Publishing Company, 1974.

MacDonald, William. *BELIEVERS BIBLE COMMENTARY.* Thomas Nelson Publishing, 1995.

[2]Millard, Catherine. *GREAT AMERICAN STATESMEN AND HEROES.* Horizon Books, 1995.

Millard, Catherine. *REWRITING of AMERICA'S HISTORY.* Horizon Books, 1991.

Morey, Robert. *Islamic Invasion.* Christian Scholars Press, 1992.

National Journal, *THE CAPITAL SOURCE.*

Scofield, C. I. D.D. *The Scofield Study Bible (KJV).* Oxford University Press, 1996.

Shelly, Bruce L. *CHURCH HISTORY in Plain English.* Thomas Nelson Publishing, 1995 2nd Ed.

U.S. Department of Commerce. *Statistical Abstract of the United States.* Bureau of Census.

Ujifusa, Michael Barone & Grant. *The Almanac of American Politics.* National Journal.

Virkler, David M. *Presidential Profiles.* Dedication Evangelism, Inc. 1967

Walton, Rus. *One Nation Under God.* Third Century Publishing, Inc. 1986

Webster, Daniel quote. *A Discourse at Plymouth*, 1820

INDEX

50 States .... - 59 -

Abortion........................... - 9 -, - 200 -

All persons born or naturalized - 15 -, - 311 -

Amendment Initiative ...... - 65 -, - 71 -

AMENDMENT IX .... - 29 -

AMENDMENT STRATEGY .. - 7 -, - 65 -

America has suffered .... - 199 -

Americans .... - 66 -, - 67 -, - 200 -

Article. V .... - 303 -

atrocity...................................... - 200 -

babies....................................... - 199 -

BILL OF RIGHTS..................... - 307 -

Both Houses of Congress .... - 59 -

Call on Congress ...... - 58 -, - 66 -, - 71 -

church .... - 71 -

citizens - 15 -, - 56 -, - 59 -, - 311 - 312 - - 314 -, - 315 -

Class Action Law Suit............... - 59 -

composition .... - 67 -

Congress............ - 4 -, - 9 -, - 12 -, - 53 - - 56 -, -58 -, - 59 -, - 66 -, - 67 -, - 68- - 71 -, - 295 -, - 296 -, - 297 -, - 298 - - 299-, -300 -, - 301 -, - 302 -, - 303 - - 306-, -307-, - 308 -, - 309 -, - 310 - - 311 -, -312 -, -313 -, - 314 -, - 315 - -316 -

Congressional prerogatives .... - 67 -

consequences........................... - 199 -

constitutional. ....- 56 -, - 57 -, - 200 - - 310 -

Constitutional Amendment- 58 -, -71 -

convene............... - 66 -, - 301 -, - 306 -

Convention.... - 58 -, - 59 -, - 67 -, - 68 - - 72 -, - 303 -, - 304 -, - 305 -, - 306 -

country...................................... - 9 -

DECLARATION OF INDEPENDENCE ....- 22 -, - 24 -

declared war on the Unborn Child .... - 199 -

delegates................................... - 68 -

Direct .... - 56 -, - 57 -, - 65 -

due process .... - 15 -, - 308 -, - 311 -

duty................................- 200 -, - 299 -

economic costs......................... - 199 -

Electors.. - 295 -, - 300 -, - 306 -, - 309 -

enumeration .... - 29 -, - 295 -, - 307 - - 309 -, - 312 -

father ....- 14 -, - 199 -

father of the Unborn Child .... - 199 -

Founding Fathers...................... - 67 -

God........................... - 22 -, - 52 -, - 74 -

grandparents .... - 199 -

incalculable costs..................... - 200 -

Independence .... - 304 -

Indirect .... - 56 -, - 57 -, - 65 -

Initiative............-56 -, - 57 -, - 58 -, - 60 - - 62- ,- 63 -, - 65 -, - 66 -, - 71 -

Initiative States......... - 56 -, - 58 -, - 62 - - 65 -,- 66 -

judicial history .... - 199 -

Law .... - 10 -

legal... - 11 -

Legislative Referendum States- 56 -

Legislative States ...- 58 -, - 65 -, - 66 - - 71 -

length .... - 67 -

liberty .... - 15 -, - 308 -, - 311 -

life.. ....- 15 -, - 200 -, - 308 -, - 311 -

limited .... - 298 -

moral.. - 11 -

mother .... - 199 -

no blacker blot .... - 199 -

nor deny to any person ...- 15 -, - 311 -

ONLY way provided .... - 59 -

percentage of votes........... - 60 -, - 62 -

persons........- 15 -, - 62 -, - 307 -, - 308 -
- 309 -, - 310 -, - 311 -, - 313 -
political .... - 22 -
Popular Referendum States.... - 56 -
Posterity .... - 295 -
powers not delegated ..... - 29 -, - 309 -
President..........- 9 -, - 59 -, - 66 -, - 296 -
- 297 -, - 298 -, -300 -, -301 -, - 302 -
- 306 -, -309 -, -310 -, - 311 -, - 313 -
- 314 -, - 315 -, - 316 -
Presidential Efforts................... - 59 -
privacy .... - 14 -
procreation rights...................... - 29 -
ProLife ....- 71 -, - 200 -
property.............. - 15 -, - 308 -, - 311 -
prophesy...................................... - 9 -
publicity..................................... - 66 -
ratification......- 59 -, - 66 -, - 68 -, - 71 -
- 312 -, - 313 -, - 316 -
ratified......- 68 -, - 303 -, - 306 -, - 307 -
- 309 -, -312 -, -313 -, - 314 -, - 316 -
Redress of Grievances......... - 58 -, - 59-
- 66 -
Referenda.......................... - 56 -, - 60 -
Referenda States .... - 56 -
retained by the people ....- 29 -, - 309 -

rights...- 4 -
Roe vs. Wade........................... - 199 -
sane motherhood.................... - 200 -
sin will find you out .... - 17 -
State.................................... - 5 -, - 9 -
State Conventions .... - 68 -
State elections........................... - 71 -
State legislators......................... - 66 -
State Legislatures...... - 4 -, - 56 -, - 58 -
- 59 -, - 66 -, - 68 -, - 69 -, - 71 -
Supreme Court .... - 14 -, - 29 -, - 66 -
timing... - 67 -
Unborn Child....... - 14 -, - 199 -, - 200 -
UNBORN CHILD AMENDMENT...- 5 -
- 9 -
un-enumerated right.................. - 14 -
United States............................... - 4 -
UNITED STATES CONSTITUTION....
.... - 295 -
vote.- 60 -, - 71 -, - 300 -, - 306 -, - 309 -
- 311 -, - 312 -, - 314 -, - 315 -
VOTER TURNOUT..................... - 60 -
VOTING POWER .... - 7 -, - 71 -
VOTING STRATEGY .... - 60 -
ways of death........................... - 17 -
We the People .... - 295 -
young mother........................... - 199 -

www.ingramcontent.com/pod-product-compliance
Lightning Source LLC
Chambersburg PA
CBHW060326200326
41519CB00011BA/1844